TRANSYLVANIA UNIVERSITY AND ENVIRON

ANTE BELLUM HOUSES
OF THE BLUEGRASS

ANTE BELLUM OF THE

THE DEVELOPMENT
OF RESIDENTIAL ARCHITECTURE
IN FAYETTE COUNTY, KENTUCKY

Published by the UNIVERSITY OF

HOUSES
BLUEGRASS

by CLAY LANCASTER

KENTUCKY PRESS, LEXINGTON

Copyright © 1961 by the University of Kentucky Press
Library of Congress Catalog Card No. 61-15624

The publication of this book has been made possible partly through a grant from the Margaret Voorhies Haggin Trust, established in memory of her husband, James Ben Ali Haggin.

To
JOSEPH CLARK GRAVES
Founder and First President of
The Blue Grass Trust for Historic Preservation

In Grateful Remembrance of
His Constant and Selfless Efforts
To Preserve Kentucky's Architectural Heritage

ACKNOWLEDGMENTS

THE AUTHOR would like to express his appreciation to the owners and occupants of the houses described for the cordial reception consistently extended to him during the many pleasant hours spent in inspecting, measuring, and photographing the buildings. The friendly warmth of landowner and tenant alike combined with the interest of the architecture to make the task doubly rewarding. Special thanks are due the following persons for their generous help and encouragement throughout the years the author has been studying Kentucky architecture: the late Mrs. Willis Field, Mr. Joseph Graves, Professor Talbot F. Hamlin, Mr. Charles R. Staples, Mr. James Maurice Roche, and Mr. C. Frank Dunn; Mrs. Maude Ward Lafferty, Miss Anne Worthington Callihan, Miss Elizabeth Watkins, Mrs. Carolyn Reading Hammer, Mrs. Amelia Buckley, Miss Virginia Hayes, Mrs. Eleanor Parker Hopkins, Mrs. John S. Gardner, Dr. Agnes Addison Gilchrist, Mrs. Eleanor H. Pryor, Mrs. Frank Dunn, Mrs. Margaret Preston Johnston, Miss Bettye Lee Mastin, Mrs. Retta Wright, and Mrs. Lucy Graves; Professor Edward W. Rannells, Professor Rexford Newcomb, Professor Everard M. Upjohn, Professor Emerson Swift, Professor Justus Bier, Professor Walter Creese, Mr. Alfred Andrews, Mr. Burton Milward, Mr. William H. Townsend, and Mr. John Wilson Townsend. Mr. J. Winston Coleman, Jr., has rendered exceptional service, not only in supplying data and photographs from his notable collection of Kentuckiana, but especially in reading the manuscript and in checking proof. The author is grateful to the staffs of the Lexington Public Library, the Library of the University of Kentucky, Avery Library of Columbia University, and the New York Public Library for their aid in research matters connected with the project.

The author also wishes to thank the Blue Grass Trust for Historic Preservation for a special grant to the University of Kentucky Press in aid of the publication of this book.

Brooklyn Heights   CLAY LANCASTER
New York
May, 1961

CONTENTS

ACKNOWLEDGMENTS	*page* vii	7 THE GREEK REVIVAL	*page* 79
INTRODUCTION	xi	8 THE GOTHIC REVIVAL	114
1 PIONEER BUILDING	1	9 THE ITALIANATE	132
2 FRAME HOUSES	11	SUMMARY	147
3 STONE HOUSES	15	REFERENCES	149
4 EARLY BRICK HOUSES	19	GLOSSARY	155
5 THE GEOMETRIC PHASE	46	ALBUM OF PHOTOGRAPHS	161
6 CLASSICISM	67	BIBLIOGRAPHICAL INDEX	175

INTRODUCTION

Fayette County is in the heart of the Bluegrass country of the Commonwealth of Kentucky, directly south of Cincinnati, the Queen City of the Ohio Valley, southwest of Maysville (called Limestone prior to 1787), the old debarkation port for settlers arriving by river from the seaboard states, and north-northwest of Cumberland Gap, the chief southern pass through the Allegheny Mountain range. Kentucky was reserved for a hunting ground by Indians living north and south of its boundaries, and the absence of aboriginal encampments meant limited opposition to colonization, which therefore took place here earlier than in surrounding territories. Fayette County became the focus of converging streams of immigration because of the beauty of its landscape and the fertility of its soil, affording choice homesites and rich farmlands.

The middle section of the county is high and open, well watered by a system of northwestwardly flowing streams that spread out like the antlers of an elk, whence is derived its name, Elkhorn, the main branches being designated South, North, and Town Fork. The southeast corner of Fayette is cut by deep valleys adjacent to a short segment of the Kentucky River, a tributary of which—called Boone Creek after the famous pioneer, Daniel Boone—forms part of the county's eastern extremity. Madison and Clark counties respectively lie beyond these two watercourses. Elsewhere Fayette is bounded by Bourbon County on the northeast, Scott on the north, Woodford on the west, and Jessamine on the south.

Fayette was one of the three original counties into which Kentucky was divided by the Assembly of Virginia in 1780. Two counties—Bourbon in 1785 and Woodford in 1788—were carved from Fayette before Kentucky was admitted to the Union in 1792, and two more thereafter, part of Clark in 1792 and Jessamine in 1798. Its present limits have remained fairly constant since 1798. Extensive land grants bestowed by the colonial and national governments upon men serving in the French and Indian War and the American Revolution brought to this area the first wave of settlers, who built the earliest permanent dwellings, surviving examples of which have served as adequate homes for successive generations upward of a century and a half.

The county seat of Fayette is Lexington. Founded on the fourth of June, 1775, it was named for the Massachusetts town in commemoration of the first battle in the struggle for American independence. By the turn of the century Lexington had evolved into the top-ranking inland cultural center north of the Spanish city of New Orleans and west of the Alleghenies. This distinction was proudly maintained for several decades, or until the fortunes of several river cities advanced phenomenally because of the rising packet trade and traffic on the Mississippi River and its subsidiaries. Described in 1828 as "the largest town on the south side of the Ohio River, above New Orleans,"[1] Lexington already was outstripped by Cincinnati in population—though not in cultural attainments—and soon by Louisville as well. The cholera epidemic of 1833, taking the lives of five hundred persons, further reduced the number of inhabitants in Lexington. But early in the nineteenth century Lexington earned the title "Athens of the West," and, in terms of land values and the enterprise and refinement of its citizens, was compared favorably with Philadelphia and other coastal cities.[2]

Fayette County's restricted size (280 square miles) makes all the more remarkable the enormous amount of building activity that took place here during the eight decades between the Revolution and the Civil War. The first city directory, published in *Charless' Kentucky . . . Almanack* for 1806, indicates that 37 of some 270 men listed were definitely engaged in building—carpenters, masons, plasterers, and painters—and another 10 to 15 are designated as coopers, laborers, and the like. This means that from one-eighth to one-fifth of the urban residents were employed in construction. Lexington at that time counted "104 Brick, 10 Stone, & 187 Frame and log Houses," besides a courthouse, jail, markethouse, Masonic lodge, an insurance office, public library, four churches, and a building housing Transylvania University. In the second directory, twelve years later, those engaged in building pursuits totaled around 90 out of a population of about 600, the percentage therefore remaining about the same.[3] After 1820 the ratio of builders to nonbuilders began to drop, so that in the third directory, of 1838, despite a continued increase in inhabitants, the builders included not more than 80 persons. By this late date, however, the professional architect had begun to replace the craftsman-builder, and soon the social breach was to widen between those who designed buildings and those who constructed them. Although the listing of professional architects remained small, there existed a vast crew of nameless individuals (both slaves and freemen) who functioned as building operators of various sorts.

The early houses of Fayette County are distinguished by quality as well as numbers. Although national trends were followed by Bluegrass builders, a provincial aspect comes to the fore, combining simplicity and originality with a high level of workmanship. This gives the buildings considerably more interest than those in areas where styles were adhered to more strictly. Builders here did not hesitate to deviate from accepted modes, and by following their impulses achieved results possessing freshness and lasting appeal. The break with authority in the matter of architectural formalities, special consideration for the properties of materials employed, and decoration derived from techniques appropriate to the implements utilized, anticipated and foreshadowed what has come to be called "modern" architecture in America a century later.

Ante Bellum Houses of the Bluegrass: The Development of Residential Architecture in Fayette County, Kentucky is devoted wholly to residential architecture as constituting a unified subject, and as being of greatest interest to the majority of people—including the writer himself. It seems, moreover, that the domestic essays in this area have more relative merit in comparison to corresponding building types elsewhere in

INTRODUCTION

America than do the civic or religious buildings, though there were several educational structures of considerable significance. Homes are more directly related to the lives of the people than any other buildings, reflecting their manners and customs, their habits and means, their aesthetic values, and the progress that is made from age to age and generation to generation. However, the chief interest of this book will be found primarily in architectural features as such, in their sources of inspiration and extent (if any) of their influence, in their physical form considered as design, and in house planning related to its functional requirements.

The houses built in Fayette County during the three-quarters of a century preceding the Civil War fall into several successive categories or periods. The earliest ones are distinguished by the construction materials: rough native logs, shaped timbers, frame, and stone in rubble and ashlar forms. After the introduction of brick as a building substance, houses may be divided according to styles. Lingering medieval characteristics are to be found throughout the first brick phase. This is followed by a period of refinement and originality. Authority from abroad next is sought during the reign of classicism, but the classic or Federal period in Kentucky is not without a decidedly local twist. Architecture next takes on a more heavy, masculine quality, as the source of inspiration shifts from the effete grandeur of the Romans to the virile simplicity of the Greeks. The Greek Revival, however, was not without its romantic aspect. The undercurrent of romanticism finally emerged and stood boldly exposed in the lacy picturesqueness of the Gothic Revival. Increased wealth and the leisure resulting from it, with its accompanying reveries, plus prosaic technical advances, made possible the opulence of the manors built during the middle decades of the nineteenth century. The irregularity of Gothic massing and restraint of Greek details came together in the Italianate villas that climaxed, and to some extent summarized, much that had preceded them in Bluegrass building. The villas also display an eclecticism foreshadowing what was to predominate architecture in this area following the sterile years of the war. In the matter of taste the South never quite recovered from the shock of invasion. The Civil War constitutes the real terminus of the first efflorescence of culture in Kentucky, and the temporary suspension of building activities during the early 1860's provides the logical stopping place for our survey.

The principal illustrations in the text that follows are line drawings. This medium has been chosen in order to present the essential features of each architectural composition free from the encumbrances of later alterations and additions which the camera cannot avoid recording. The illustrations are, in fact, compilations derived from reliable descriptions obtained through interviews with former residents, from modern and old photographs, and from personal investigations, including the measuring of existing monuments for plan and elevation sketches. Supplementing these text figures is an album of photographs, which give color and texture contrasts that cannot be interpreted in line drawings, and thereby help to round out the visual material.

PIONEER BUILDING 1

THERE WAS nothing that could be called architecture, and little that might be considered legitimate building, in Fayette County at the time the white man arrived. A previous race had constructed earthworks and stone pyramids, described, respectively, by the scientist Constantine Rafinesque (*Western Review,* 1820) and the historian John Filson.[1] Catacombs containing embalmed bodies were reported in Thomas Ashe's *Travels* of 1806.[2] But these remains made no contribution to the construction program that was to follow.

Pioneer building grew out of very humble beginnings. The first scouts erected flimsy shelters intended only for a night's occupancy. These consisted of a roof and one or two windbreak walls made of any available materials, such as sticks and leaves. Determined settlers followed close upon the heels of roving scouts, and the first structures built with any degree of permanency were log cabins, which began to appear around the middle of the eighteenth century. The American log cabin has an interesting history. Today it is fairly well known that the earliest English colonists of Virginia and Massachusetts did not live in log houses, because there was no antecedent for them in the British Isles.[3] In Europe the log house is native to Scandinavia, Russia, Switzerland, and parts of Germany, and it was introduced into the New World by the Swedes, who settled along the Delaware River in 1638.[4] About 1710 it began to be used independently by the Germans. The Scotch-Irish were the first English-speaking people to employ it, but not until after 1718. By the time of the American Revolution the log house had become the ubiquitous frontier dwelling, adopted by all nationalities, including the American Indian.

The log house presented many features desirable to the pioneer. It was readily constructed from indigenous materials, trees that had to be removed in clearing the land for cultivation, loose surface rock and mud for closing up the chinks between the timbers. The log structure provided a comfortable place of habitation. With its big fireplace and the natural insulation of the thick, all-wood envelope, the log house could be made warm in winter; and it was cool in summer. Construction was not complicated, requiring no extra framework to sustain the walls, and the simplest kind of triangular truss for the roof. In their eagerness to erect a house as quickly as possible, the first settlers made use of newly felled tree trunks, stripping off the branches and notching the ends of uniformly measured logs, which were laid horizontally on a rectangular plan, overlapping alternately at the corners. The fireplace was fashioned of stone, the chimney of small logs, lined with a coating of mud which was hardened to the consistency of pottery by the fire's heat. The floor was tamped earth, the roof covered with shakes or split shingles. Door and window openings were protected by batten shutters that swung on leather or wood hinges. Such houses were erected singly or clustered together to make a community, the latter often surrounded by a palisade of contiguous upright logs for protection against beast and savage. Because of the perishability of the unseasoned wood that went into these primitive log houses, no examples of the type have survived in Fayette County. A facsimile may be seen in the reconstructed (1926) Fort Harrod at Harrodsburg in Mercer County, some thirty miles to the southwest of Fayette.

Certain advances distinguish the second phase of log construction from the first. The timbers were allowed to season properly, and they were squared for a more finished-looking and workmanlike job. Two systems of fitting the logs together at the corners were employed in central Kentucky. One was adapted from the notching used earlier, in which the log end was cut away to form a rooflike peak running length-

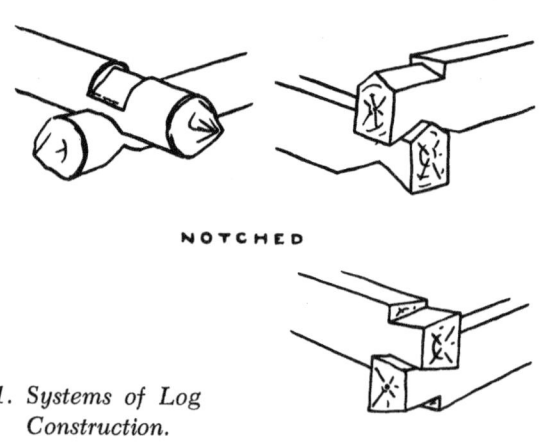

1. Systems of Log Construction.

wise on top, with a saddle joint on a cross axis carved into the underside (*Fig. 1*). The alternative may be described as a modified half dovetail, the indentations made on a slope in such a way that the weight of the logs locked them in place. Old log houses in the highlands of south Germany, using this exact method, indicate a likely origin. The extremities of the timbers in both types were self-draining of rainwater. The notch system was employed in the Patterson, Cleveland, and Watts cabins and the saddlebag cabin, to be discussed below, as well as in a cabin at Winton on the Newtown Pike and the north end of the ruins of the Harp house on the Harp and Innes Road. Examples using the half dovetail are the Bowman cabin on the Woolfolk place at South Elkhorn, and the smaller cabin (presumably used as a storeroom) near the saddlebag cabin on the Armstrong Mill Road. The majority of log houses are weatherboarded over so that their joinery cannot be determined. Among the exposed buildings the predominance of the notch and saddle indicates this to have been the favorite device for locking logs in Fayette County.

Surviving log houses are to be found mostly around the perimeter of the county, where they have remained untouched by building operations in or near Lexington; but this is no indication of the original distribution. Log houses generally were built close to the more important streams, where the first land claims were staked. They may be divided geographically into five groups:

(1) those along the lower end of the Richmond Pike and Jacks Creek Road, near the Kentucky River and Boone Creek, in the southeast corner of Fayette; (2) those built overlooking the various tributaries of North Elkhorn, which extends down through the northeast section of the county to below the Winchester Pike; (3) those on South Elkhorn, that cuts into the southwest corner of Fayette; (4) those on East Hickman Creek, flowing southwardly midway between Lexington and the Kentucky River; and (5) the group on the principal branches of the Elkhorn, including Town Fork that traverses Lexington. The first house to be discussed was located here. Composed of a single room, it represents the minimum in frontier housing.

PATTERSON CABIN   Built probably before 1780 in what was to become downtown Lexington, the log cabin of Colonel Robert Patterson —one of the founders of the community in 1775— was moved to the Patterson property between High and Maxwell, Lower (now called Patterson) and Merino streets about 1783. Later Patterson went to live in Dayton, Ohio, where he died in 1827. Purchased by his descendants, the cabin was taken to Dayton in 1902 and set up in a public park. It was returned to Lexington in 1939 under sponsorship of the State Highway Department and given a site on the campus of Transylvania College, of which institution Robert Patterson had been a trustee. The house is nearly square (*Fig. 2*). It has a door in the

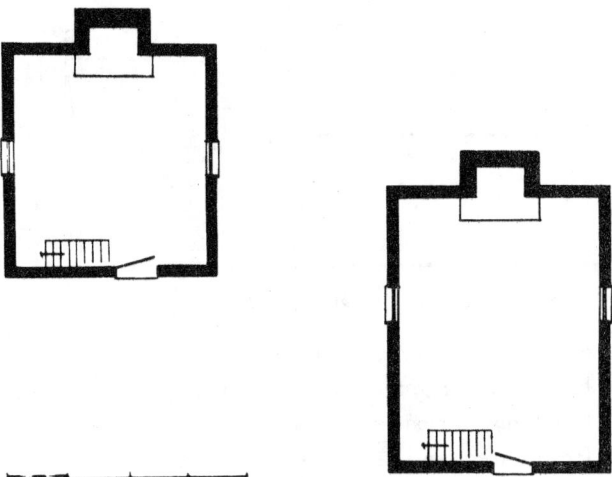

3. Plan of Cleveland Cabins.

front and a small window in the back wall. Another window, lighting the garret, is in the gable opposite the chimney. As reconstructed, the cabin has a plank floor raised off the ground, a stone foundation, and a large stone chimney, the sides of which slope inward above the fireplace, supporting the flue of small notched logs. The ends of the ceiling joists project slightly and those of the two plates farther beyond the wall planes, which is a feature normal to log construction. The roofing is of split wood shingles.

The remaining single-room cabins in Fayette County are not numerous. One is to be found on the Moore place near Bethel. The original section of the northern Harp house (previously mentioned), on the Harp and Innes Road, is another, enlarged into a two-story frame and brick residence. Two stone chimneys on the Watts place above Athens mark the sites of two others, with an existing log stable nearby. The cabin without a chimney on the Berry farm (Armstrong Mill Road) has been noted. A similar structure, also probably used for storage, is at the Carter place on the Military Pike. The two Cleveland cabins, in the first geographic division, are the best preserved in the county.

CLEVELAND CABINS   Eli Cleveland obtained 740 acres of land between Boone Creek and the Richmond Pike in 1786, and probably built shortly thereafter the two cabins standing

2. Patterson Cabin as Set Up on the Transylvania Campus.

4. South Side of Cleveland Cabins.

east of the later main house. Approximately half again larger than the Patterson cabin, these buildings measure 18 by 19 and 18½ by 23½ feet in area, and are placed 14 feet apart, oriented alike, but not set on an axis, undoubtedly for privacy and a wider vista from the windows (*Fig. 3*). Each has a shouldered chimney entirely of stone, a door opposite in the gable end, and a single window, now provided with glazed sashes, in each sidewall (*Fig. 4*). A steep, ladder-like stairway to the side of each door gives access to the loft, where sleeping quarters were provided for the younger boys. The building of a second cabin similar to the first constitutes the simplest mode of pioneer expansion; in this case it is possible that the smaller structure housed the slaves. A large log barn with flanking lean-tos also is on the Cleveland farm, and another like it is to be found at Locust Grove, five miles west of Lexington north of the Leestown Pike.

The one-story house divided into more than a single room was the next advance in building. The cabin on the south side of the Iron Works Road, halfway between the Newtown and Cynthiana (Russell Cave) pikes, contains two rooms, with an enclosed staircase to the garret adjoining the dividing wall. Shallow gun closets flank the chimneypiece in the west room. The Fry cabin on the Paris Pike at Hughes Lane and the servants' cabin back of the Hunter house at the county line on the Tates Creek Pike have two rooms and two terminal chimneys.

The ruins of a log house with a central chimney and the foundations of a pair of long cabins with end chimneys mark the site of a group once known as Bird Hill, which stood a mile directly west of the Cleveland farm on a prominence overlooking the deep valleys bordering the Kentucky River. Here is virtually a miniature settlement (*Fig. 5*). An arrangement resembling Bird Hill apparently existed in the early log buildings at Winton on the Newtown Pike, and it was translated into more substantial materials with the construction of the main pavilion of brick in 1823, the log units continuing to serve as subsidiary buildings until after the Civil War.[5]

WATTS HOUSE   A distinctive log house is that standing on the extensive land holdings acquired by David Watts in the Boone Creek area (about four miles north of the Cleveland tract) between 1790 and 1824.[6] The structure presumably was put up soon after the first acquisition in 1790, which constituted 100 acres, unless it was already standing when this land was purchased from Charles Morgan. The deed included the word "premises," indicating some sort of improvement existing at the time of the transfer. The house has a full second floor, which signals a decided advance in frontier home building, people now being provided with the added protection and privacy of going upstairs to bed. The outstanding external feature is the immense stone chimney, over four feet deep and almost eight broad, with a stack rising above its outer edge—at present of brick, undoubtedly originally of small logs—well removed from the gable as a precaution against fire (*Fig. 6*). A

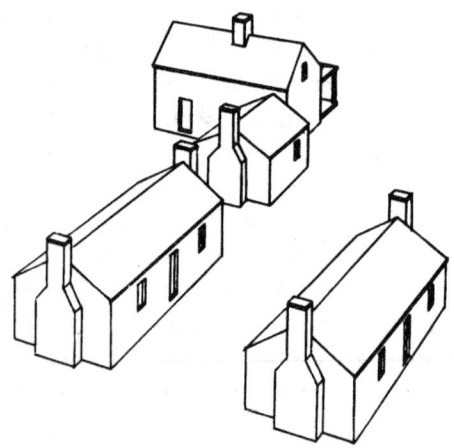

5. Bird Hill. Conjectural Restoration.

6. *Watts House. Somewhat Restored.*

single large room (17 by 22 feet) occupies most of the ground floor, reminding one of the medieval hall in serving all living purposes. A large fireplace, rectangular in plan, disclosing its primary function to have been cooking, is centered on the wall at one end of the hall in the great chimney. In the front corner across the room there is a boxed-in double staircase, composed of two flights of steps twenty-eight inches wide that rise in opposite directions to the floor above, which was divided by a partition into two chambers, entered only by means of their separate stairways (*Fig. 7*). At the present time all obstructions have been removed from the upstairs. A slanting casing was probably built over the steps to the larger chamber, permitting light to penetrate into the smaller room from the front window. A tiny low opening at the head of the outer stairway (which, incidentally, terminates only a few inches short of the sidewall) can be considered little more than a lookout hole. The larger chamber also has an opening of similar size and shape, but placed higher in the wall alongside the small fireplace. Presses under the stairways furnish storage space. A frame wing was added at this end of the log house, continuing across the back, probably about 150 years ago. It shows considerably more deterioration than the original structure. Now used only for storing hay, the building has not been lived in for several decades.

Externally resembling the Watts house are the Beatty and Henderson houses above the Muir Station and Bryan Station roads, the Pearson cabin west of the Elkchester and Redd roads, the forepart of the Foster house on East Hickman Creek north of the Richmond Pike, the eastern

8. *Muldrow House. Restored.*

portion of the Barr house a mile northeast facing Todds Road, and one in Athens.

MULDROW HOUSE   A house about equal in size to the Watts house is the log dwelling built by Colonel Hugh Muldrow about 1787 in the extreme west end of the county, midway between Rice Road and South Elkhorn Creek. The Muldrow house has chimneys at the ends, straight stone shafts that slope inward on three sides at the lower eaves level, and which probably had superstructures of small logs, replaced today by brick stacks (*Fig. 8*). Each story is divided

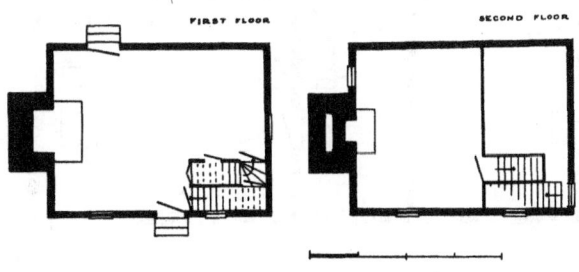

7. *Plans of Watts House. Restored.*

into two rooms. An enclosed staircase is fitted into the front corner of the smaller room (near end of our illustration), and irregularities in the ceiling plaster indicate the former existence of a companion in the front corner of the larger room as well, an arrangement that may be found also in stone houses, as in the Boggs house (1784), near Athens, and the Frederick Shryock house (1804), near Avon (*Figs. 26, 27*).

The neighboring Worley house, directly southward, is almost a facsimile of the Muldrow house. Other structures resembling it are the McLear house on the Nicholasville Pike at the Wilson-Downing Road, one on the Jacks Creek Road Extended, and a third near the northernmost tip of the county.

RANKIN HOUSE   One of the oldest houses in Lexington is at 215 West High Street. It is now clapboarded over, the lower front windows have been enlarged, and the building has been given modern conveniences and additions. The core of this structure is the log house built in 1784 for the Reverend Adam Rankin, the pioneer minister who established the First Presbyterian Church. The distinguishing feature of the residence is the separate stairhall connecting the 13- by 18-foot main room below with the three small chambers on the second floor (*Fig. 9*). The staircase has a closed stringer masking the ends of the steps in the manner of stairways in seventeenth-century houses on the east coast, with square banisters and newels fastened together with wooden pins. The batten door to the closet under the lower flight is equipped with pewter H-L hinges, crudely shaped. A larger family room and a master chamber over it were built later adjacent to the stairhall. Both floor levels are a step higher than in the original portion, and the roof is lower, so that the upstairs room has a sloping ceiling. The two end chimneys, accommodating fireplaces on both floors, are neatly built of brick, the breadth exceeding six feet, the depth about two (*Fig. 10*). A rear porch, overlooking Town Fork and the

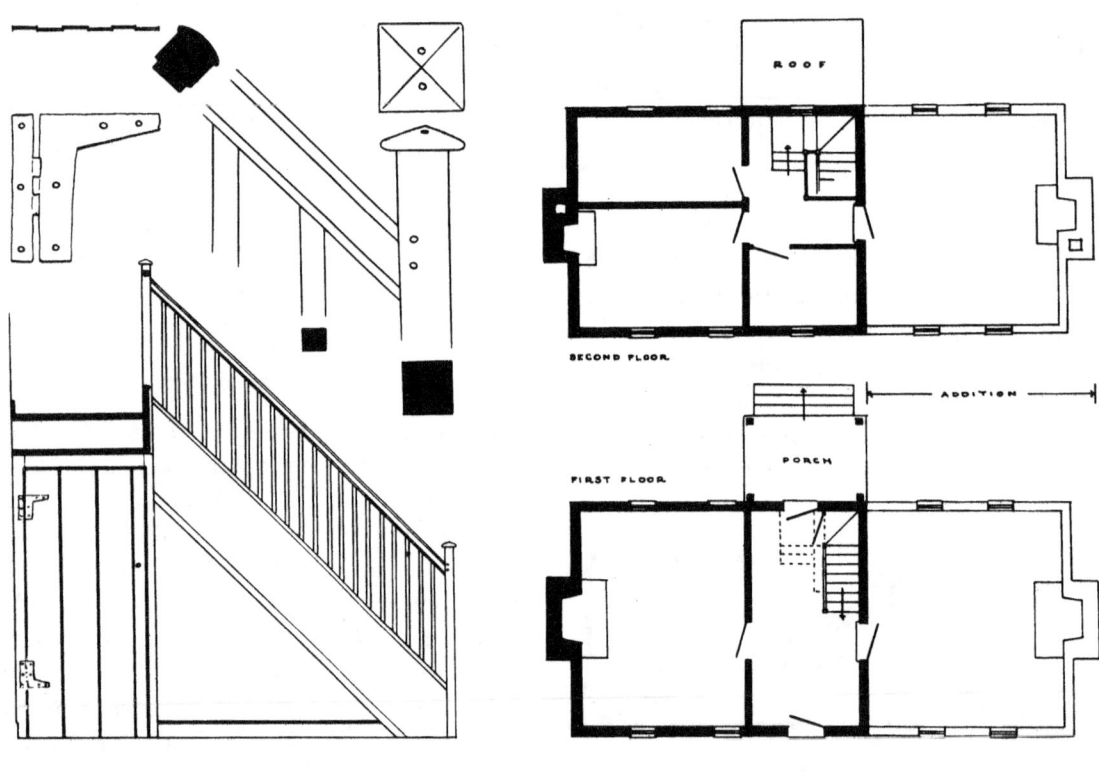

9. *Plans, Restored (right), and Stairway Details (left) of Rankin House.*

10. Street Front and West End of Rankin House. Restored.

11. Evans House.

town beyond, had chamfered posts—with lambs' tongues forming the transition from square to octagon—upholding the roof. The kitchen, in all likelihood, was in a separate building, the splayed sides of the fireplaces in the house proper denoting that no cooking was intended here.

The practice of enlarging the house through adding rooms resulted in long and varied shapes. Some builders strove for unity by covering their rectangular plan with continuous roof planes. The Carr house overlooking Shelby's Branch on the Tates Creek Pike, the Barr house on Todds Road west of the Chilesburg, and the Nutter house on the Lemons Mill Road near the Innes place have varying ceiling heights inside for the sake of achieving external regularity. The roof compensates for a slight setback in the front plane of the Evans house near Bird Hill (*Fig. 11*). Having one chimney within the outline of the house and the other protruding, as here, became a frequent device in early brick residences such as the Woolfolk and Keen houses in the west corner of Fayette County (*Fig. 50*).

Other owners were not so squeamish about having their houses avoid the look of being "added to." The resulting asymmetrical compositions sometimes are pleasantly picturesque, as in the case of the Stone house on the western stretch of Stone Road, the Clemens house two miles south on the Higbee Mill Road, the Bates house near the intersection of the Spurr and Yarnallton roads, above Locust Grove, and the Caldwell house on the Cynthiana (now Russell Cave) Pike.

CALDWELL-WILSON HOUSE Only a portion of the corner pavilion remains of the L-shaped log house begun about 1788 by Matthew Caldwell on his 400-acre tract on the upper branch of North Elkhorn Creek. The three sections running parallel with the stream were two storied, although the ceilings upstairs were quite low in two of them. The wing thrown out at right angles was single storied (*Fig. 12*).[7] A tall chimney was attached to the corner unit and a smaller one terminated the low ell. The upper chambers evidently were reached individually by stairways in the corners of the rooms. The property is designated "Wilson" on the Hewitt map of 1861, and is remembered today as the Sam Wilson place.

12. Caldwell-Wilson House. Restored.

13. Bowman Cabin.

Kentucky's geographic alliance with the southern states—despite the severity of her cold winters—is reflected in the appearance here of several types of log house the openness of which is reminiscent of semitropical planning. Chosen for discussion are three key examples.

BOWMAN CABIN   The cabin behind the Woolfolk house at South Elkhorn is believed to have been built by Colonel Abraham Bowman, who settled here shortly after establishing Bowman's Station six miles east of Harrodsburg in 1779. The half-dovetail log walls and stone basement provide single rooms on three levels, with cellar or garret reached by steps from ground level sheltered beneath an overhanging gable on the northeast end of the house *(Fig. 13)*. The outside stairways afforded more privacy to the room on the main floor, which alone has a fireplace. It also has two windows, on opposite walls, whereas the rooms below and above have but one each *(Fig. 14)*. Equipment and provisions were suspended from long wooden pegs driven into the wall beneath the overhang, and undoubtedly hung on the upper stair railing as well. The external stairway appeared on later brick buildings, on kitchens at Rose Hill on North Limestone Street in Lexington, Union Dale near the intersection of the Cynthiana (Russell Cave) Pike and Lemons Mill Road, and Grassland on Shelby Lane, as well as on the main pavilion at Winton, built in 1823 *(Fig. 79)*. Back of the Bowman cabin stands a small barn of

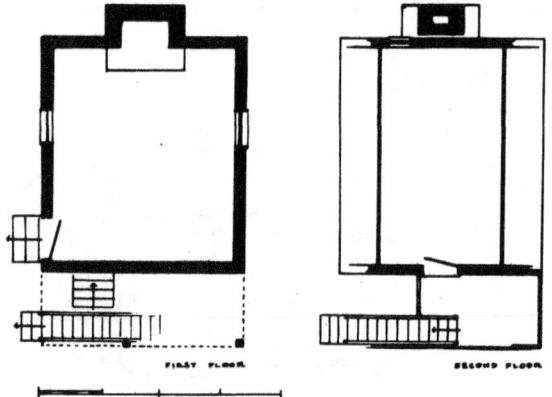

14. Plans of Bowman Cabin.

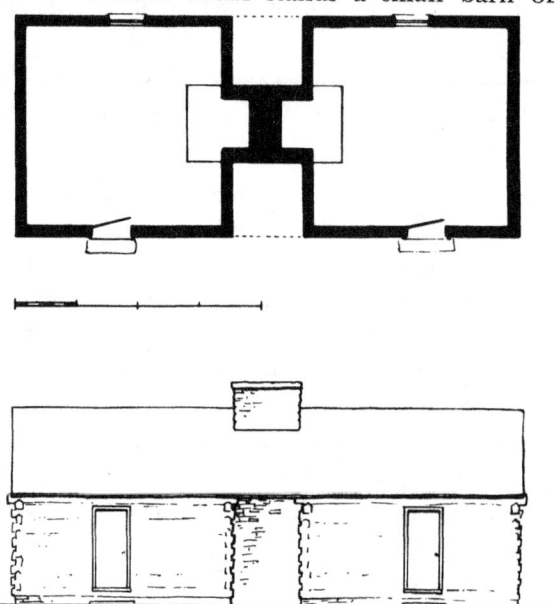

15. Plan and Elevation of Saddlebag Cabin. Restored.

squared walnut logs, with a breezeway between two enclosures.

SADDLEBAG CABIN   At the Berry farm on the Armstrong Mill Road, bounded on the west by Squires Road, is the remains of David Crenshaw's saddlebag log house of 1788. Of a type common to North Carolina,[8] although rare in the Bluegrass region, this one is composed of two approximately sixteen-foot-square rooms attached to opposite faces of a six-foot stone chimney, with open spaces to either side between the rooms *(Fig. 15)*. The recesses were large enough to stable several head of livestock, and must have had slat gates to keep the animals penned up at night. Construction here is of the notch variety, yet another small log structure (mentioned earlier) about 75 feet from the saddlebag house has half-dovetail joints.

DOGTROT HOUSE   The breezeway scheme employed in the log barn on the Bowman place also was incorporated in dwellings. The log house at Winton built during the 1790's is said to have consisted of a one-room and a two-room cabin connected by a porch open at both sides, called a 'possumtrot, dogrun, or dogtrot, which characterizes our third southern type. Dogtrots were incorporated in two-storied as well as in smaller structures. The Jones house, at the end of the Jacks Creek Road Extended, was composed originally of two square blocks of superimposed single rooms—only one of which was provided with a chimney—connected by porches, open on both levels, containing the stairway. The most notable dogtrot house in Fayette County stands on the Darnaby farm facing a tributary of North Elkhorn and the old Chilesburg (now Royster) Road. It may have been in existence when the land passed from George to Francis Smith in 1798.[9] The early form of the house was that of an inverted L, with the dogtrot crossing the midsection of the plan, a single room in the stem and two rooms in the base of the L on each floor (*Fig. 16*). A thin batten partition separates the adjoining rooms, each room having its own fireplace. Ascending from the open dogtrot, the stairway itself was enclosed, and probably the upper hall was closed too. The remarkable feature about the second story is that the walls above windowsill level are constructed of vertical logs (*Fig. 17*). The English had built entire houses in palisade fashion along the James River during the late seventeenth century.[10] Coming closer home, the French also built in this manner in the Mississippi Valley during the early eighteenth century, as instanced by the courthouse (*ca.* 1737) at Cahokia, Illinois.[11] A possible explanation for the use of vertical timbers in the Smith-Darnaby house may be that the full second story was created by lifting the roof several feet above its original position, and the upright log sections were inserted as logical and convenient

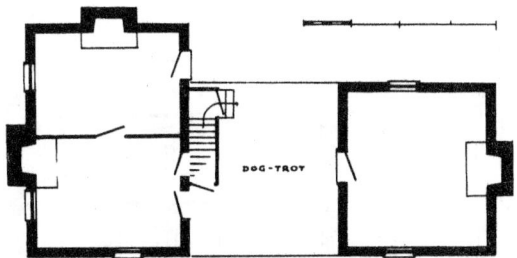

16. First Floor Plan of Dogtrot House on Darnaby Farm. Restored.

props. Flooring in each of the three chambers is of a different kind of wood,—poplar, ash, and wild cherry. The house has been remodeled several times. It was surfaced with clapboards and a low portico set before the walled-in dogtrot around the middle of the nineteenth century. Later a brick kitchen was attached to the rear of the single room, the back window made into a door, and a window opened next to the fireplace; the stairway was reversed and the entire house redecorated about 1930.

The final type of log house was built on a plan comparable to that of the better early brick houses of two stories, with an ample hall encompassing an open well containing a staircase, and large equisized rooms to either side. On the Gess farm, the house set farther back from the Walnut Hill and Chilesburg Road is a five-bayed example. The lower half of the end chimneys are stone, the upper half brick, perhaps signifying the addition of the second floor. The walls are boarded over, and wood pilasters at the corners denote midcentury remodeling.

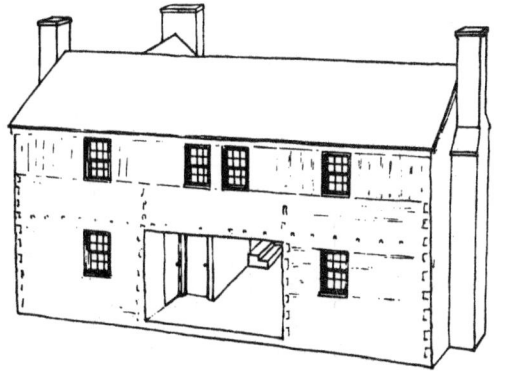

17. Dogtrot House. Conjectural Restoration.

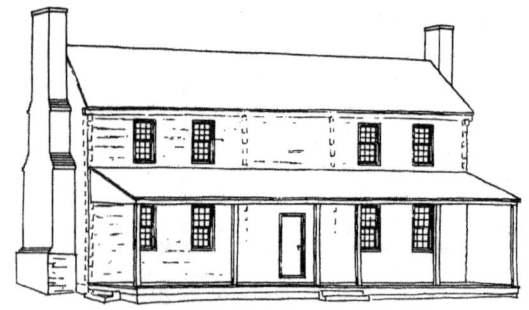

18. Webb House. Restored.

WEBB HOUSE   The Charles Webb house, built about 1790, on the Ware Road in the eastern corner of the county, catches one's attention by its handsome pair of chimneys, which are seven feet broad at the base and rise almost thirty feet. They have a four- to five-foot stone plinth, with shafts of fine Flemish-bond brickwork that are double-shouldered and admirably proportioned *(Fig. 18)*. The stairway rises on the righthand side of the central hall to a landing over the entrance, continuing on the left up to the second floor. There is no window in the front wall of the upper hall. The house has been covered with shiplapped boards and converted into a sort of chalet, with deep overhanging eaves. Plate glass sashes replace the early panes.

The log houses described date from about 1780 to 1815. Not many, however, were built after the turn of the century. Most of the log houses still standing have been weatherboarded and enlarged, some greatly so, like the rambling Alberti house on the Winchester Pike, which will be discussed in a later chapter. In other cases the log house became the service ell to a new front mass, one instance being the Darnaby house situated a mile northwest of the Alberti house, and another the O'Neal house below the crossing of the Leestown Pike and Yarnallton Road. Changes at Winton have been noted as similar. Some of the old log houses were relegated to the slaves after landowners had completed new brick residences for themselves, as on the Cleveland and Bowman farms. The rest were left to the tender mercies of the elements, and those that have disappeared are lost for all time. With the exception of Bird Hill and the Caldwell house, reduced to mere ghosts, most of the examples described stand a chance of surviving for several more decades. Fayette County is blessed with a presentable array of log houses, and their fate should not be left to chance. Definite steps need to be taken to insure their preservation, that future generations may have the opportunity of becoming familiar with authentic pioneer dwellings and other structures.

FRAME HOUSES 2

Log houses by 1800 were considered passé, and people living in them began to have them covered with siding of shiplapped boards and painted. Besides a stylistic effect, this provided protection from the weather. It is a remarkable fact that wind- and water-powered sawmills put in an appearance in America long before they were operated in England, where they were eschewed for promoting unemployment.[1] In the enterprising colonies, production was given first consideration, plenty of work being available for every industrious individual. Sawmills existed in New England prior to the second quarter of the seventeenth century. By the mid-1790's, mills were already beginning to change hands in Kentucky, as indicated by advertisements in the *Kentucky Gazette*. Offered for sale were one on Dick's (Dix) River, about twenty miles south of Fayette County, one on Salt River, fifty miles west, one on Grier's Creek in Woodford County, and another on Silver Creek in Madison County, each of the last two within eight miles of Fayette.[2]

With the accessibility of clapboards, houses no longer needed to have walls of solid timber. A framework could be erected of uprights and horizontals, braced by diagonal members forming rigid triangles, sometimes filled, and then sheathed. The structural system was identical to the half-timber construction of medieval Europe, whence it came. The European practice was to fill the voids of the frame with wattle-and-daub, which was then plastered over. The exposed structural timbers created a decorative pattern outlining geometric areas. Colonists, both in Virginia and Massachusetts, found that the climate in America demanded a protective covering, and generally used overlapped horizontal planks,

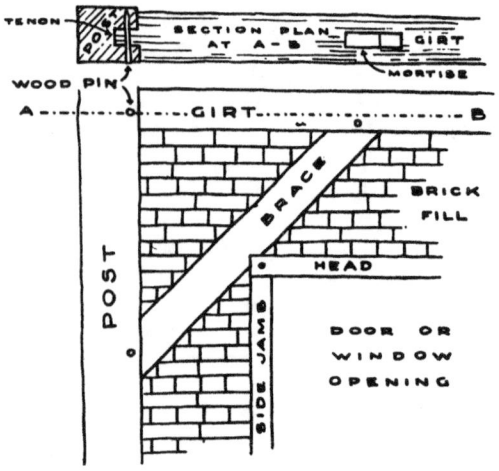

19. Elements of Typical Early Framing.

though sometimes shingle siding. In Kentucky the choice invariably was the former, and the filling here often was soft-burned bricks, which had begun to be manufactured locally during the 1780's. Bricks were inserted dry or with a mud binding, laid in horizontal rows of headers or bonded by alternating tiers of headers with stretchers. The latter method is known as English bond (*Fig. 19*). Affixed at short intervals were thin vertical strips of wood, called studs, onto which the clapboards were nailed.

John Bradford's newspaper during the late 1780's stated that Lexington, the "budding metropolis," was made up of "about fifty houses, partly frame and hewn logs, with the chimneys outside."[3] In *Charless' Almanack for 1806* Lexington is reported to contain "104 Brick, 10 Stone, & 187 Frame and log Houses," indicating the majority to have been built of wood.[4] Evidently frame houses once were plentiful in and around Lexington, but there are not many left. Their vulnerability to fire has reduced their numbers, either from conflagration itself or from fear of it, prompting replacement.

It is usually difficult to ascertain the age of frame houses. Those of various periods are similar in construction and have few applied details, which are easily replaced. An early frame house may be identified by small-paneled doors, as opposed to those having tall upright panels common after 1840. Further indications are the presence of chairrailing, and delicacy of tooling on mantels, stairways, and door and window frames, if these exist. However, in frame houses especially, such elements may mean merely the belated use of features outmoded elsewhere. The Barker house on the Cleveland Road above Athens, although built in 1846, has chairrailing in the living room, perhaps a concession to the exquisite mantel, which is said to have been taken from a house on East Main Street in Lexington standing in the vicinity of the present railroad tracks.

Selected for discussion are two houses in the southeast quarter of the county, a two-storied and a single-storied example.

MCCANN HOUSE   A typical frame house, originally of modest proportions but expanded into a sizable building, is the one nine miles from Lexington on the Todds Road, probably begun by Neal McCann about 1797. It is a two-storied rectangular block with brick end chimneys. Flanking a central stair hall are equisized sitting and dining rooms (measuring 12½ by 23½ feet) on the first floor. There is no extended well about the staircase, which is of the simplest type, having a chamfered post at the upper end and a crude column newel at the base of the railing. The doors downstairs are of the six-panel variety, with the exception of the front door, which has eight. On the second floor a large chamber adjoins the stairway; two smaller ones are opposite, with a hall chamber at the front. An enclosed stairway leads from the upper hall to the garret. Fireplaces in the basement attest to cooking having been performed below. A later detached brick kitchen, dating from the first quarter of the nineteenth century, is located about thirty feet to the rear and a little beyond the plane of the east end wall (*Fig. 20*). The two pavilions were connected by an L-shaped frame addition that seems to belong to the 1840's, though baluster posts suggest a prior date for the galleries (*Fig. 21*). A single rail between the posts, a yard above floor level, evidently served as a temporary rack for saddles, blankets, garments, tools, and other equipment.

Additional two-storied frame houses include the five-bayed McConathy house five miles south of Lexington, which originally had a detached two-storied frame kitchen, and the John Wilson house (1825) a mile southwest, on the Tates Creek Pike; the Berry house on the Armstrong Mill Road; the east end of the Devore house near the sharp bend in the Kentucky River; the back wing of Cedar Grove, on the east side of the upper extremity of the Cleveland Road; the Sidener and Coons houses on the Muir Station Road; the southern portion of the Moore house near Bethel on the opposite side of the county; the front block of the Arthur O'Neal house (1810) below the crossing of the Leestown Pike and Yarnallton Road, which is built over a stone-vaulted winecellar entered from the outside at the east end of the structure; and Elk View, George Caldwell's residence of 1793, below the Frankfort Pike near the Woodford County line. Elk View is composed of a four-bayed principal mass to which is attached a long, straight low ell at the rear having an open gallery along its northern flank.

LOCUSTON   At the far end of the row of primitive houses bordering the north side of the Jacks Creek Road Extended is a one-story frame dwelling that was designated Locuston on the Hewitt map of 1861. The present structure seems to have been built as the front to an older house

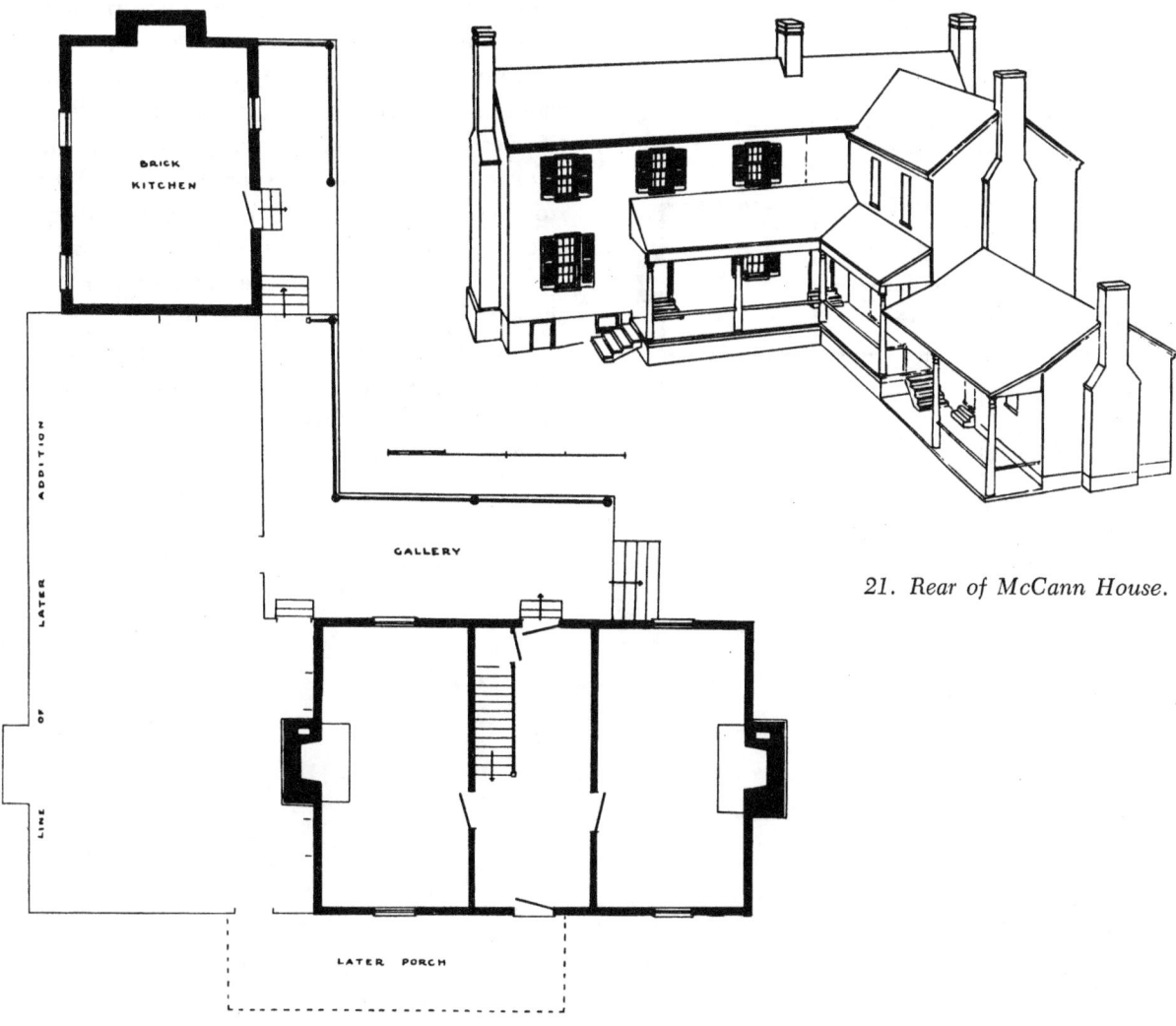

21. Rear of McCann House.

20. First Floor Plan of Neal McCann House.

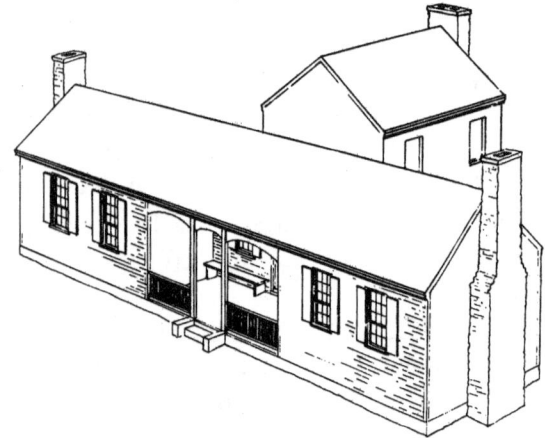

22. Locuston. Restored.

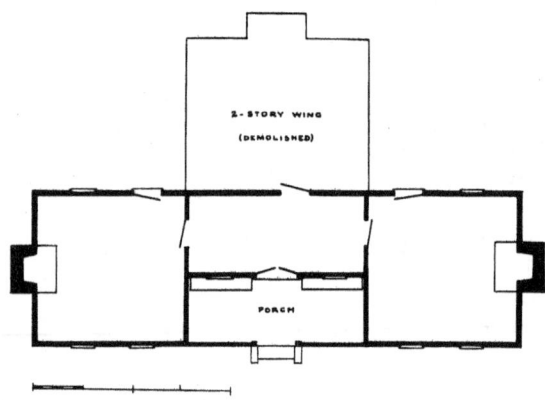

23. Plan of Locuston.

said to have been two-storied,[5] probably of log construction, occupying a larger foundation than the existing part. The long mass with which we are concerned is difficult to date, and can only be guessed as belonging to the decade between 1825 and 1835 on the basis of the reeded moldings enframing the front double doors, and the segmental arches that enliven its recessed portico (*Fig. 22*). The porch is eighteen feet broad and half the depth of the house, with railings, plank benches, and a crude cove running along the inner side of the plastered ceiling, making a pretense at refinement. The posts are spaced close together at the entrance, which seems to be a regional characteristic, as in contemporary brick houses, like the former Gist-Peck house on Maxwell Street (*Fig. 80*). A pair of stone blocks terminate the step ends. Single rooms, sixteen feet square, adjoin the middle section, each having three windows and an outside door, and a fireplace in a simply built, shouldered stone chimney (*Fig. 23*). The windows throughout are fifteen-paned. One might expect flush boards on the walls of the recessed porch, but shiplapping was used consistently.

A few ante bellum houses of later periods were of frame construction, but this system came into its own only during the impoverished years following the Civil War.

STONE HOUSES 3

THE DIRECTORY for 1806 informs us that only ten out of about 300 houses in Lexington at that time were of stone. Because the manufacture of brick began soon after the founding of the town, the small percentage of stone building is not surprising. Stonework seems to have been more in demand for the beautiful and excellently laid fences for which the Bluegrass is famous, and for foundations and chimneys of early timber houses, than for walls of dwellings. Yet stone houses did and do exist; they are to be found, like the log houses, mostly along the larger streams that flow through Fayette County. The land is plentifully supplied with limestone, and not a little skill was displayed by the masons in laying the gray blocks in smooth, true walls.

A small stone house which stood until 1957 near Lexington on the north side of the Old Frankfort Pike was called "Kentucky's Oldest House," the claimant contending that it was built by James McConnell about 1780.[1] The building was low and had flush chimneys (later with brick stacks) at each end. The centered front doorway was flanked by single windows obviously enlarged about the middle of the nineteenth century. Square openings (perhaps not original) were in the upper gabled ends. The house had little distinction, other than its questionable claim to priority.

A few years after the date ascribed to the McConnell house, Colonel Robert Patterson moved to his High Street property west of Lower (now Patterson) Street, where his first cabin was transported. He lived here twenty years, first building a two-storied log house on Main Street, and afterward a two-storied stone house farther south.[2] Two stone walls, presumably part of the

24. Rear of Patterson House. Appearance in 1939.

latter, are incorporated in the rear wing of the house at the summit of the hill on Patterson Street, now partly frame and attached to a front brick pavilion of about 1815 (*Fig. 24*).[3] The stone walls measure about 12 by 34 feet (left end and far side of the house in our view). The building they enclosed contained two rooms, with fireplaces opposite one another. Unless the wall height has been reduced, the structure in question cannot have been more than a story-and-a-half house, but of course it is not known what the present brick section may have replaced. The house, as it looked prior to remodeling during the 1940's, made an interesting composition of wood, stone, and brick, having that fresh quality that accompanies casual expansion.

BOGGS HOUSE   About eight miles southeast of Lexington, reached today from the Athens-Walnut Hill Road, a substantial and attractive stone house was built by Robert Boggs in 1784.[4]

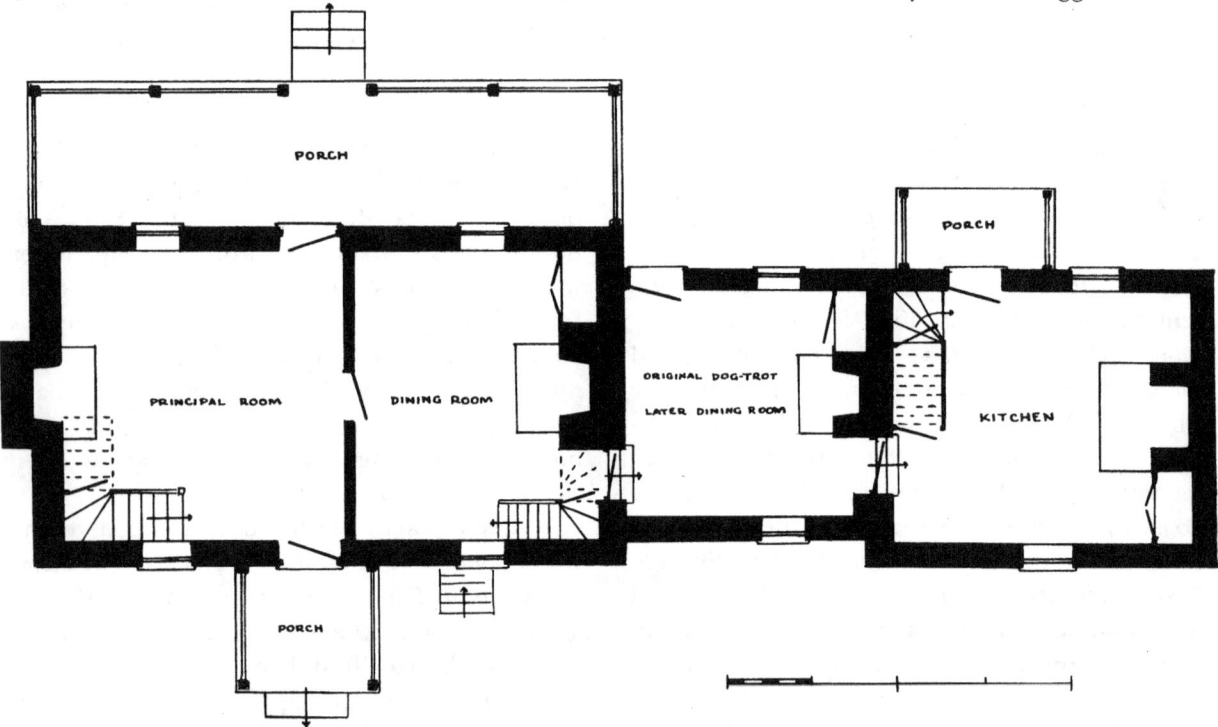

25. First Floor Plan of Boggs House.

The main portion housed two rooms on the first and two on the second floor, the pairs of rooms connected vertically by separate staircases (*Fig. 25*). A stairway over the larger pair continued to the garret. Porches at front and rear have chamfered posts five inches square, with slender square banisters to the railings, matching those of the corner stairways inside. A story-and-a-half stone kitchen was connected to the south wall by an open dogtrot, which—probably around 1800—was enclosed to make a new dining room (*Fig. 26*). Following the slope of the site, one mounts

the addition of cornices inside the two main rooms.

A stone house resembling the main block of the Boggs house is currently used as a guest house at Poplar Hill Farm on the Cynthiana (Russell Cave) Road. It was built by Robert S. Russell in 1791 on his half of his father's French and Indian War grant. The building has been altered. A second example is the house built by Frederick Shryock (brother of the builder, Matthias Shryock) on the Briar Hill Pike.[5] The date "1804" is incised in a circular stone set in the

26. Boggs House.

three steps from the kitchen to the later dining room, and three more from this room to the main portion of the house. The back service porch has chamfered posts four inches square. A kitchen stairway is enclosed by a batten partition, the chamber above lighted by a pair of dormer windows, a rare feature in the Kentucky area. The flush and protruding end chimneys on the principal block recall the Evans log house. The downstairs windows in the main block are fifteen-paned, the rest twelve-paned. The porch doors are nine-paneled, that between the main rooms six-paneled, and the one under the stairway next the former dogtrot is four-paneled. Modern changes to the Boggs house include the transfer of the basement stairs to the back of the house, the installation of plumbing conveniences, and

north gable. The Shryock house is slightly larger than the two-story pavilion of the Boggs house, the elements more regularly disposed, the chimneys similar, the stairways of equal size, and the windows all alike, both upstairs and down (*Fig. 27*). The chamber fireplaces are placed slightly off center to allow for the passage of flues from the lower fireplaces. A third house is Stoneleigh, below Sandersville on the Greendale Road, built by John Bell in 1810. It differs from the others in having four bays instead of three; the two innermost openings downstairs are doors to the equisized rooms, with an enclosed stairway adjacent to the front door in the west room. Cooking was done in the basement prior to the construction of a brick kitchen behind the low rear ell, probably in the 1840's. A building resembl-

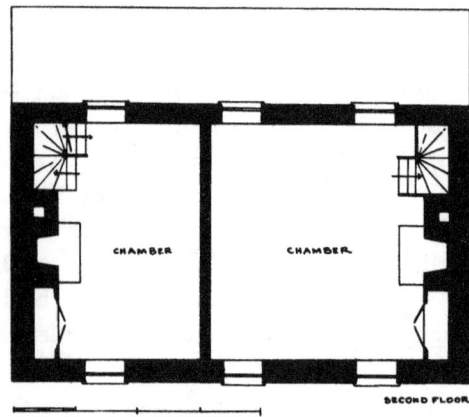

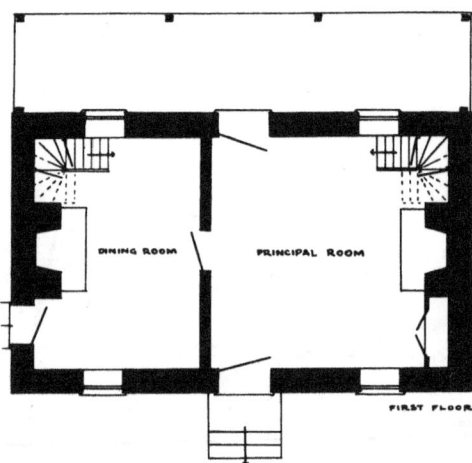

27. Plans of Shyrock House. Porch Conjectural.

28. West Front of Grimes House.

ing Stoneleigh is the inn beyond South Elkhorn Creek at the old bend in the Versailles Pike at Slickaway (now Fort Springs).

Other stone examples in the county are Piscatorial Retreat, an L-shaped one-storied house overlooking Town Fork near the county line, south of the Leestown Pike; and the west section of the two-storied Devore house, near Bird Hill.

GRIMES HOUSE The finest stone house existing in Fayette County is situated overlooking Boone Creek on the Grimes Mill Road. This house, built in 1813 by Charles Grimes, consists of a five-bayed, two-storied principal mass, with a lower wing, also of two floors, at one end, and a low ell attached to the latter at right angles (*Fig. 28*). The windows in the main block are tall, indicating high ceilings. The stonework is laid with exquisite care, especially the facade toward the stream, with alternating square and horizontal blocks reflecting the pattern of contemporary Flemish bond brickwork. The wood trim inside is finely detailed. In the parlor off the transverse stairhall the fireplace is flanked by shallow niches enframed by an archivolt springing from reeded pilasters, matching those of the mantel (*Fig. 29*).

Domestic building in stone had a short career in Fayette County. Not until after more than a generation had elapsed was another noteworthy house to be built of this material, and then it was to be a solitary example—the little romantic villa called Botherum, dating from 1851. As a matter of fact, stone played a minor role even in public buildings erected before the Civil War. In short, the use of stone ran far behind that of brick in early masonry construction in the Bluegrass.

29. Parlor Detail, Grimes House.

EARLY BRICK HOUSES 4

WITH THE advent during the 1780's of brick, which became the prevalent wall medium from this time onward, houses cannot be characterized according to the building substance. The use of brick, a processed material, signified that an advance had been made beyond the resources of pioneer days. Houses no longer were built only for shelter, but began to assume certain stylistic refinements made possible by the availability of a growing variety of materials, both imported and of local origin.

Brickmaking headed the list of home industries pertaining to building. One hears everywhere from the tenants of old houses in this locale the persisting tradition of bricks burned on the place, shaped from earth excavated for the foundations. In some instances (as at Sugar Tree Grove on the Winchester Pike) the report is substantiated by the remains of a pit in which the burning is thought to have occurred. The tonal variations of the dark red brick, indicating relative degrees of hardness, depended largely upon the intensity of heat achieved in the firing process. A notice on the front page of the *Kentucky Gazette* for March 31, 1791, announced that the subscriber was looking for a brickmaker, ending: "Enquire of the Printer," the equivalent of the box number used today in anonymous paid advertisements. Bricks also were procurable from brickyards, such as that of John Bob, who sought additional hands through the columns of the *Gazette* on February 25, 1797.

Quarried limestone was obtained in and around Lexington from very early times for use in foundations, stoops, copings, chimney caps, date corbels, and modeled keystones, and also sometimes for outside steps and windowsills,

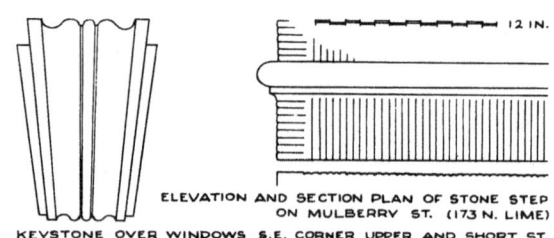

30. Cut Stonework Details.

where a material more permanent than wood was desired (*Fig. 30*). Brick was never employed for outside steps or windowsills, although it is frequently misapplied for these purposes in modern imitations of colonial houses. Stone sills and steps had a rounded molding called a nosing, derived from the shape of a wooden tread, overhanging the riser, which in stonework was tooled with upright ribbing.

Masonry was laid with thin joints of mortar composed of lime and a binder of fine "pike dust," gathered from the roads where the metal rims of wagon wheels scraped and pulverized rocks.[1] Lime was burnt in Lexington, and sold in 1797 by a merchant bearing the architectural name of Laurence Lintel. Stone lime brought nine pence per bushel, and slacked lime, used in plastering, marketed at six pence.[2]

Although the vertical construction of the house from this time on was formed primarily of brick, the horizontal and sloping members remained mostly of wood, including floors, inside stairways, and roofs. Indigenous woods cut into planks were ash, poplar, cherry, and walnut, according to a commercial notice of 1813; in one of 1820, pine was substituted for the hard ash.[3] Ash, as indicated, is to be found mostly in the earlier houses, and because of its rich golden yellow color is as beautiful as it is durable for flooring. By midcentury, the softer, green-grained poplar superseded it for this purpose. Wild cherry was prized for parts that were to be delicately worked, especially those to be kept unpainted, such as stairrails. It also was much used in cabinetwork. Walnut served for woodwork of larger scale, for baseboards (known contemporaneously as "washboards") and for solid wood dado panels, as in Fairfield.

Although wooden pegs played an important role in the assembling of the framing and woodwork, nails were indispensable for securing shingles, clapboards, and flooring. Nail-cutting machines had come into use in America during the Revolution, and some of the demand in Kentucky was supplied from the seaboard states, especially Maryland and Virginia. Yet as early as 1788 a shopkeeper in Lexington offered "a quantity of Nails of different sizes, of his own manufacture . . . [and at] as moderate terms as possible for Cash, Indian Corn, Tobacco, Butter, Tallow and Hogs lard." The local inventor, Edward West, who successfully ran a small steamboat on Town Fork fourteen years before Fulton's *Clermont* moved under its own power on the Hudson, seized the opportunity of devising "a *Machine* for the CUTTING OF NAILS," calculated to "cut one thousand pounds of Iron into Nails of any size, in twelve hours," warning those who had witnessed his model that he had taken the proper steps to obtain a patent on the invention. Confronted with such evidence of early mass production, one is surprised to find advertised as late as 1815 nails wrought by hand at the penitentiary, perhaps providing occupational therapy for the prisoners. At the turn of the century, cut brads and nails were available in 12-, 10-, 8-, 6-, 4- and 3-penny sizes.[4] Lexington supplied Cincinnati with nails, and purchasers came from as far as two hundred miles for them.[5]

Business houses selling nails also carried bar iron, some of it smeltered at the Bourbon Furnace in Bath County. Hand-tooled metal preceded cast work, which required heavier and more specialized apparatus than wrought iron; yet facilities for casting were established at an early date, a proprietor in 1790 seeking builders to work at the "Slate-creek Iron-works," the plant itself presumably being under construction or enlargement. The bulk of the castings of the first furnaces consisted of kettles and stoves, the age of architectural cast-iron work not coming into its own until the 1840's. The forger of decorative wrought iron was known as a whitesmith, the more menial blacksmith being occupied largely in shoeing horses. A newcomer opening his place of business at the corner of Limestone and Water streets advertised in 1809 that he engaged in "WHITSMITH'S [sic] WORK," including the making of "All kinds of plain and ornamental Railings . . . screens of different kinds, and smith's work in general. [signed] Thomas Studman."[6] During this period, iron building fittings were made to order.

The one article that invariably was imported into Kentucky was window glass, just as formerly it had been imported into the eastern states from England. Glassmaking did not become a commercial success in this country until after 1790, although, of course, transparent windowpanes had been in common usage for a century and a half before this time.[7] In 1792 the firm of Elliot & Williams announced the arrival of a shipment of "WINDOW-GLASS 8 by 10." No source of the import is given here, but later announcement (concerning a price reduction) discloses that one place of manufacture was New Geneva in southwest Pennsylvania. Later notices indicate nearby Pittsburgh to be the chief center supplying Bluegrass builders with glass. Before the close of the eighteenth century, windowpanes could be had in the following sizes: 7 x 9, 8 x 10, 9 x 11, and 10 x 12 inches.[8] These were set in sashes usually three across, two or three deep, sometimes four across and in three —in rare instances in four or more—vertical rows.

Hardware was another item generally shipped from beyond the mountains. The firm of Alexander and James Parker offered for sale in May and June of 1788 an assortment of "H & HL hinges," as well as cupboard and chest hinges, "Nob and pad locks," and also locks for furniture doors and drawers. The lion-and-unicorn seals found on several early nineteenth-century doorlocks (as at Stoneleigh) show that they originated in England. But mechanical aptitude in Kentucky was not limited to Edward West; in the Upper Street shop of James Lowry, "Door Locks and Locks of all kinds" were made and repaired during the 1790's.[9]

The bringing in of improved tools made possible more and better work in housebuilding and detailing. The Parker brothers' store in Lexington carried carpenters' tools, including "Chisels and gouges . . . Turners tools & wheel-irons Files & plane bitts . . . Saws assorted," as well as bolts and nails. William Leavy classified saws in his store as "Mill, Pit, Cross-cut, Hand, Tenon, Dove tail, and Compass."[10]

Color pigments also were imported, although in 1793 Edward Howe's Lexington mill was pressing linseed and flaxseed oil for use in paints. During this same year, Joseph Hudson listed a stock of "Prussian blue, Rose pink, Patent yellow, Red and White Lead, Lithage [lead monoxide], Spanish Whiting and Verdigrease." Robert Holmes in 1795 carried all but the last color, but in addition had "Yellow Ochre . . . Spanish Brown, Lamp-Black." In the second decade of the nineteenth century the selection was increased with "French Virdigris, Chinese Vermillion," "Terra de Sienna," "MINERAL GREEN," "TURKEY UMBER," "BLOOD LAKE," "Stone Ocher, Dutch Pink . . . King's Yellow, Spanish Brown . . . and Ivory Black." The Lexington White Lead Manufactory, beginning operations in 1815, claimed its "Dry White Lead . . . superior to any imported from Europe," and assumed a program of producing "White Lead ground in oil, Red Lead, Lithage, Patent Yellow and Sugar of Lead." Most painters' brushes undoubtedly were imported into Kentucky; however, James C. Ramsey advertised in 1802 that he would pay "Eighteen Pence per pound . . . for COMBED HOGS' BRISTLES" to go into the making of brushes, and admonished his compatriots "to encourage manufactures in their own country."[11] Paint was used mostly to cover wood, interior plaster walls generally remaining white. Exterior brick walls were invariably left unpainted up to the Revival periods.

Upon the introduction of brick the warm red of the houses lent a new architectural color note to the Kentucky landscape. The first brick houses are to be appreciated for their forthright design, the cubic forms given accent through use of bands or moldings of wood—painted in

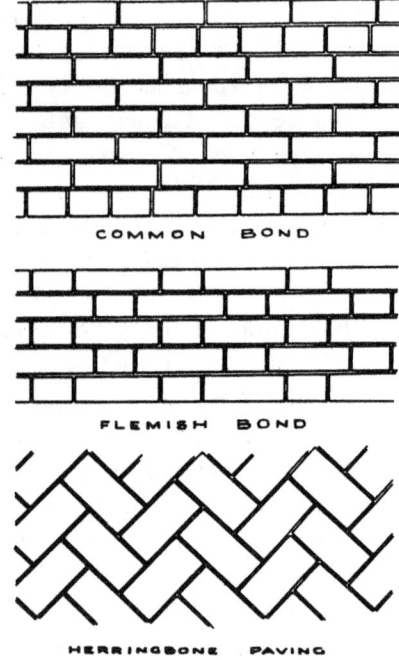

31. Early Types of Brickwork.

high values in contrast to the deep rose-hued brickwork—enframing rectangular doors and windows, and projecting as a cornice at the summit of the walls. Roofs usually were single-pitched with gable ends. Dormers were rare, light and ventilation for the garrets coming through windows in the gable ends.

The laying of bricks throughout the early period followed one of two modes. Walls several bricks thick were keyed together—bonded—by placing specified bricks crosswise. The simpler type consisted of a row of headers to several rows (usually four) of stretchers, which is designated *common bond*. It was, as the name signifies, the more generally employed of the two. The second type, alternating headers and stretchers in each course, produced a more attractive surface pattern. Called *Flemish bond* after the country of its origin, it was reserved for more important walls, such as the principal facade (*Fig. 31*). Pavings of brick were put down in a zigzag pattern known as herringbone. The usual size of bricks used in the Bluegrass area from the beginning up to the end of the nineteenth century was 2¼ x 4 x 8¼ inches.

Many of the early two-storied dwellings have a projecting stringer or belt course at the level of the upper floor. This is typically an eighteenth-century feature, yet it persisted at least as late as 1815. An existing elevation for the new three-storied academic building of Transylvania University, inscribed with that year's date, displays belts at the two upper floor levels.[12] Two-storied belted houses include Ellerslie (now demolished) on the Richmond Pike, the oldest part of the neighboring Christian or Price house, the William Gibson (1791) and McMahan houses, the house at the bend of the Walnut Hill Road, Spring Valley, Baxter (second floor removed) and Prather houses on the Jacks Creek Road and its extension, Shady Grove, the James Martain (1810) and Berry houses and Retreat (1792—razed 1955) on the Tates Creek Pike, the John Hart place (before 1813) on the Armstrong Mill Road, the Gist house on the Clays (Mill) Road southwest of Lexington, the Isaac Wells house (1794) near South Elkhorn, the Bryan house at the head of the Military Road, Hazel Dell (now destroyed) on the Harrodsburg Pike, the Hall house, Rose Hill and Stony Point on the Parkers Mill Road, Valley Retreat (altered) and Locust Hill (1790) near the west county line, part of the Moore house near Bethel, the Cooper house (at Spindletop Farm) on the Iron Works Road, and the Johnson house (altered) on the Cynthiana (now Russell Cave) Pike.[13] In Lexington a few houses having the horizontal stringer were the Matthias Shryock residence (1809) that stood north of the old Opera House on North Broadway, the house on the southeast corner of Upper and Short streets facing the courthouse, the Colonel Thomas Hart house (1798—demolished 1955) at Second and Mill, the Dr. Frederick Ridgely house a block east on Market Street, the Samuel Ayres house (1814) at High and South Limestone, and the Captain N. G. S. Hart house on Mulberry or North Limestone above Fourth Street. The center block of the Thomas January—later Tobias Gibson—house on West Second Street also has a belt course across the front. Belts seldom encircled the entire building. They logically appeared only on opposite sides, on those walls into which the main joists were thrust, but as often as not they are to be found on adjacent walls, as at Ellerslie (front and northwest side) and the Moore house (front and northwest end) in the county, and the corner Hart and Ridgely houses (the belts on the street walls) in town.

The belt is a survival of a medieval elaboration sprung from a structural source, as opposed to the more purely decorative devices inspired by classic design proper to the Renaissance. Early houses of Fayette County displayed other features traceable to origins in the Middle Ages. Conspicuous is the parapet wall surmounting the roofline at the gable ends and over party walls of contiguous houses, its existence between houses prompted by its convenience for either of the "parties" wishing to build on an additional story without having to disturb the adjoining roof. Such parapets once could be seen on dozens of old houses facing Vine and Water streets, between Limestone and Broadway, and north on Broadway to Main Street, the superstructure walls forming brick ridges connected with the chimneys, the flangelike front ends, supported on brick corbels, overhanging the plane of the facade (*Fig. 32*). A liking for brick elaboration often extended to the use of a horizontal brick cornice like that shown here. Cornices of brickwork also were used on county houses, such as the two-storied Bryan house between the Harrodsburg Pike and Military Road, the Featherstone house on West Hickman Creek below the Tates Creek Pike, the cottage on the north side of the Old Frankfort Pike facing the Elkchester intersection, the main part of Union Dale on the Cynthiana (Russell Cave) Pike, and the north end of the Dr. Dudley house just beyond the Lexington city limits on North Broadway extended, where parapets similar to those on the city row houses complete the gable extremities of this tiny pavilion.

A variation of the sloping parapet is the crowstep gable. The one existing Bluegrass example terminates the rear wing of the Doland house, facing Harriets Mill Road (now part of Bethel Road) in the northwest corner of the county. It is reminiscent of seventeenth-century Dutch houses in New Amsterdam and Albany, or of Medway, the South Carolina house built in 1686 by the Dutchman Jan Van Arrsens. Another southern example is the Newport Parish Church (1682) at Smithfield, Virginia, which, with its trussed interior, square tower, buttresses, tracery windows, and crowstepped east gable, is the most thoroughly Gothic building in America. The Arthur Allen house ("Bacon's Castle"—*ca.* 1655), in Surry County, Virginia, probably had parapets over the entrance pavilion, and certainly had curvilinear Flemish gables at each end, a further elaboration of the simple stepped type.[14]

While our attention is directed toward the housetops, it may be noted that the roofs of

32. *Parapets of Row Houses, West Side of Broadway South of Main Street.*

houses were generally more steeply pitched during the early period than in later times, the advance of the classic tradition causing roofs to become less in evidence—more nearly flat—with gables transformed into low pediments. The same principle of gradual reduction applies also to chimneys. Those showing the most direct inheritance from the Middle Ages were conspicuous, external, complicated forms, such as the east chimney of Locust Hill (1790) on Redd Road, its double shoulders resembling those belonging to the log Webb house. With few exceptions, chimneys remained on outside walls up to the time of the romantic influx, though after the beginning of classic domination they did not break through the wallplane and stacks became incidental in size and design. It should be mentioned that absence of built-in ovens is a regional peculiarity.

Another medieval feature was the decorated metal boxes that hung on the upper wall of buildings. These were funnels into which rainwater falling on the roofs was gathered and emptied into the slender downspouts. Often these heads were embellished with cast eagle reliefs, rosettes, and stars, as on the South Broadway row buildings (*Fig. 32*). A particularly handsome bombé downspout funnel, formerly on a West High Street house having a horizontal parapet concealing the roof, displayed the date of its manufacture—1835 (*Fig. 33*). It may be looked upon as a late example, but such funnels were still being made two decades later, as can be seen at Cedar Hall on the Bowmans Mill Road (*Fig. 139*). They became less noticeable among heavier Greek Revival ornaments, and—like most of these medieval elements—came into their own again during the Gothic Revival era.

A nonclassical element recurring in early houses was the porch support without base or capital, consisting of a square post, chamfered above rail height to within a few inches of the top. The transitions from four- to eight-sidedness were achieved through use of a reverse-curve notching designated lamb's tongue. We have come across it on the Rankin log house and Boggs stone house; among brick houses it occurs in the front porch of Hurricane Hall on the Georgetown Pike (*Fig. 34*), in the side gallery of the Farra house on the Versailles Pike (*Fig. 45*), in the original galleries of Locust Grove north of the Leestown Pike, in the back porch of a small house on the west side of Limestone three doors below Third Street, and in the rear gallery to the Norton (later Woolley) cottage that stood on High Street east of Limestone in Lexington. The porch on the Boggs house is the only one in good condition; most of the others are completely destroyed. Plain square posts also were used, as on the Isabella Lake house (*Fig. 48*) on North Limestone, and Stony Point (*Fig. 40*) on the Parkers Mill Road.

The lack of emphasis around openings was another medieval, as opposed to classic, architectural characteristic. Some of the fine eighteenth-century Kentucky houses northwest of Fayette—such as Liberty Hall (1796) in Frankfort and Federal Hill (1795) outside Bardstown—had boasted columned doorways and Adam-type mantels. But in the area with which we are concerned, the clean-cut opening was given preference. A case in point is the Hunt-Morgan house in Lexington, where a side door and service entrance were pedimented and the great front door was not (*Fig. 64*). The fanlight doorway with leaded glass in geometric patterns is a direct descendant from medieval architecture.

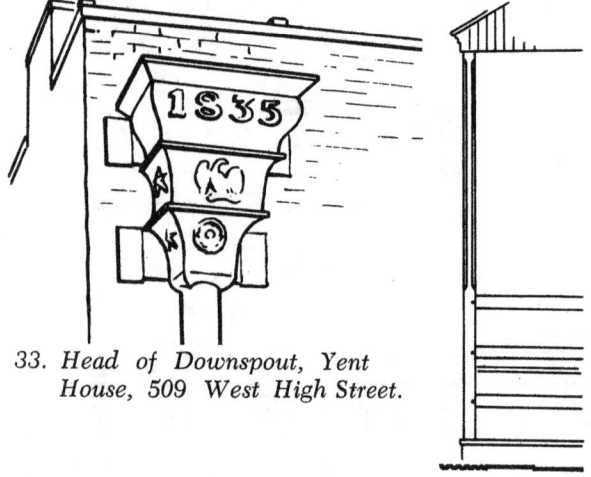

33. *Head of Downspout, Yent House, 509 West High Street.*

34. *Porch Detail, Hurricane Hall.*

The disregard for absolute symmetry in most ante bellum Bluegrass houses is another trait reflective of the Middle Ages. Service wings were placed off axis from the main block, and as a rule, detached dependencies were not disposed according to an axial layout. The few exceptions in which symmetry prevailed were made possible by relegating the service rooms to the basement, as in Mansfield and Corinthia, both of which belong to the later Greek Revival period. The outstanding earlier examples were by the eastern architect Benjamin Henry Latrobe, one being Ashland, where the service wing balances a chamber wing on the opposite side of the main mass. In Latrobe's design for the John Pope house, the kitchen was included on the ground floor in the continental manner, but the house as built provided for cooking in the usual Kentucky ell to one side at the back (*Figs. 71, 72*).

The prominence of the stairway is the most medieval feature of the interiors of these early houses. One recalls how, at Jefferson's classic home, Monticello, the stairs are narrow and tucked away in alcoves. In the house of the feudal ages, distinguished from that of antiquity by its verticality, the stairway acquired architectural importance. In the two most distinguished Fayette County residences antedating 1800—Ellerslie and Hurricane Hall—the staircase is in a sort of living hall, the second example having originally a fireplace in the hall itself, making it less a passageway connecting rooms than an important reception center in its own right. The lower floor of the front mass of early nineteenth-century Locust Grove is divided into two rooms, of two and three bays' breadth, with the staircase against the division wall in the larger room. Both interiors have fireplaces, and both have entrances from the offcenter front porch. Somewhat the same scheme was followed in the Keen house (1805) on the Versailles Pike and Woolfolk house on the Bowmans Mill Road, with the difference that in this pair the rooms are equisized and the stairways (now removed) were enclosed, undoubtedly for the practical reason of conserving heat in winter (*Fig. 50*).

Classic elements already had put in an appearance in Kentucky architectural details before the close of the eighteenth century. During the early period of the building up of Fayette County, therefore, the classic could not have the stimulating impact of something freshly introduced from the eastern states to become the latest fashion rage. It amounted, rather, to a quiet symbol of refinement determining the elaboration of mantels and doorways, niches, arched hallway screens, chairrails, external cornices (rarely, if ever, used in rooms), and porticoes. The focus of the room was the fireplace, upon the enframement of which the greatest care and artistry were lavished. Pilasters or colonnettes usually supported a mantel shelf for displaying the best candlesticks, clock, or china, the shelf often a breakfront or serpentine cornice, the edge sometimes intricately carved, the panels of the flat frieze below embellished with sunbursts, star and lozenge shapes, ovals and circles, swags and interlacings, reeding, fluting, roping, and a variety of other carved and gouged shapes (see *Figs. 51, 67*). The nongeometric motifs, such as floral forms and figures, were not likely to be carved from wood but cast in pewter, lead, or other white metal, nailed in place, and painted (see *Fig. 94*). Carving on doorways, arches, and chairrailings was similar to that on mantels (*Fig. 74*). External work generally adhered more to orthodox elements than that inside, cornices, for instance, being composed of cyma moldings, modillions, and dentils (*Fig. 35*). Some of the more profusely decorated house cor-

35. *Cornice Detail, N. G. S. Hart House, North Limestone above Fourth Street.*

nices are also the earliest, as on the original block of Hurricane Hall (*Fig. 45*).

Carving was performed by a craftsman other than the builder. Although there were resident specialists to be sure, a good portion of the work was executed by itinerants, who carried samples of their skill with them as they traveled about seeking employment wherever houses were being built. Woodwork was composed of small sections that were assembled and painted. Out of the general anonymity of this craft emerges the name of one carver whose artistry was of the highest order. He was Mathew P. Lowery, who settled in Mercer County about 1800, and practiced in and around Harrodsburg for three or four decades. He is credited with the front doorway and mantels at Clay Hill (1812) near the Harrodsburg city limits on the Danville Pike, and his name has been linked with the woodwork of Mount Airy, the Andrew Muldrow house in Woodford County, unfortunately burned on October 8, 1945.[15] Comparable work in Madison County is to be found in Castlewood (razed in the mid-1940's),[16] and in the Ezekial Fields house now incorporated into Gibson Hospital in Richmond. It must be admitted that existing carving in Fayette houses does not measure up to the best in surrounding counties, the most eligible contestant being that in Mount Hope on Gratz Park, if indeed the mantels in this much-remodeled residence can be accepted as original. Attention is called to the reeding on the front window frames of Mount Hope, with the identical profile lathe-turned in the corner blocks, a refinement also used at the Gist-Peck house on Maxwell Street and Woodlands—both demolished —and related to fluting used in a number of elliptical fan doorways, including that of the Hunt-Morgan house (*Fig. 63*), Poplar Grove (*Fig. 76*), the McCoy house north of Lexington, and Norton cottage (*Fig. 90*). The last two are no longer in existence.

Workers in stone made a bid for some of the carved mantel trade. At the opening of the nineteenth century a team announcing itself as "PETER PAUL & SON, STONE CUTTERS from LONDON, . . . living on the Woodford road, Lexington," informed the "public at large" that they performed all sorts of jobs requiring stone, which included, besides memorials, "Polished MARBLE CHIMNEY PIECES, and FREESTONE ditto."[17] The stonecutter, of course, carried on a trade quite distinct from that of the stonemason. There are remains of exterior detailing in stone, but the author has not come across a stone mantel in Fayette County predating the Greek and Gothic Revival periods. Certainly Peter Paul remained in Lexington, building a home for the son at 220 Market Street in 1816, and perhaps someday one of his chimneypieces will come to light.

Early stucco work is as scarce as marble mantels, although it, too, is known to have been available. During the second decade of the nineteenth century an artisan styled Robert H. Armstrong, from Charleston, South Carolina, professed to execute "Stoco-work, plain Plastering; cornices, plain or ornamented; centre pieces, plain or ornamented."[18] His address was "Mr. William Clark's Hotel, at the corner of Mulberry and Short Street," signifying that he was not settled. One suspects that he did not remain here long, for his name does not appear in the 1818 city directory. Except for enframements around openings and paneling—both of wood— three-dimensional interior detailing, so far as is known, did not appear above chairrail level until cornices and entablatures and fancy centerpieces became popular during the Greek Revival era. If Robert Armstrong's handiwork could in any wise measure up to that of other Charlestonians, such as Ezra Waite, who produced the exquisite reliefs in the Miles Brewton house (1769),[19] it would seem a pity that his talent was not put to better use in and around Lexington.

Pictorial ornament apparently was more favored. The cheaper and more readily obtainable form of mural was wallpaper, which was sold at the emporium of Joseph Hudson—along with paints—at least as early as 1793, advertised as "stampt paper for rooms." A few years later an art and decorating concern, F. Downing & Co., besides cutting profile likenesses with the "physiognotrace," engaging in gilding and japanning, and restoring and repairing old looking glasses, undertook house and sign painting "in all its branches," including "*Papering,* and decorating apartments in the most finished style." George Ruth in 1809 advertised "PAINTING GLAZING AND PAPER HANGING." Wallpaper designs that reached Kentucky are indicated by the subjects available in the stock of Downing (perhaps F. Downing ?) & Grant, recorded in the *Kentucky Gazette* in 1816.[20] The 1818 city directory locates the store on Short Street. Downing & Grant had "just received an elegant assortment of *French and American Paper Hangings.* . . . Among them there are a few sets of the Monuments of Paris, Views of the City and Bay of Naples, with an elegant representation of Mount Vesuvius, Captain Cook's Voyage in the Pacific Ocean, and a representation of his death by the Owyhee nation, a view of the chase, Paul and Virginia, and some views in India, They also have received a few handsome figures for chimney boards." The scene designated "a view of the chase" may have been that of the paper hung on the walls of Woodlawn in Madison County. Although the house was not built until 1822, the paper is said to date from 1814.[21] It bears the mark of Jacquemort and Bénard, the successors of Reveillon, the outstanding French wallpaper manufacturer of the late eighteenth century. Other sets of this hunting scene are on the walls of the John A. Andrews house (1818) in Salem, Massachusetts, the Haverhill parlor—from a Massachusetts inn built in 1818—in the Metropolitan Museum of Art, and fragments in a Virginia room near Washington, D. C.[22] The amusing story is told in connection with the Kentucky house that the walls were too tall for the wallpaper and the paperhanger had to wait the better part of a year for "more clouds" to be sent from Paris. The paper was sold and removed from the walls in 1929.

Antique wallpaper is preserved in the parlor of Hurricane Hall, where it was hung to celebrate a wedding in 1817. Presses to either side of the chimneybreast were removed to provide sufficient surface for full display of the scene. In fact, the extra space proved to be a little superfluous, and the situation was remedied by inserting on the right side of the chimney—somewhat out of context—the fragment cut out for the hall door. The subject is an Italian pastoral panorama with Roman ruins in the foreground, and glimpses of a body of water and a Renaissance city in the background. Scattered about are figures and domesticated animals. Considering the date, one wishes to identify the scene as "the City and Bay of Naples" listed among the Downing and Grant stock; but there is no "elegant representation of Mount Vesuvius," though the ruins may suggest those in the vicinity of Pompeii. The rolls of paper are said to have arrived wrapped in tinfoil. The colors are remarkably bright and fresh after fourteen decades of exposure.

Painted murals likewise figured in the decorative scheme in central Kentucky. During the late 1820's and 1830's, Alfred Cohen, from southern France, painted nostalgic, primitive Mediterranean landscapes on the parlor walls of Pleasant Lawn, Airy Mount, and the McConnell house in Woodford County.[23] In Fayette, Horace E. Dimmick, proprietor of the Great Western Manufactory, makers of furniture, venetian blinds, mattresses, featherbeds, etc., at 15 Hunt's Row (Water Street between Mill and Upper), offered his services in executing "*Landscape Painting* on walls or fire boards, in oil or distemper colors," as well as any other kind of "ORNAMENTAL PAINTING as may be wanted."[24] On the dining room mantel at Vaucluse on the Georgetown Pike are two painted frieze panels depicting stiff allegorical figures in dark landscape settings, believed to have been conceived by Oliver Frazer's daughter Bessie (1841-1910) during her early years. Oliver Frazer was one of the leading portrait painters in central Kentucky from the late 1830's to the time of his death in 1864.[25]

The medium that tended both to elaborate and standardize architecture in provincial districts was the builder's handbook. Several sources provide us with information concerning the exact volumes known or used in Fayette County, which apparently made some contribution to house design here in the late eighteenth century and opening decades of the nineteenth. The earliest record is an advertisement of books for sale at John Bradford's bookstore. In the June 27, 1795, issue of the *Kentucky Gazette*, Bradford listed three volumes: "Swan's Architecture," "(*Paine's*) [*sic*] Architecture," and "Town & Country Builder."

The first refers to one or the other of two books by Abraham Swan: either *The British Architect*, originally published at London in 1745 and republished at Philadelphia in 1775—the first book on architecture printed in America—also reprinted at Boston in 1794; or *A Collection of Designs in Architecture*, London, 1757, and Philadelphia, 1775.[26] "Swan's Architecture" also was offered for sale by MacBean, Poyzer and Company at Main and Cross streets (Broadway) in 1798.[27]

The second book mentioned by Bradford undoubtedly is one of the small publications by William Pain, *The Builder's Pocket-Treasure*, London, 1763, and Boston, 1794, or *The Practical Builder*, London, 1774, and Boston, 1792 (a reprint of the fourth London edition of 1787). Or it might conceivably be either *The Practical House Carpenter* or *The Carpenter's Pocket Directory*, published in London during the early 1790's, though not reprinted in this country until 1796 and 1797 respectively at Boston and Philadelphia. The *Pocket-Treasure* was advertised by title at Johnson & Warner's bookstore, corner of Main and Mill streets, in 1810.[28]

The third item in the Bradford advertisement was John Norman's *The Town and Country Builder's Assistant*, produced in Boston around 1786. In addition to delineations showing architectural treatment of special features, as in the other books, it contained designs for stairs in various polygons and diagrams for building odd-shaped roofs. Plates XLVI and LIII suggest the forms of the flankers on Woodlands (*Fig. 70*).

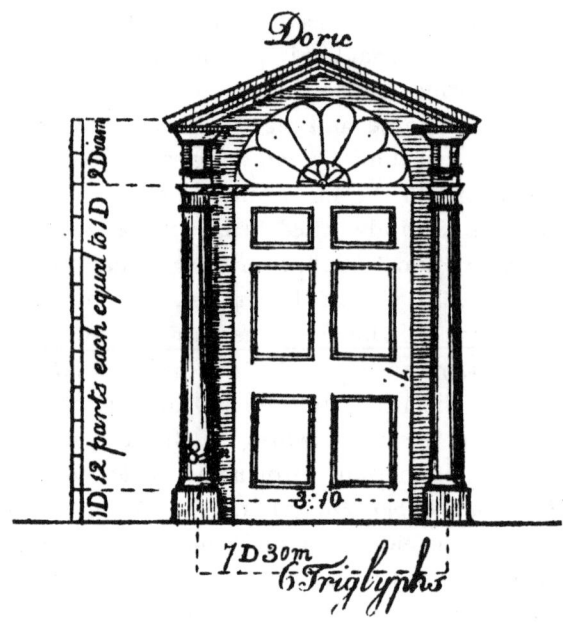

36. Design for a frontispiece. Asher Benjamin, The Builder's Assistant (Greenfield, 1800), plate 12 (detail).

Two books by Owen Biddle were listed as available during the second decade of the nineteenth century. Johnson & Warner announced a copy of "Biddles Architecture" in 1810, and Daniel Bradford the "Carpenter's Assistant" in 1813.[29] These are assumed to refer to *The Young Carpenter's Assistant*, the first edition gotten out in Philadelphia in 1805 and a second one in 1810. Doorways with half-moon transoms in the *Carpenter's Assistant* suggest those of Vaucluse (*Fig. 61*), Coolavin (*Fig. 92*), and Ashland (*Fig. 188*).

Conclusive evidence of the ownership of an early guide by a Lexington builder is offered by an extant copy of Asher Benjamin's *The Builder's Assistant* (1800) which was a third edition of *The Country Builder's Assistant* (1797), both produced in Greenfield, Massachusetts. The book belonged to Matthias Shryock and is now owned by Mr. Frederic L. Morgan of the Louisville architectural firm of Nevins and Morgan. Among the designs for architectural details is plate 12, for a frontispiece, with fanlight remarkably close to that of the front door of the classic cottage on Main Street (*Fig. 36*—compare *Fig. 106*). This enframement resembles those of Vaucluse and Coolavin, mentioned above. Plate 29 in the same book represents the facade of a two-story house with a belt course and a Palladian doorway suggesting those of the 1816 main building of Transylvania University (*End Papers*), and the front doors of a small house on the southeast corner of Second and Jefferson streets in Lexington (recently obliterated), and of Winton on the Newtown Pike. Plates 31 and 32 give the plans of a house with octagonal and pavilions attached to hemicycles, each with its own chimney, a feature in common with the Woodlands flankers, but differing in having low-pitched pyramidal roofs instead of bonnets, and in enclosing circular rooms within the polygonal forms.

Although the early city directories give us the names of men in the building trade, we have scanty information as to what buildings were executed by them. David Sutton has been named designer of the 1806 three-story brick Fayette County courthouse, built by Hallett M. Winslow and Luther Stephens.[30] Latrobe designed and Asa Wilgus built the John Pope house east of Rose Street, 1811-1814. Samuel Long is said to have constructed the house on the northeast corner of Market and Second streets for General Thomas Bodley about 1815.[31] Some of Matthew Kennedy's work has been identified and some of Matthias Shryock's is known, and will be discussed later. But on the whole, the builders of early residences remain anonymous. At least a few buildings of this period came into existence from previously prepared drafts, as indicated by a notice in the local newspaper in 1804, which reads: "DRAWING. Ground plans, elevations, and sections for buildings of any description, in the most plain and elegant style; also Bills of materials, and estimate of expenses, to execute such plans, as will be given, may be had at a small expense, by applying to. O. P. ROBERTS, at Mr. John Keiser's, Lexington."[32] Keiser was the proprietor of an inn on Short Street. Roberts' name does not appear among those of residents in the city directory issued two years later, and one assumes he did not remain here long. Then, as now, the person wishing to build a house could obtain graphic representations and estimates before ground was broken, but it is unlikely that the drawings often included more than floor plans.

The best known surname in Kentucky architecture is Shryock—originally Dutch, Van Schrieck—associated with several members who distinguished themselves as builders. The founder of the family in Kentucky was Matthias Shryock (1774-1833). He came from Frederick County, Maryland, and then returned to fetch a bride in 1798. In 1809 he built a home on the west side of North Broadway, between Short and Second streets.[33] The double-storied brick house, two rooms deep and three bays wide, had a belt course, parapets at each end, with a stone corbel inscribed with the date, and carved keystones above the windows.[34] Matthias Shryock erected an Episcopal church on Market Street about 1820, the predecessor of the present Christ Church building that replaced it twenty-seven years later.[35] He also constructed a house on North Limestone, where Lexington Junior High School now stands.[36] His name is listed as having worked on the old Transylvania Company building once located in the north end of Gratz Park.[37] Matthias Shryock died during the cholera epidemic in June of 1833, and his body was interred in the Episcopal Cemetery on East Third Street, the grave marked by a monument in the form of a miniature Greek temple, erected by his son Gideon. Gideon Shryock and a younger brother, Cincinnatus, followed their father's calling.

The builder Michael Gough (1778-1855) was closely associated with Matthias Shryock, both professionally and through marriage ties, Shryock having married Gough's sister. The two men from Maryland practiced as partners, and Michael Gough lived in the same block. His carpentry shop was located in the alley west of Broadway. Michael Gough built a house adjacent to the north side of the Shryock home for his son Jerry, and constructed another for a second son, Perry, on the same side of Broadway two doors beyond Third Street.[38] Neither of the sons entered the building profession. Michael Gough was buried in the Episcopal Cemetery on East Third Street.

Since settlers of Kentucky had come primarily from the eastern states of Virginia, Maryland, Delaware, the Carolinas, Pennsylvania, and New Jersey, as expected we find the architecture of these areas reflected in the initial brick houses of Fayette County. Like the average eastern example, they are simple in form, plan, and decoration. We shall see that the evolution of Bluegrass architecture is a growing away from these early characteristics. However, it is to be remembered that the log house had advanced to being two full stories in height, which was carried over into frame construction and stonework, thence into houses built of brick. Thus we shall find some of the earliest brick dwellings of quite ample proportions, preceding others of smaller dimensions prompted by a later and different ideal.

ELLERSLIE   Begun five years before Kentucky gained her statehood, Ellerslie (razed in 1947), on the Richmond Pike, looked the way one would expect a good-sized, late eighteenth-century house built in the wilds of western Virginia to look. Built about 1787, it was perhaps the first brick house in Fayette County. The original residence of the Honorable Levi Todd was a rectangular mass 22 by 63 feet, containing three square interiors on the first floor. The middle division featured a staircase of two long flights without open stairwell in one corner. The western chamber upstairs approximated the size of the room below, whereas the balance of the second floor was subdivided into a T-shaped hall, stairway to the garret, and three small chambers (*Fig. 37*). The five-bayed facade was pierced by small windows, those above of lesser height than the ones below (all enlarged at a later date), and having, like the wide, transomed doorway, projecting keystones. The front and right flank walls were belted at the second floor level (*Fig. 38*). The house was doubled in size, probably in 1792, when a hundred acres were added to the property of Levi Todd from the estate of his brother John, who was killed at the battle of Blue Licks. The addition deprived the two smallest upstairs rooms of outside exposure, but three large rooms were gained on both floors, besides a considerably larger garret. The new second floor suite was entered across a platform bridging the topmost steps of the first flight. The final plan bore some resemblance to that of Prestwould, in Mecklenberg County, Virginia.[39]

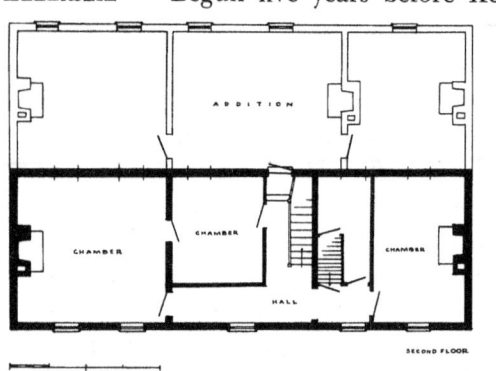

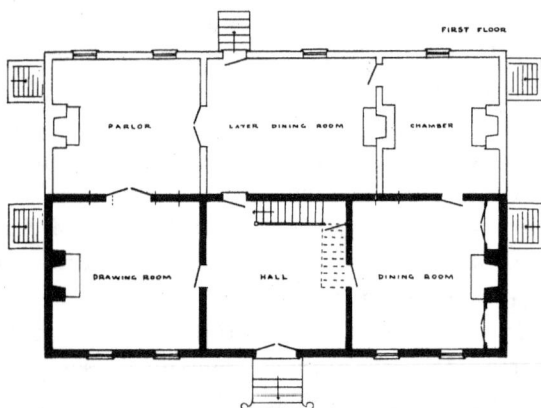

37. *Plans of Ellerslie. Unshaded portions indicate later addition.*

Levi Todd was the first clerk of Fayette County, and he kept the county records in a small stone house in the yard. It burned on January 31, 1803, destroying many of the documents and injuring others. Copies made from these remnants are still referred to as the "Burnt Records." The clerk died soon afterward, and Ellerslie went into the possession of John Todd's widow, who married Robert Wickliffe. At the time of the Civil War it was owned by Mrs. Margaret Preston. The house itself, after a long period of abandonment, was razed in 1947.

STUART HOUSE   A house patterned after

38. Ellerslie. Restored.

Ellerslie is that east of the intersection of the Athens-Boonesboro and Walnut Hill-Chilesburg roads, built for the Reverend Robert Stuart on a tract of 168 acres presented to him by his father-in-law, Levi Todd, about 1805.[40] Like Ellerslie, it is five bays wide, but the Stuart house was two rooms deep from the beginning, with a central stairhall traversing it from front to back. There is no belt course. The lower windows are 18-paned and those above 15-paned. The only unusual feature was the entrance motif: the front door, composed of double leaves with side lights and a wide transom, was sheltered by a small porch, the steeply pitched roof of which necessitated the elimination of a center window in the upper wall. The house now has been made to face in the opposite direction, with the porch removed and the old entrance boarded up.

PRICE HOUSE Geographically and in other respects closer to Ellerslie than the Stuart house is the Price house, built by Pugh or Williamson Price during the first decade of the nineteenth century, located a little over a mile northeast of the Todd house. It was originally a three-bayed, belted structure having two rooms on each of its two floors, the stairway in the smaller interiors, and a pair of additional rooms (the far one a kitchen) in a low wing.[41] Like Ellerslie, this block was enlarged, although separated from the new part by a narrow passageway containing a steep flight of steps. An imposing stairhall was added, at right angles to the corridor, spanning the entire north end of the house (*Fig. 39*). Possibly these improvements occurred

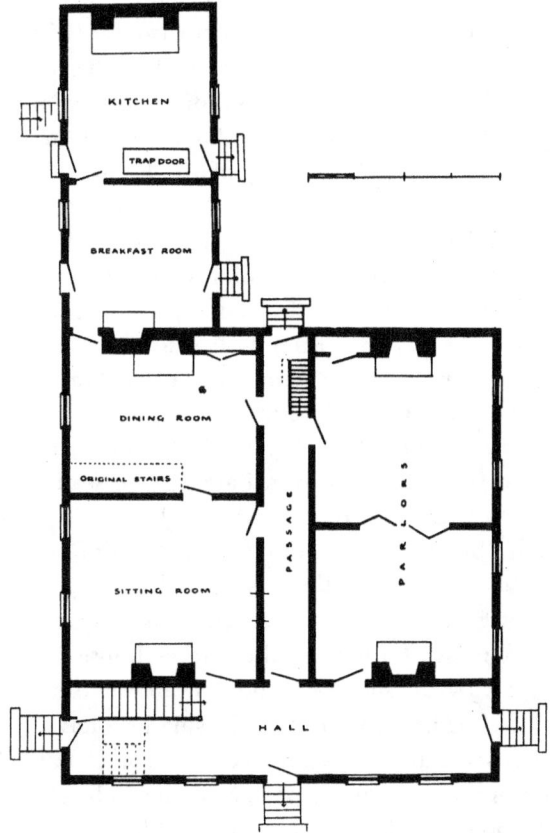

39. First Floor Plan of Price House.

40. Stony Point. Gallery Restored.

after Williamson Price sold the house in 1817.[42] The building was not built near a road. The new hall made a pretense at facing the Winchester Pike, yet doors at front and back showed preparedness for alternative orientation. However, the road that later was cut through (Liberty Road) came closest to the rear end of the service wing, the only side of the building not accessible from the grand stairhall. There are 18-paned windows to the main story of the house and 15-paned windows above. The later walls are not belted like the early walls. The original structure bore a strong resemblance to Locust Hill on Redd Road near the west county line, and a lesser likeness to Spring Valley and the Baxter house (second floor removed) at the branching of the Jacks Creek Road.

STONY POINT   Parkers Mill Road takes its name from Captain John Parker, who settled on South Elkhorn Creek in the early 1780's. The main block of the house built by him, in all probability within the next decade, is typical of early Fayette brick residences. Like the original front mass of Ellerslie, the Parker house is five-bayed, with shorter windows above the belt course (*Fig. 40*). But it is smaller, having a narrow transverse stair hall set somewhat off center, with a square parlor on the right side of the house and a lesser room for dining on the other. A plain, deep porch spans the rear of the building. The east wing probably was an early addition, containing a secondary passage with stairway and a single room on each floor, plus a shallow front gallery (*Fig. 41*) which now is removed, leaving an overhanging roof. The heaviness of the portico before the main entrance assigns this feature to the later Greek Revival period. The house is not placed at the summit of a hill in the manner usual to early country residences, there being a rise of ground behind it. A double-fireplace stone chimney to a cabin (perhaps of the saddlebag type) survives in a barn a short distance behind the house, possibly the remains of Captain Parker's first house and subsequent kitchen. A modern ell now provides service and other rooms.

Stony Point undoubtedly served as model for some of the neighboring houses having similar lines. The Isaac Wells house (1794) four miles upstream and the Hall house three miles nearer town on the Parkers Mill Road are two, differing only in having external chimneys and wings at the rear instead of to the side. The Johnson house (much altered) on the Cynthiana (Russell Cave) Pike, the Cooper house (at Spindletop Farm) on the Iron Works Road, the William Gibson (1791) and McMahan houses on the Richmond Pike, Retreat (1792–demolished 1955) on the Tates Creek Pike, and the Captain N. G. S. Hart house on North Limestone above Fourth Street in Lexington also should be mentioned as similar.

Two-storied, five-bayed brick houses with central hall but without the belt course include Fairview (1810) and the Robert Wilson house (1792—enclosed stairway off hall, as at Locust Hill) on the Iron Works Road, Welcome Home (1816), the Thomas M. Allen house on the Lemons Mill Road, the Bush house, the original part of Mount Brilliant (1790) and Pine Grove (considerably altered) on the Cynthiana (Russell Cave) Pike, Cedar Grove, the Kenney house (1804—built by Colonel Abraham Bird), and Morgansa (1814—by Major Gabriel Tandy) on the Paris Pike, Anchor and Hope (1808) on the Greendale Road, White Cedar Springs, the Price and Jackson (constructed for Major Henry Payne in the 1790's) houses on the Old Frankfort Pike, the two houses on the north branch of the Bowmans Mill Road, the Bryan house at the east end of the Military Road, the Falconer (built by Richard Allen, James Lane Allen's grandfather) and Gist (1795) houses on Clays (Mill) Road, the Headley (1798—built by Joshua Brown) and Haligan houses on the Tates Creek Pike, and the John Hart house (1813) at the intersection of the Armstrong Mill and Squires roads.

HURRICANE HALL   The most engaging residence in Fayette County of which a part predates 1800 is Hurricane Hall. Located on the upper stretch of the Georgetown Pike, it stood on the 190-acre farm purchased by Roger Quarles from David Laughed (or Laughead, or Lawhead) in 1805.[43] The original house was a two-and-a-half story square brick block. The first floor was divided into a parlor with presses flanking the chimneybreast, a dining room, and a stairhall almost equal in size to the two rooms combined (*Fig. 42*). A fireplace was in the front section of the hall. Three chambers were on the second floor, and the staircase continued to the garret, which probably was the sleeping quarters for the houseservants. Presses adjoining the fireplace in the chamber over the parlor were enriched with dangling pilasters alongside the paneled doors over a series of drawers which included a pull-out writing shelf at chairrail level (*Fig. 43*).

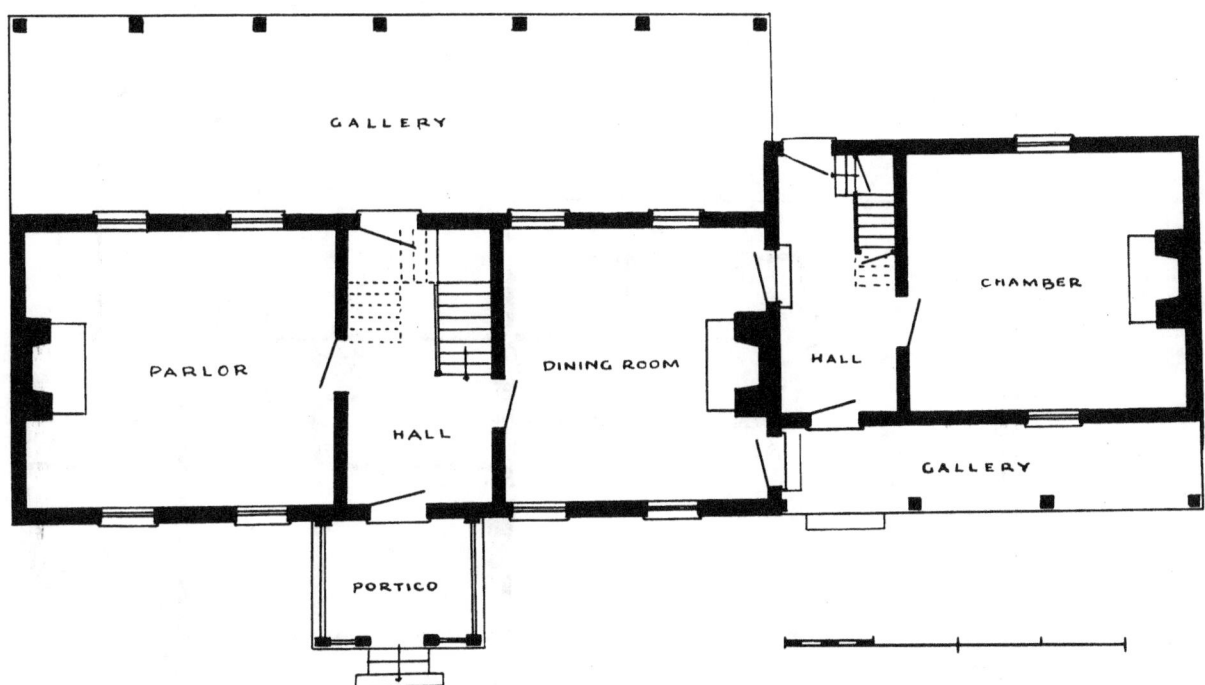

41. *First Floor Plan of Stony Point.*

The house was four bays across the front and three across the rear, the windows 24-paned downstairs and 15-paned above. Placing smaller upstairs windows on axis was an old Virginia practice, as at Westover on the James River, Elsing Green in King William County, and the Wythe house in Williamsburg; only in the Old Dominion houses it involved a subtlety in dimensions rather than in the number of window-panes.[44] The kitchen, in a detached pavilion, probably was contemporary with the house itself.

The additions dating shortly after 1805 in-

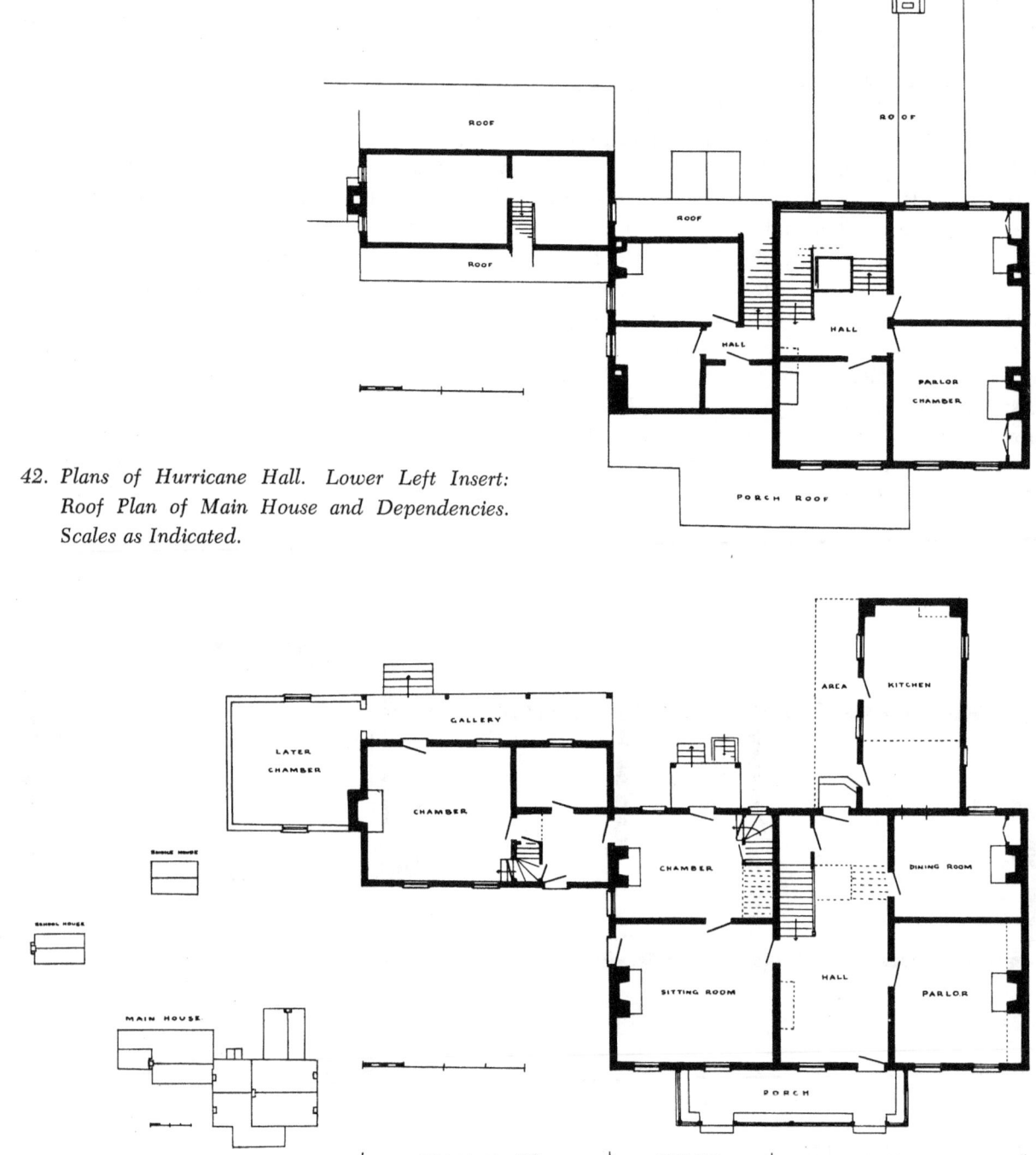

42. *Plans of Hurricane Hall. Lower Left Insert: Roof Plan of Main House and Dependencies. Scales as Indicated.*

43. Mantel, Presses, and Built-in Drawers in Northeast Chamber, Hurricane Hall.

clude an extension of the kitchen connecting it to the main block of the house, and the story-and-a-half wing beyond the hall *(Fig. 44)*. In this section a stairway between walls leads from the back room up to the small chambers above *(Fig. 42)*. The new front porch was encompassed by benches, its roof supported by chamfered posts *(Fig. 34)*. Another addition dates from the 1840's. It also is one-and-a-half stories, and is so placed that the two upstairs rooms are lighted by windows in the gable ends. A wing housing a single room was built adjacent to it about a decade later. The latest wing was entered only from a rear gallery. This part no longer exists, and the front porch has been replaced. The paneled presses in the parlor were removed upon installation of the French wallpaper that was hung to celebrate the wedding of Sarah Jane Quarles to William Z. Thompson in 1817. The wallpaper in the stairhall, imprinted with motifs representing early steam rail and water transportation, probably dates from around 1840. Of the number of dependencies that once stood to the west of the house, only the schoolhouse and huge smokehouse retain something of their original outlines (insert, *Fig. 42*). Traces can be found of the foundations of slave cabins beyond.

FARRA HOUSE Resembling Hurricane Hall externally was the Farra house on the Versailles Pike, having two chimneys on one gabled end and a single one on the other *(Fig. 45)*. A wing was at the rear, and along the right flank of the house extended a long gallery with closely spaced chamfered posts and railing. Five 12-paned over 15-paned windows and a central front door were crowded in the facade facing Lexington. The plan consisted of a narrow transverse hall, with two rooms on the north side and a single large room on the south, a stairway behind the last. There were two rooms on each floor of the ell. The building was razed in 1941 for construction of the Bluegrass Field airport.

44. Hurricane Hall in mid-1840's. Restored.

45. *South View of Farra House.*

STEEL'S RUN   Equally as picturesque as Hurricane Hall is a house called Steel's Run, overlooking a creek of that name west of the Elkchester Road. The forepart of the house is a story-and-a-half block with end chimneys, five bays across, a good-sized dormer containing a window of three lights over the entrance. Attached to the southeast corner is a two-story wing that once had an addition beyond it. An open gallery extends westward along the back of the principal form, and turns at right angles with a long, low ell, two rooms deep at the end. Steel's Run, however, lacks the charm and refinements of Hurricane Hall.

FAIRFIELD   John Bradford, a native of Fauquier County, Virginia, came to central Kentucky in 1785 as a surveyor. He established his family in a log house built on his landholdings west of the junction of the Iron Works Road and Cynthiana (Russell Cave) Pike. Early in 1787, John and his younger brother Fielding went to Philadelphia to purchase a printing press and, back in Lexington, on the eleventh of August of that year drew from it the first issue of the *Kentucky Gazette*, which was to continue in publication until 1840. Soon afterward, John Bradford is thought to have begun construction on a two-story brick house on his farm, which was given the name Fairfield. The house has a central stairhall flanked by a room to either side downstairs and containing three chambers upstairs. The kitchen was in a separate structure, perhaps the earlier cabin. Single windows light the main rooms at front and back, and there are fireplaces on the end walls. The parlor mantel is neatly carved with reeding in arched shapes in the five-paneled frieze beneath the serpentine shelf. A paneled wainscoting of black walnut encircles the room, and the doorway is enframed in pilasters and an entablature matching that of the mantel opposite (*Fig. 46*). The staircase rising on the south side of the hall has a square newel and closed stringer, not unlike the stairway in the Rankin log house in Lexington (compare *Fig. 9*), but Fairfield has turned banisters rather than square ones. Paneling is applied beneath the railing to the stairway wall and is superimposed over the chairrail on the front plane of the stairs. Presses flank the chimneybreast in the south room. The main cornice of the house is decorated with coved consoles alternating with carved rosettes. The small-paned windows (probably 15 downstairs and 12 above) have been exchanged for plate glass. A wing and entrance porch have been added to the house by the present owner.

Houses resembling Fairfield in having a central front door, usually opening into a narrow stairhall, a single window to rooms right and left, a full second story, without belt course, are: a house near the county line on the Cynthiana (Russell Cave) Pike, and another similarly placed on the Mount Horeb Road, the David Morris (before 1822), Cole (doubled in size by an addition) and Henderson houses on the Leestown Pike, the Sidener and Coons houses on the Muir Station Road, Royster and Darnaby houses below the Hornsback Mill Road (now the Briar Hill Road), the front of Cedar Grove on the Cleveland Road, the Watts house on the Sulphur Well Road, the house at the lower end of the row in Athens, Woodland on the Squires Road, the Riley house on the Delong Road and two houses in the vicinity on the Walnut Hill Road, the Featherstone house on the Tates Creek Pike, two (Elbert and Downing houses) back of Hazel Dell on the Harrodsburg Pike, and two more (one the Berry house) in the extreme west corner of the county on Frogtown Lane and near the end of Dedman Road. In Lexington the house at 263 North Limestone falls in the same category.

LAKE HOUSE   The Isabella Lake house on Mulberry Street (173 North Limestone) in Lexington was built about 1800.[45] Although situated on a lot thirty-three feet wide, its front measures only twenty-one feet across. It is a typical small town house three bays wide. The front door opens into a narrow hall on the south end, where a staircase rises to the second floor. To the right are two rooms on axis, though the rear one is smaller by reason of presses alongside the mantel and an offset to the hall (*Fig. 47*). The flues from the fireplaces come together in a single broad chimney centered over the north gable. Both rooms were lighted by a pair of windows. The house was about half again as deep as it was wide (*Fig. 48*). The kitchen and smokehouse were in a separate building that later was extended to form a new, long and narrow dining room, which blocked up one of the original back windows.[46] The old rear wall with the new one adjacent to it acquired double thickness. The annex evidently antedates the wing of the neighboring house, which is built against the lot line, leaving only a one-foot space between them. A gallery extending along the north side of the ell had a nearly flat roof supported on square posts, with horizontal boards serving for railing. The kitchen chamber was reached by an outside staircase next to the smokehouse. Front windows of the Lake house were 15-paned, and the entrance steps were of cut stone (see *Fig. 31*). Changes have been made in the fenestration, the front door has been replaced, and the smokehouse, porch roof, and backstairs have been demolished.

The layout of the Lake house was utilized with variations in other early Lexington houses. The Colonel Thomas Hart house (1798–razed 1955) on the southwest corner of Mill and Second streets (*End Papers,* left foreground) is one. Others are the Captain John Stark house (1812)

46. Parlor Door and Staircase, Fairfield.

48. East View of Lake House. Restored.

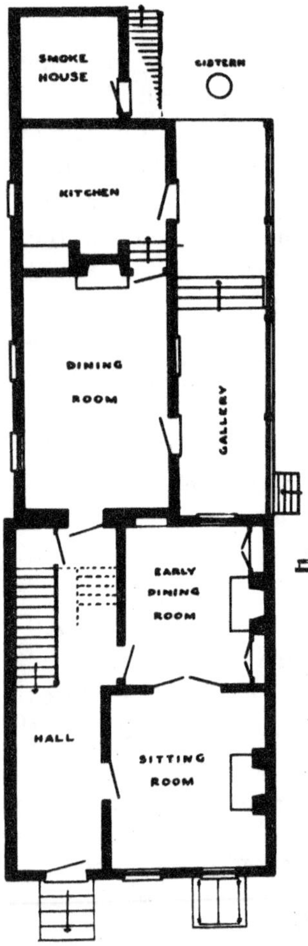

47. First Floor Plan of Lake House. Restored.

on Market Street at Mechanic (*End Papers*, fourth house up on right), and the two houses next going north. Mrs. Wheelock's house and the adjoining John McMurtry house (1837) on Broadway below Second Street (both built by McMurtry; both demolished) were similar examples having greater complexity in the service parts. The back wing of the Wheelock house was accessible only by means of an open gallery at the end of the stairhall. In the McMurtry house the wing was connected to the main block by a vestibule, with a secondary stairhall before the dining room and serving rooms between dining room and kitchen. The same basic scheme carried over into Greek Revival townhouses, such as the Butler house, a later McMurtry project on South Broadway (*Fig. 152*).

RIDGELY HOUSE   The two-storied house on the southeast corner of Market and Second streets was built for Dr. Frederick Ridgely between 1794 and 1806, when it was sold to Dr. Elisha Warfield. Having a basement stringer,

49. Ridgely House. Restored.

belt course at the second floor level, steeply pitched roof, and small, narrow windows (original width indicated by voussoirs), the house is eighteenth-century in style (*Fig. 49*). It is two rooms deep, and, as in the Lake house, the flues of front and back rooms on the left side rise to a single chimney. The interior has suffered many changes; like the Farra house, it seems to have had a narrow transverse hall with the stairs off to the side, here accessible from Second Street. The house has recurringly served physicians, and it is now the office of the Christian Churches of Kentucky.

WOOLFOLK HOUSE Built overlooking South Elkhorn Creek for Sowyel Woolfolk before 1820, this two-story house features large rooms while reserving a minimum of space for stairways and passages. The facade is six-bayed downstairs, each of the main rooms having two windows and a door, but only a single window surmounted the twin entrances. There is no stairhall. The stairs were between walls, with doors opening from both the drawing room and dining room (*Fig. 50*). A closet under the stairway and presses flanking the chimneybreast were in the dining room. In the drawing room opposite, the fireplace is flush. Its large breakfront mantel has reeded insets and straight shafts substituting for colonnettes as side supports, with bases composed of square plinths, and four little carved balls on each holding up a paneled block on which the shafts rest (*Fig. 51*). The breakfast room in

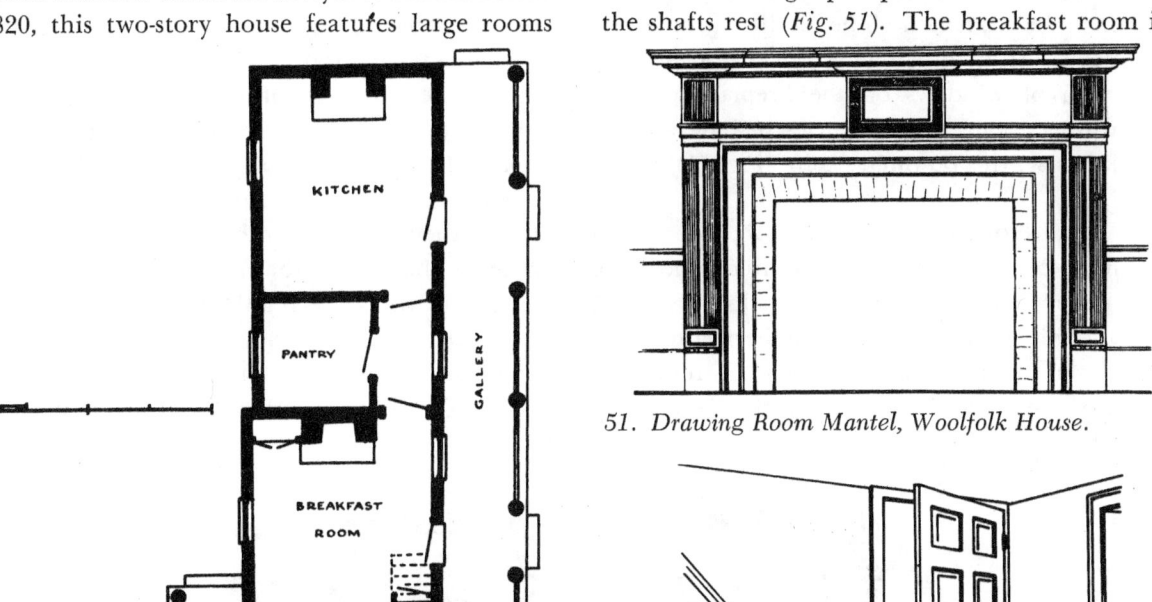

51. *Drawing Room Mantel, Woolfolk House.*

50. *First Floor Plan of Woolfolk House. Restored.*

52. *Enclosed Stairway in Corner of Breakfast Room, Woolfolk House.*

the wing adjoining the dining room encloses a secondary stairway in one corner, leading up to the vagrant's chamber over (*Fig. 52*). The pantry and kitchen behind are in an ell that was given an upper floor probably not long after the house was built. The gallery on the west side of the wing has round piers of wedge-shaped bricks with a banistered railing (now replaced by a later one) between. A similar pier sustains the roof sheltering the door to the drawing room. One assumes other such supports in a front porch or portico as well. This area is now occupied by a stairhall of the 1890's, contemporary to the columned veranda across the front of the drawing room and east end, and the chambers adjoining the stairhall. The addition of three rooms necessitated the removal of the presses and insertion of windows on the fireplace wall of the dining room. Dependencies include a brick smokehouse, the Bowman cabin (*Fig. 13*), and a log barn.

KEEN HOUSE   The Woolfolk house is a facsimile of a house three miles directly north of it on the Versailles Pike, built by John Keen in 1805. This earlier building has been altered to a greater extent than the Woolfolk residence. Both of the original stairways in the Keen house have been taken out and replaced by one occupying most of the breakfast room, and French doors abound. The facade has been given a mock Mount Vernon portico and low terminal pavilions resembling those on Jackson's Hermitage near Nashville. The Woolfolk house has higher foundations, yet a thorough examination reveals that the two structures originally had all main points in common. Mrs. Sowyel Woolfolk and Mrs. John Keen before their marriages were Sally and Mary Bowman, daughters of Colonel Abraham Bowman, which may explain the duplication of their domiciles.[47]

Twin front doors side by side is a characteristic encountered at Stoneleigh (1810), and Locust Grove, both north of the Leestown Pike. We find it again in the story-and-a-half Forest Home, near the Woolfolk house on the Harrodsburg Pike at the county line, in the two-storied Foley house nearby, and in the house that resembles the last, called Cove Spring, on the Lane Allen Road. Another is the house by the river at the end of the Tates Creek Pike. Two others on the same road that are similar—these are four-bayed but have actually only one front door—are the James Martain house (1810) and Shady Grove, both belted. The house at the

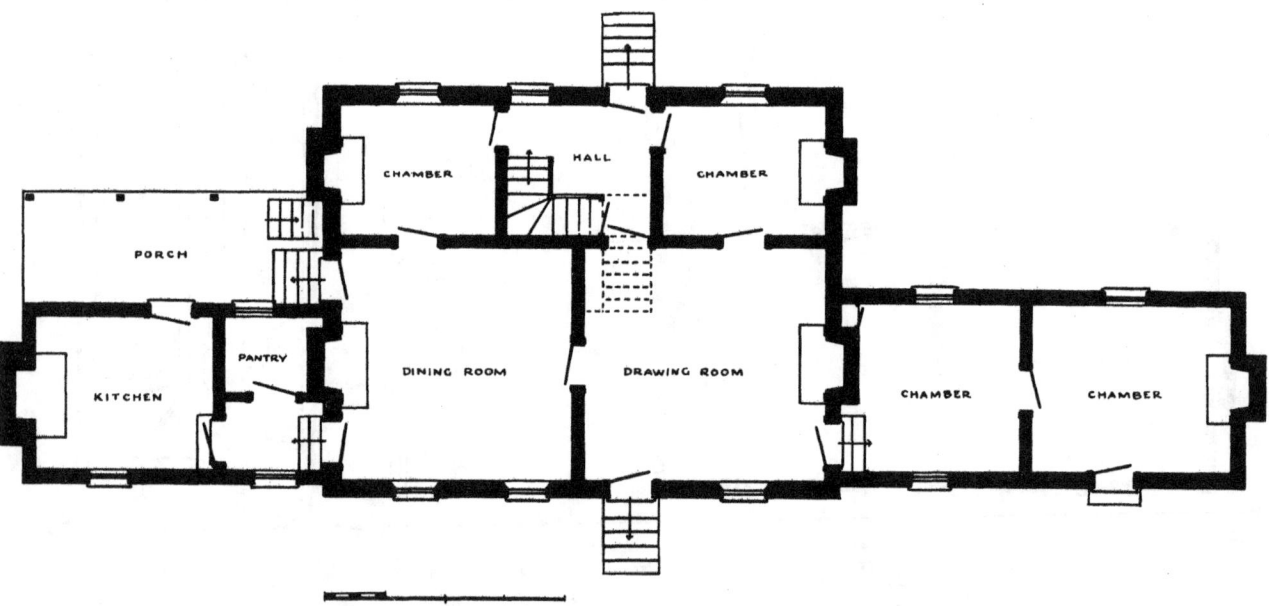

53. *First Floor Plan of Woodstock. Restored.*

54. Woodstock. Restored.

upper end of the row in Athens also is two-storied and four-bayed; however, its doors alternate with windows in the front wall.

Before concluding this discussion of early houses that are more than a story-and-a-half, mention should be made of brick examples that may be described as being a story and three-quarters. We have seen one in the early nineteenth-century front mass of the Patterson house on the hill in Lexington (*Fig. 24*). Others are the Sidener house on the upper stretch of Russells (Greenwich) Road, and Manchester, built probably by Richard Gray *ca.* 1810, near the Keen house, facing Rice Road. Manchester has been enlarged to two full stories and recently enveloped by a portico of exaggerated scale.

WOODSTOCK Below the intersection of the Todds and Cleveland roads, William Hayes built a story-and-a-half brick house containing large drawing and dining rooms and two small chambers with a stairhall between on the first floor of the main block, and two additional chambers upstairs. A low wing on the east side houses a pantry and kitchen that opens onto a broad porch. A brick in the southwest chimney, which is one of four flanking the center mass, is inscribed with the owner's initial and date of construction, "H 1812." The chimney at the end of the later west wing also includes a brick correspondingly marked "H 1820." The large rooms of equal size at the front of the house and the arrangement in the service wing recall corresponding elements of the Woolfolk house (*Fig. 53;* compare *Fig. 50*). The stairway is like those in many small houses in Maryland, and it is from there that William Hayes came. The six-panel doors in the principal rooms are of normal proportions, but unusual in having panels flush with rails and muntins. Windows here are 24-paned, whereas those in the wings are 12-paned (*Fig. 54*). All the chimneys are external; the four on the main block are not centered on the gables, due to differences in room sizes. An old gate at Woodstock, equipped with wrought-iron strap hinges and hook, has orbiculated tops to the end posts and slender square upright bars,

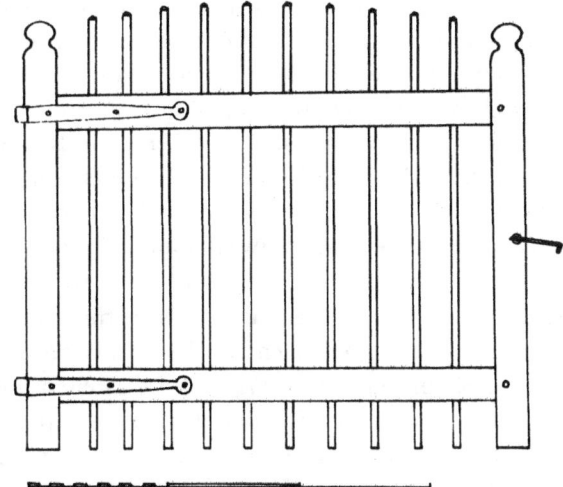

55. Gate, Woodstock.

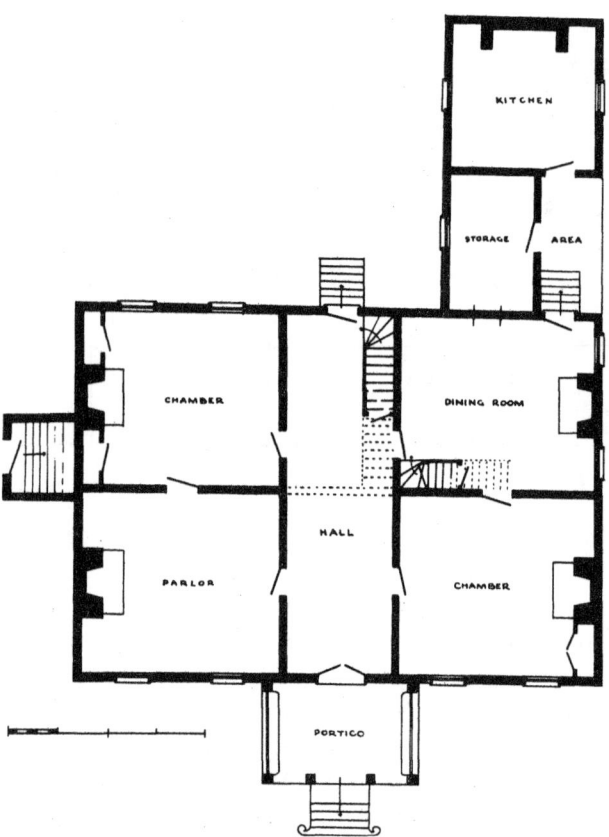

56. *First Floor Plan of Cleveland-Rogers House.*

the peaks of which describe a low convex arc (*Fig. 55*). In 1943 the mantels and other woodwork were restored, cornices added inside the rooms, and the wings rebuilt on a modified plan.

CLEVELAND-ROGERS HOUSE   Returning to the Boone Creek region, about fifteen to twenty yards due west of the Eli Cleveland cabins stands a brick residence constructed about the time the property was sold to Joseph and Jeremiah Rogers in 1819.[48] Like Woodstock, the house is a story-and-a-half type, only more conventional in plan, with a wide central hallway bounded by pairs of rooms equal in size to the two large rooms of the Hayes house. The staircase is in the rear of the hall, and a smaller enclosed stairway ascends from the dining room (*Fig. 56*). A kitchen and storage room entered from a sheltered paved area at ground level constitute the rear wing. On the west side of the house is a brick pent built over basement steps, an appendage the like of which, to the writer's knowledge, did not occur again in Fayette County until the rebuilding of Ashland in 1857. Windows in the Cleveland-Rogers house are 18-paned downstairs, the front ones with carved reeded frames not unlike those of Mount Hope in Gratz Park in Lexington. The portico set before the entrance has benches to either side, like the porch at Hurricane Hall (*Fig. 44*). It is pedimented, with a large fanlight in the tympanum (*Fig. 57*). The supports are slender Tuscan columns mounted on pedestals of railing height, four at the front, and two—also full round—placed against the brick wall, such as one finds in the portico of Homewood (1798-1800) near Baltimore.[49]

The Cleveland-Rogers house can be compared to Mount Airy, the Andrew Muldrow house on Grier's Creek in Woodford County, considered to date from 1817. The general layout is similar, but the stairs in the Muldrow house were in twin compartments to either side of the rear of the hall, and the kitchen was to the side, connected to the house proper by a dogtrot. Palladian windows were in the gables, lighting the upper rooms, and in the front wall to right and left of an arched portico.[50] The carved woodwork in Mount Airy was exceptionally fine. One of Kentucky's greatest architectural losses was its destruction by fire in October of 1945.

Other story-and-a-half houses, two rooms deep, in Fayette County include the Waller Bullock house (1813), about halfway between the Cleveland place and Lexington on the Delong Road, the Fields house a mile or so nearer town on the Richmond Pike, Harmony Hall (1810) a mile due west near the reservoir, the Cassell

57. *West View of Cleveland-Rogers House.*

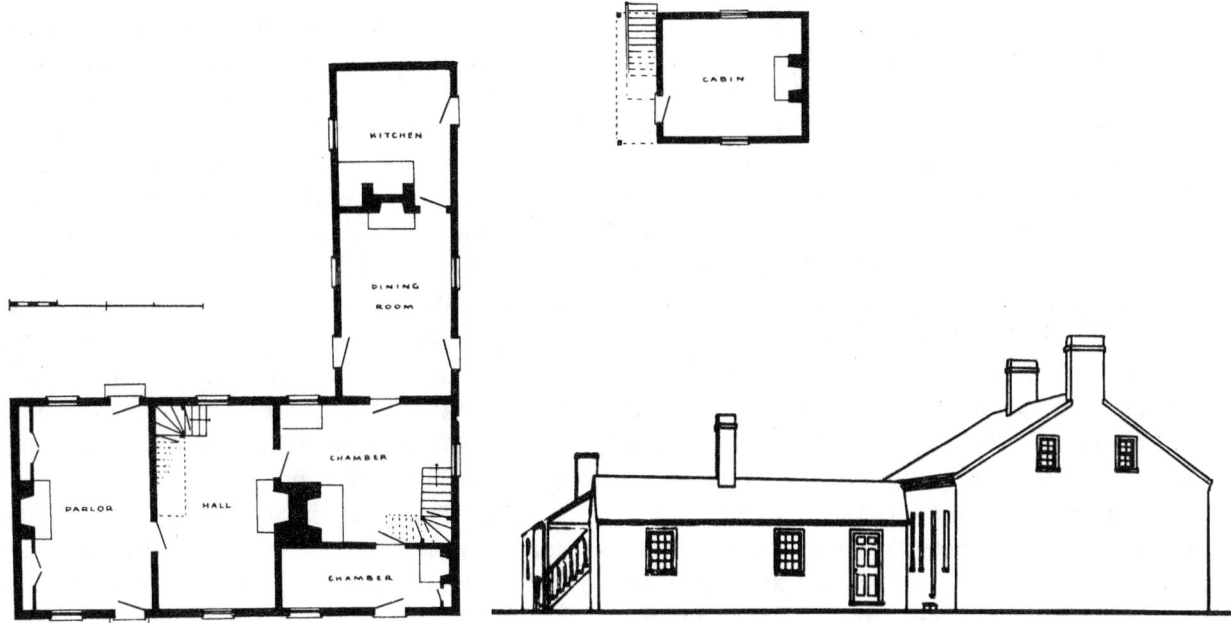

58. Plan of Union Dale.

59. Union Dale.

house facing the Nicholasville Pike (below Wilson-Downing Road), the Doctor Dudley house at the northern outskirts of Lexington, Forest Home at South Elkhorn (already mentioned), Harmony Grove—one of the largest—above Hurricane Hall on the Georgetown Pike, Pleasant Retreat (built for Stark Taylor, 1813) southeast of the crossing of the Newtown Pike and Iron Works Road, the James Innes house (1800) four miles northeast, the Dudley house on the Winchester Pike and the house on Spring Hill Farm (Glen Rose) on the Frankfort Pike, the last two having chimneys between rooms cutting awkwardly through the upstairs volume. Glen Rose was remodeled in the Gothic Revival style. There are also several houses in Lexington of equal size, such as the house at 628 West High Street, the house at the southwest corner of Pine and South Upper streets, and the Jacob Ashton house (1834) on East High Street facing Rodes Avenue, to be discussed later. The house on Upper and the Ashton house were given Greek Revival facade alterations.

UNION DALE   A house that is small but endowed with some distinction is Union Dale, in the northern corner of the county on the Russell Cave Pike below Carrick Road. The main block is 22 by 45 feet, containing a parlor at one end, a hall—unusual in having no outside door—with an enclosed stairway in one corner, a square room next (also with a stairway, the upper half enclosed), and a small, narrow chamber or storage room (*Fig. 58*). A long dining room and kitchen are in a low extension. Each room has a fireplace. Upstairs chambers are lighted by narrow windows in the gables (*Fig. 59*). Horizontal cornices at front and back of the principal block are of brick. A brick cabin located about twenty feet north of the kitchen has an outside stairway to the loft like the Bowman log house (see *Fig. 13*). Union Dale is interesting for its casualness and diversity of room shapes despite its size limitation.

Several Fayette houses that are strictly one room in depth, hence providing very little space in the garret under the sloping roof, still boast a full-scale staircase in a central hall. The Joseph Rogers house (1794), or Bryan's Station, has a stairway that curves up in one corner of a large square hall, with a fireplace opposite. Hilldale, at the intersection of the Lemons Mill and Huffman Mill roads, has a more narrow hall, and yet its proportions are those of a full two-storied house. Over the front door is a pediment pierced by a miniature Palladian window. Other contemporary houses of about the same dimensions are the Marshall house, closer to town on the Huffman Mill Road, the Rodes house (below Morgansa) on the Paris Pike, Maplewood (1812 —demolished 1953) on the Newtown Pike, the Williams house (built by Robert Tilton during the 1790's) on the Frankfort Pike, two others in this vicinity, Greenwood on the Redd Road, the Bryan house below the Winchester Pike, and Mountrose on the Richmond Pike. Somewhat larger than the others was the Wallis house on the Sulphur Well Road at Boone Creek, which burned during the late 1950's. An attractive little house is Sugar Tree Grove beyond the Cleveland Road on the Winchester Pike, built by Horace Coleman about 1815. A wing on the west end has an arched opening to the dogtrot.

WHITE HOUSE   The property three miles east of Lexington north of the Winchester Pike, was originally called Tuckahoe during the late eighteenth century, when it was owned by Joseph Royal Farrar. Afterward it was known as White House, and then designated Patchen Wilkes from the end of the nineteenth century to the present time. Farrar died in 1797, and his heirs sold the place to William Smith, who probably constructed the first of the existing structure, disposed around three sides of a court. The facade is eight bays across, two doors separating three sets of windows in pairs. The earliest section of the house seems to be the westernmost, consisting of a central transverse passage with a room to either side, between end chimneys, and a wing that terminated in a smokehouse (*Fig. 60*). The 15-paned windows in this portion of the front block are smaller than those in the balance, which are 12-paned. The existing window frames throughout are of the narrow variety proper to the Greek Revival period, indicating installation after the late 1830's, though we can assume the form of the house to have been determined prior to the era of Greek influence, details being readily subject to replacement. A single room deep, circulation about the house depended largely upon the use of the open

60. *North View of White House. Restored.*

gallery bordering the court, extending the entire length of the southeast wing, across the front block, and partially along the northwest wing. Inasmuch as the land slopes down toward the rear, the end of the northeast wing is double storied, and the last segment of the wing opposite is a relatively tall smokehouse, its division wall built up into a parapet to prevent the spread of fire that might arise here. White House, as completed, is the logical conclusion of the one-story house in Kentucky. It bears a striking resemblance to the Spanish colonial *rancho* or *hacienda* (farm) house of the Southwest, which began to appear on the California landscape during the first decade of the nineteenth century, built of sun-dried adobe rather than of burnt bricks. White House compares favorably with Rancho Camulos (1839-1849), the setting for Mrs. Helen Hunt Jackson's novel, *Ramona,* in Ventura County, California.[51] The modern ranch house in the Bluegrass can look for a suitable prototype right at home, in White House.

There were, and are, other single-story cottages in Fayette County, but none attained the definitiveness of White House. Perhaps the most admired in Lexington is the Reverend James McChord house (1815) on North Limestone below Fifth Street. Alterations in 1924 resulted in the installation of antique woodwork from several other houses, a new fan doorway, the walls rebuilt from windowsill level up, and the connection of a two-storied pavilion at the rear to the main part of the house. Nearby Thorn Hill may have been a twin to the McChord house before it was remodeled in Gothic Revival style during the middle of the nineteenth century.

VAUCLUSE   Now called Malvern Hill, formerly known as Eothan—when it was the home

61. Vaucluse.

of the Redds and Frazers—the little house a mile from Lexington off the Georgetown Pike was built by the Reverend James Moore about 1798. It was originally named Vaucluse after the adopted home town of Petrarch near Avignon in southern France. The builder, first minister of Christ Church Cathedral and president of Transylvania College, figured in James Lane Allen's story, "Flute and Violin." The focus of his house was the square, high-ceilinged parlor designed for musicales. The room was flanked by two chambers opening onto a recessed portico, an arrangement not unlike that of Locuston (see *Fig. 22*). Soon after 1800 the portico became an enclosed hall, with a central fan doorway and arched windows. The frontispiece has been pointed out as similar to a design in Asher Benjamin's *The Builder's Assistant* (1800—*Fig. 36*). The columned porch in front probably dates from around 1840 (*Fig. 61*). The parlor is lighted by two large windows on the north wall, the fireplace between having a marble mantel contemporary with the front porch. In a wing behind the west chamber, adjoining the parlor, is the dining room, on the wood mantel of which is painted the allegorical scene mentioned earlier in this chapter. A wing has been added to the east side of the house.

THE GEOMETRIC PHASE 5

During the second and third decades of the nineteenth century in Kentucky, the characteristics of the early brick buildings described in the preceding chapter came to be regarded as archaic. Two new trends arose as offshoots from the early brick architecture, and they may be traced in two distinct groups of houses built during this transitional period in Fayette County. The first of these represents an imaginative architecture based upon simple organizations of geometric forms—an architecture local in character and almost unconcerned with style. The second was a provincial reflection of the American classic style known as Federal, which was to lead directly into the flowering of the Greek Revival. Though quickly superseded by Federal classicism, the almost styleless geometric phase was the best expression of the creative spirit of the Bluegrass builders, and has left us some of the finest and most attractive examples of Fayette County architecture.

Enumerated in the preceding chapter were some of the features of medieval architecture that reappeared literally in early Kentucky building. One of these, it will be remembered, was the leaded glass window or fan doorway. The front door of Vaucluse, the one example recently looked at (*Fig. 61*), like the design in the Asher Benjamin book (*Fig. 36*), is flanked by elongated colonnettes, which, although classic in form, are gothic in their attenuation. Other doorways have clustered piers, trefoil in plan, the shafts interrupted by horizontal bands, an obvious acknowledgment of the source of their origin. The one most frequently admired is the entrance to Mount Hope on Gratz Park (*Fig. 62*). The house is directly on the sidewalk and the doorway is exposed, rather than shaded by later porches,

ANTE BELLUM HOUSES

62. Entrance to Mount Hope.

as at Rose Hill on Limestone Street (*Fig. 85*). The pattern of the side lights at Mount Hope repeats that of the earlier Hunt-Morgan house doorway in the same block (*Fig. 63*), perhaps because the leading in the Mount Hope doorway was replaced in modern times. The door itself, with its low pyramid panels, bears little relationship to the balance of the scheme. The simple, low mass of the stoop, thrust boldly forward, with its delicate wrought-iron railing, contributes much to the appeal of this frontispiece. The main entrance of the Hunt-Morgan house, which is of exceptional size, is more typical of central Kentucky doorways (*Fig. 63*). Its stanchions and cross bars are innocent of any reference to formal architectural orders, but are articulated instead with running bead moldings, that signify the function of these members to be enframements rather than load-bearers. The fan doorway in the Bluegrass figured as an imposing center of interest in facade design, and symbolized the hospitality for which Kentucky is justly famous.

HUNT-MORGAN HOUSE   The house on the northwest corner of Mill and Second streets in Lexington was commissioned for John Wesley Hunt, a native of Trenton, New Jersey, who became the first millionaire in the Bluegrass. One of his twelve children, Henrietta, married Calvin C. Morgan, and for a while lived in the house with her son, General John Hunt Morgan, who distinguished himself in the service of the Confederacy. In addition to its impressive doorway the Hunt-Morgan house has other exceptionally fine features. It was built on a lot approximately 200 feet square, purchased in February, 1814.[1] The facade is offset by a small front yard surrounded by a low coping and a wrought-iron fence. Superimposed over the main doorway are a Palladian window with leaded side lights and fan, and an arched window in the gable. The right flank of the house is adjacent to Second Street and once had a columned doorway to Mr. Hunt's office. The service court at the rear is screened by a six-foot wall extending to a carriage house and stable at the west end of the property (*Fig. 64*). One enters the court through a pedimented gateway, and a carriage gate is next to the stable.

The rooms are well disposed. A central entrance hall connects the stairhall in the northeast corner, the office directly opposite, and the drawing and dining rooms behind (*Fig. 65*). The squarish stairhall contains a graceful staircase with curving flights ascending to the upstairs chambers and third-floor playroom. The bedroom over the dining room retains the only noteworthy original mantel (*Fig. 66*). Reeded jambs with circular motifs in the corner blocks repeat

63. Front Doorway of Hunt-Morgan House.

64. General View of Hunt-Morgan House.

the design of the door frames in the main part of the house, supporting here a breakfront frieze and serpentine mantel shelf. Marble chimneypieces, ceiling centerpieces, and sliding doors between the drawing and dining rooms downstairs date from the midcentury period. In the drawing room, original stone sills at floor level indicate that the pair of tall windows may have been furnished with triple sashes, like those of the principal rooms at Jefferson's Monticello, those in the entrance hall at Ashland (*Fig. 188*), and one in the drawing room at Rose Hill (*Fig. 87*). Or they may have had hinged panels beneath double sashes, to permit one to step out into the garden. A transverse passageway through the second floor of the principal block connects the front hall with the service wing.

The service wing is divided into four equal parts, one of which functions as a stairhall. A deep porch upstairs, supported on brick piers rising above the screen wall, shelters the court on Second Street. The kitchens were located in the basement. A two-storied, detached building for servants behind the service wing was added, probably during the 1840's. The structure terminating the wall was a combination carriage-house, with double doors at both ends, and stable, providing two stalls, with a stairway to the hayloft above. It is one of the best preserved period structures of its type in central Kentucky.

Changes to the exterior of the Hunt-Morgan house include the replacement of the office doorway by a late nineteenth-century, double-storied bay window. A contemporary porch (since removed) was centered on the Mill Street facade. The front windows and the two upper windows on the Second Street side have been enlarged, and most of the sashes in the house fitted with large panes of plate glass. The cornices were made deeper and placed on consoles. A later iron fence replaces the original, which was like that across the park in front of the Bodley house.

In 1955 the Hunt-Morgan house became the headquarters of the Foundation for the Preservation of Historic Lexington and Fayette County, now the Blue Grass Trust, and is maintained as a museum. In the convenience of room disposition, the interest of adjoining room shapes, and ease of circulation, the residence is outstanding among early nineteenth-century American townhouses, with few equals outside of New Orleans,

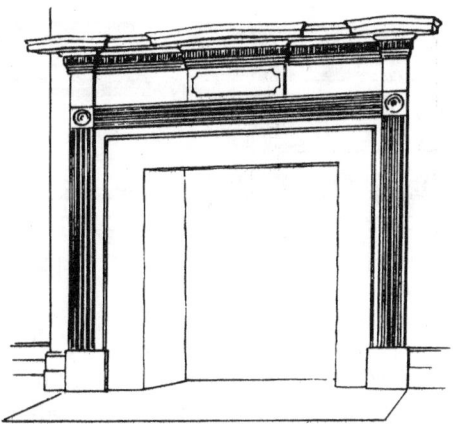

66. *Mantel in Chamber over Dining Room, Hunt-Morgan House.*

where the house plan was transplanted directly from continental Europe.

MOUNT HOPE Sharing the Mill Street block with the Hunt-Morgan house, Mount Hope was built *ca.* 1819 for General John M. McCalla, as a standard central-hall residence, two rooms deep. The two smaller rooms to the north side of the transverse hall are separated by a subsidiary stairhall opening toward an alley now known as New Street. The rear portion of the main hall originally contained the principal staircase, probably rising against the north wall to a landing at the back, continuing on the south side up to the second floor. Mantel details in this house are especially attractive. Carving on them includes sunbursts, stylized acanthus, reeding, a chain motif and elaborated dentils (*Fig. 67*). The frames of the triple window in the second story over the fan doorway, and pairs of single windows to either side, are beaded like interior woodwork. The frontispiece (*Fig. 62*) probably dates from the regime of Benjamin Gratz, who acquired the house in 1824. An enlargement was added across the rear of the house in 1841 by the builder John McMurtry.[2] A dining room is to the south and a kitchen to the north of the extended passageway, which is somewhat more narrow than the front hall. The two sections probably were divided by a partition, but now they are separated by a carved arched screen matching that bisecting the original hall.

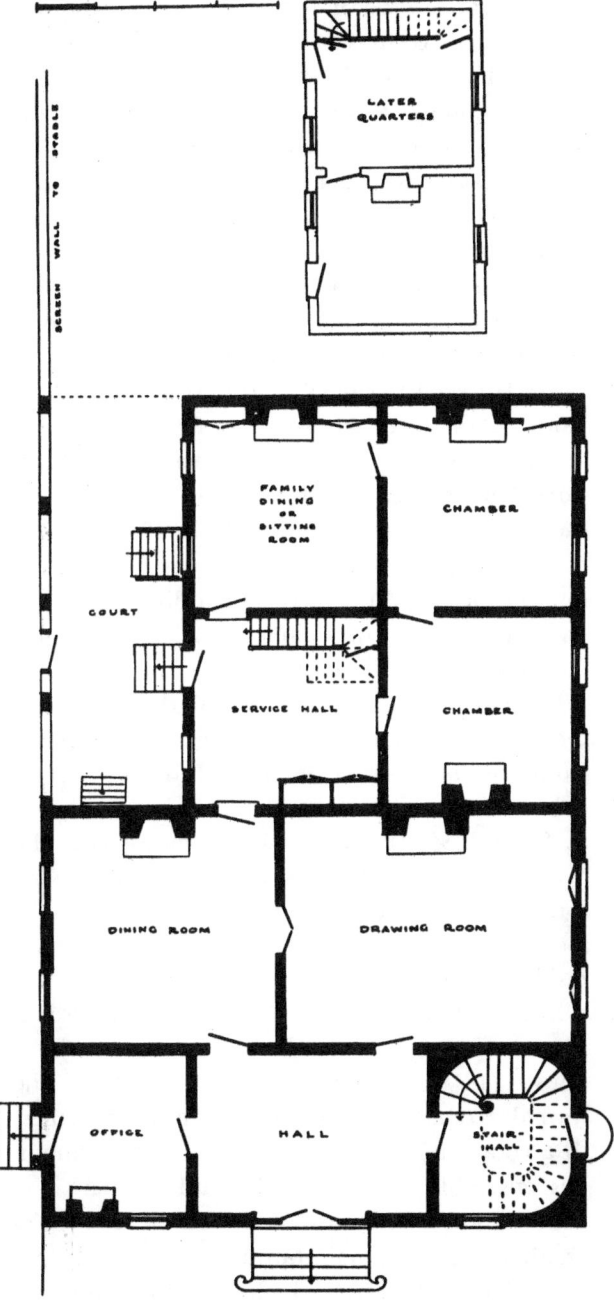

65. *Plan of Hunt-Morgan House. Restored.*

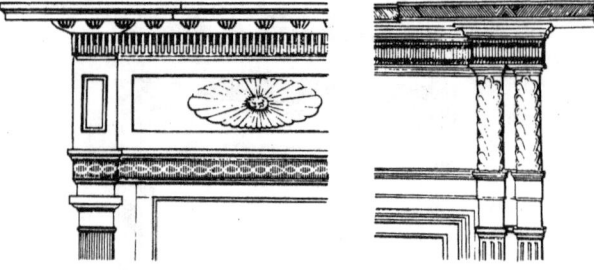

67. Details of Mantels at Mount Hope.

Galleries were erected on the south side of the house, made accessible through new, tall French windows. Although considerable alterations have changed the side and rear walls, the unpainted front of Mount Hope betokens the outstanding craftsmanship of early Kentucky brickmasons. The house has remained in the hands of a single family for some thirteen decades.

BODLEY HOUSE   On the northeast corner of Market and Second streets, facing the Hunt-Morgan house and placed similarly, stands the residence built by Samuel Long for General Thomas Bodley, who purchased the property on November 5, 1814, for $10,000.[3] The plan of the Bodley house has some features in common with its neighbor, but the stairhall originally spanned the entire front of the first floor, with the principal doorway (probably having a fan and sidelights) centered on the west front, and subsidiary doors at the north and south ends. A Palladian window—the arch itself perhaps blind—with convex reeded panels and bead molds composing its frame, was directly over the main doorway, lighting the upstairs hall. The first and fifth windows of the second floor, and the first below, are blind. At the garden end of the hall an elliptical open-newel stairway soars upward with exceptional grace. As in the Hunt-Morgan house, the staircase connects three floors. Also, the two main rooms on the first level adjoin the hall; the dining room, however, is on the garden side. An alley behind the house takes the place of a service court. A long ell, containing service and servants' rooms runs parallel to Market Street. The Bodley house is shown at the extreme right of the *End Papers*.

Midcentury alterations include the addition of a Doric entrance porch, modeled after that on the Woolley house (*ca.* 1841) diagonally across Market and Second streets. The squaring of the doorway and Palladian window conforms to the Greek Revival style, which eschews arches. A horizontal cornice continued across the front gable creates a pediment, and a colossal-order Tuscan portico has been added to the north flank. The Second Street door was converted into a window, and the south end of the hall made into a separate room having its own fireplace. Plate glass replaces small panes in all windows. As noted earlier, the wrought-iron fence around the dooryard is a facsimile of that once belonging to the Hunt-Morgan house.

The block between Mill and Market, Second and Third streets, was the campus of Transylvania University, site of the Transylvania Company's plain brick building of 1792, which was at the upper end, and of the elaborate, three-storied main building built near the center of the block by Matthew Kennedy in 1816. A pair of low pavilions, on the east and west sides of the lot, set between the larger buildings on axis, created a college quadrangle. Below the south facade of the main hall stretched a wide lawn (*End Papers*). The symmetry of the group extended to surrounding buildings. The similar fronts of the Hunt-Morgan and Bodley houses balance one another across the university green at Second Street. The Ridgely house, on the corner south of the Bodley house, balanced the former Colonel Thomas Hart house (1798—demolished 1955) across from the Hunt-Morgan residence (lower left corner of illustration). On a line with the front of the Kennedy building, Mount Hope balances the Captain John Stark house (1812) at Market and Mechanic. The formal arrangement of this square bears witness to a cooperative endeavor achieving a harmonious ensemble which may be said to mark the culmination of the early period of Kentucky architecture. The main building of Transylvania burned in 1829, after which the university purchased the property north of Third Street and constructed a series of buildings in the Greek style. Today the only remaining structure of the early college group is the low pavilion on Market Street. The old lot changed owners several times, and finally became Gratz Park upon presentation to the city of Lexington in 1884. The public library was erected in the lower section in 1904.

CAVE PLACE   The home of David Bryan was built in 1821 four miles southwest of Lexington, facing a road connecting the Harrodsburg Pike and Parkers Mill Road. It is called Cave Place from the cavern that runs under the house back into the hillside. With the mouth of the cave close by, an ample natural cooling chamber is provided for foodstuffs during the warm months. The house had a five-bayed central block with small twin wings, all of two stories, and a single-storied service ell extended back from the right flank. The one element of the house that distinguishes it from the usual county residence of the first quarter of the nineteenth century is the dual-leaf front doorway, with leaded fan and side lights, opening into the central stairhall (*Fig. 68*). The property passed to a son, General William Bryan, upon the death of the father in 1834. Probably about a decade later, the square-piered porches were attached to the front of the house, one before the fan doorway and one to each wing. Alterations in 1916 included the lengthening of the wings, with octagonal ends, the centering of a new colossal-order tetrastyle portico, eyebrow dormers lighting the garret to either side of the pediment, and the building of a large living room across the rear of the principal mass.

The developed fanlight in Kentucky was not merely a segment of a circle, but half of an ellipse, or a three-centered arch shape, the complexity of which required more than average technical skill to execute. Fanlights appeared on houses less impressive than Cave Place, such as the Neil McCoy house (1811), perhaps best described as of a story-and-three-quarters, that stood on the Cynthiana (Russell Cave) Pike near the Lexington city limits. Its doorway was remarkably similar to that of the Bryan house, and a Palladian doorway to the second floor opened onto a balcony over the fan door.

The application of unusual geometric forms in architecture was not restricted to arched doorways and windows, but was manifested horizontally in layouts as well, in polygonal and cylindrical rooms, as will be seen in the following group of four houses.

PLANCENTIA   Colonel Lewis Sanders, owner of several three-storied commercial buildings on Main Street in Lexington, began construction of a large residence for himself two miles north of the city in 1815. A contemporary description of the house published in the newspaper reads: "It fronts the Georgetown road—an oval room

68. *Cave Place prior to 1916.*

69. *Plancentia in the Late Nineteenth Century.*

in the center, 26 by 30 feet, with a dome ceiling —two octagonal rooms, connected with the oval room by saloons: back, and adjoining of which is a two story Brick House, 55 by 58, with a 10 foot passage, having six rooms on each floor. The basement of the back building is of stone, nearly the whole of it is above ground, with several convenient rooms, and passage as above; also cellars under the whole of the front."[4] The house, together with a nearby village under construction, was being advertised for auction to be held on May 15, 1815. The residence was unfinished, but the notice stated that it could be completed in four months. It was to have been called Plancentia. The purchaser was Colonel James Morrison, who willed the property to Robert Scott, the latter leasing the building about 1825 to Elijah Noble for a tavern, known as "The Sign of the Golden Eagle." According to extant photographs, the front section, containing oval and octagonal rooms, was not retained for the tavern; and perhaps it was never finished. In its place a pedimented portico with a range of six columns *in antis* occupied the space immediately in front of the two-storied cube (*Fig. 69*). Later, the portico itself was removed, and new windows to the upper chambers were inserted in the wall facing the Georgetown Pike, when the building again became a private residence. Twin parlors on the south side of the central passage are lighted by arcuated windows, the leading of the fans identical in pattern to that of the Hunt-Morgan house doorway. The stairway originally occupied the small space to the rear of the parlors, but recently was moved to the transverse hall. The truncated hipped roof held a reservoir.

WOODLANDS Woodland Park in Lexington is the site of an unusual old house that was razed soon after 1900. The building served as the agricultural school of Kentucky Agricultural and Mechanical College (later the University of Kentucky) during 1868-1880. In the next decade, its grounds became a public park, taken over by the city in 1902. Woodlands, as it was called, was the James G. Trotter place. Trotter's family owned the land from 1794 until 1829, when it passed to Elijah Warner, and thence in 1831 to Colonel James Erwin, who was listed as its proprietor in the MacCabe directory of 1838. The conspicuous features of Woodlands had been intended or realized at Plancentia. The main mass was two-storied, with chimneys placed between rooms—a rare feature in Fayette County, although found in Liberty Hall (1796) at Frankfort and Federal Hill (*ca.* 1795) outside Bardstown. The bizarre elements of Woodlands were the octagonal flankers capped by bonnets with baroque finials, stationed at the four corners of the house, and the rounded, protruding entrance hall centered on the main facade, connected to the front flankers by rectangular rooms, with a balustrade above the cornice encircling the flat roof (*Fig. 70*). The fan doorway inserted in the

70. Woodlands. Restored.

curved entrance hall was a remarkable construction. Enframements of this opening and of the triple windows in the connecting units and second floor chambers were beaded. The front suite is similar to that described as unfinished at Plancentia. If the entrance hall indeed were elliptical, it would have penetrated the front wall of the two-storied block. This is entirely possible. There was a precedent for it at Ashland, the neighboring home of Erwin's father-in-law, Henry Clay, where an octagonal hall formed a projecting bay. The rounded entrance lobby reminds one of the cylindrical entrance pavilion of the Octagon House (1790) at New York Avenue and Eighteenth Street in Washington, D. C.[5] The flankers recall the rectangular corner rooms at Mulberry (1714) in South Carolina, with curvilinear crowning turrets.[6] It is possible that the Woodlands appendages were later additions, perhaps dating from the Erwin regime, to a plain rectangular house. Octagonal *garçonnières* were common in Louisiana, Erwin's home state. Although the total effect of Woodlands lacked refinement, it cannot be said to have been without distinction.

The highwater mark of early Kentucky house planning owed something to trained alien architects, and Fayette County was indebted to one in particular: Benjamin Henry Latrobe (1764-1820), son of an English clergyman and an American mother. At one time he had been a member of the German army, and at another, of the London architectural firm of Samuel Pepys Cockrell. He came to America following the death of his wife, landed at Norfolk, Virginia, in 1796, and within two years had established a practice in several coastal cities. A versatile engineer as well as architect, Latrobe was responsible for the construction of the Philadelphia waterworks—machinery as well as architecture—before 1800, and he superintended steamboat building at Pittsburgh in 1813-1814. Both before and after the latter project he worked on the United States Capitol in Washington. His influence upon building in the United States was tremendous. He introduced both the Greek and Gothic Revival styles, and trained some of the best younger architects of his generation. Latrobe died of yellow fever in New Orleans in 1820.

Although never in Kentucky, Benjamin Henry Latrobe submitted a plan for a Transylvania building in 1812,[7] designed some buildings in downtown Lexington for Henry Clay,[8] planned the wings to Clay's Ashland, and designed the John Pope house. Bluegrass homeowners once attributed to Latrobe most of the fine fan doorways and winding staircases, but the fact is now established that he did not use that type of doorway, and seldom made stairways prominent in his schemes. Although his influence here was slight, the two domestic enterprises with which Latrobe dealt directly are of interest in themselves.

POPE HOUSE   The two-storied residence of

ANTE BELLUM HOUSES

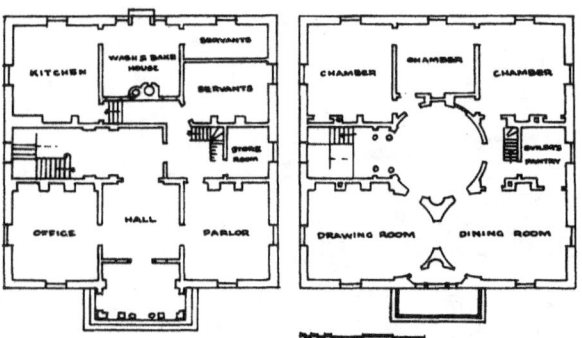

71. *Basement and Principal Floor Schemes for Pope House Redrawn from Latrobe's Plans.*

Senator John Pope, built by Asa Wilgus[9] on the large lot southeast of High and Rose streets (now on Grosvenor Avenue) from plans drawn by Latrobe in 1811, was unique in that it sat low to the ground, and the rooms on the second floor were more important than those below. Had Latrobe's design been executed faithfully, these characteristics would have been even more pronounced. As it was, the Lexington builder adhered only to the room arrangement, practically disregarding the architect's elevation drawings. Latrobe conceived a house fifty-four feet

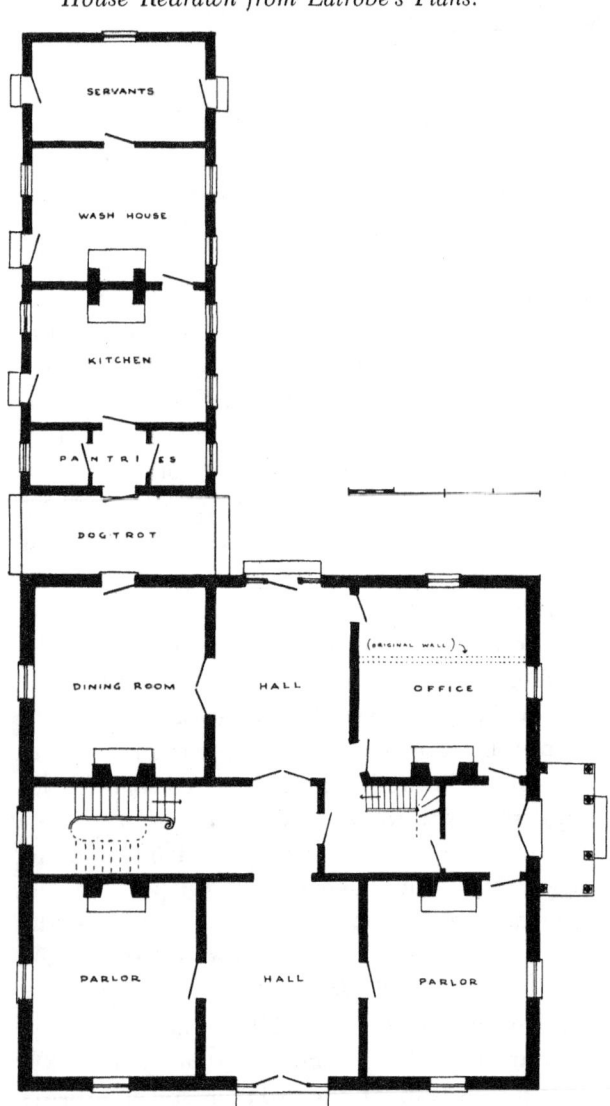
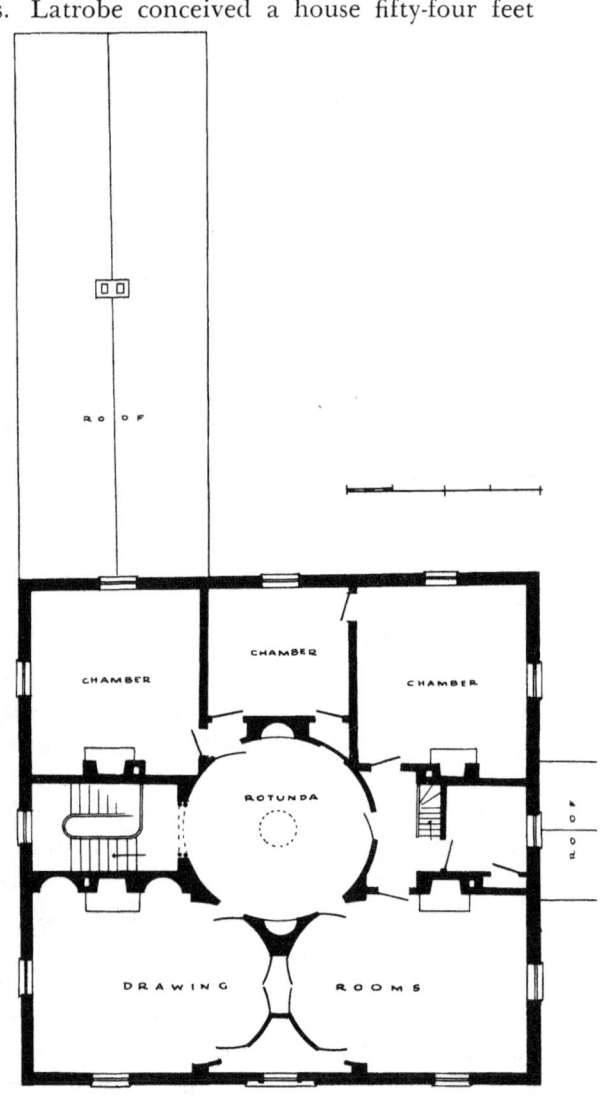

72. *Plans of Pope House with Wing. Conjectural Restoration.*

73. Pope House as Designed by Latrobe (left) and as Built (right).

square, having a portico and recessed entrance at ground level, the lower floor containing an office and parlor, stairhalls, and service rooms. The main floor was the upper one, with drawing and dining rooms at the front, a domed rotunda in the center lighted by a skylight and flanked by stairs and a butler's pantry, and three large chambers at the rear (*Fig. 71*). In an alternative drawing by Latrobe, an attic story supplied additional bedrooms. The house as built in 1814 probably was faithful to Latrobe's plan, perhaps diverting the bakehouse to other purposes, but at an early date it acquired the long service wing at the rear, housing kitchen, pantries, washrooms, and servants' rooms. The lower floor of the main block thus was left free for living and dining purposes. The upstairs provided twin drawing rooms (rather than one for dining), but the design was carried out as conceived (*Fig. 72*). Having the principal rooms above the ground floor was quite continental but not unique in Kentucky. Liberty Hall (1796) at Frankfort originally had a sizable drawing room on the second floor. The portico was omitted from the Pope house, and a fan entrance opened into the hall without recession (*Fig. 73*). The height of the two stories was made about equal, which nullified the basement effect, yet no cellar was dug under the lower floor. The fenestration was the same for both stories. A cupola at the apex of the pyramidal roof replaced the skylight within the balustrade of the truncated pyramid intended by Latrobe. Niches alongside the fireplace in the west drawing room show unconcern for academic detail, having convex panels with reeded borders (like the woodwork of the triple window in the Bodley house) on the pilaster shafts, fluting and stars on the abacus, and a punched meander pattern on the face of the archivolt (*Fig. 74*). The wooden keyblock resembles the stone sometimes used over windows (compare *Fig. 31*). A frieze of cast-metal leaves encircles the niche below the springing. The niche frames here and in the rotunda, and the mantel in the northeast chamber, constitute the only original carving remaining in the Pope house. Several slender Corinthian colonnettes, probably belonging to a screen separating ro-

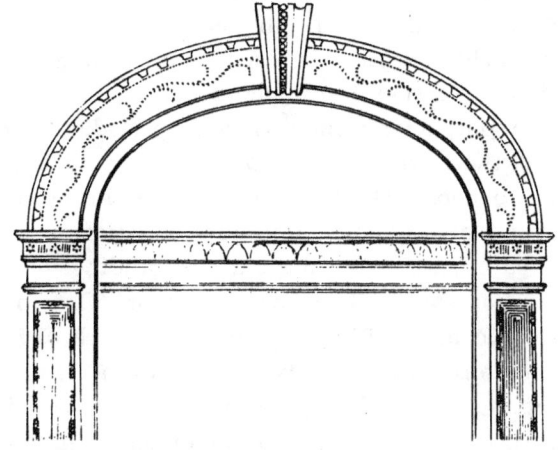

74. Detail of Upper Part of Niche in East Drawing Room, Pope House.

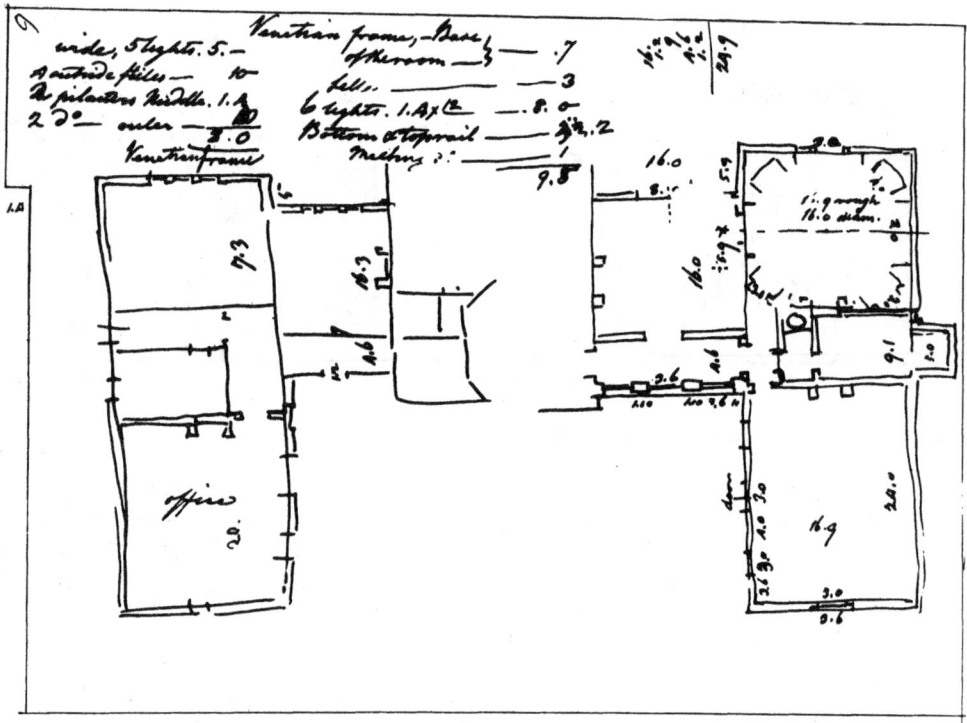

75. *Latrobe's Sketch Plan for Wings of Ashland.*

tunda and stairhall, parts of the stairrailing, and five or six of the curved doors to the drawing rooms were being stored in the basement of a house on Transylvania Park in 1940.

The Pope house has suffered drastic changes. Pope sold it in 1836 to Catherine Barry. It was remodeled for the Woolfolk family by Thomas Lewinski (see below Chapter Nine), in 1865, acquiring banks of arched windows, an indented doorway, a cast-iron porch across the front, and low-pitched gables on each side, with wide, bracketed eaves. The stone mantels in the drawing rooms date from this same period. After 1900, the service ell was razed and a short wing of two floors rebuilt on part of the site. Conversion of the house into four apartments resulted in extensive damage to the building.

ASHLAND The home of Henry Clay on the Richmond Pike is known to us through numerous contemporary engraved and lithographic views, which show that the house followed the plan and form of the present Ashland, rebuilt on the same site several years after Clay's death. The original Ashland introduces us to a type of elegant country house with low, equally disposed wings flung out right and left from a central mass of two stories. The effect is not unlike Brandon (*ca.* 1765), the residence of Nathaniel Harrison in Prince George County, Virginia, thought to have been designed by Thomas Jefferson.[10] Both houses are seven-part compositions. In the Virginia example, only the centermost unit is two-storied; whereas in Ashland three sections are combined in the middle block (*Fig. 188*). The entrance bay has a colonetted fan doorway in the front plane and a tall window in each splayed side, triple-sashed like those in the drawing room of the Hunt-Morgan house, with a balustrade over the cornice and a Palladian window upstairs in the pedimented pavilion. The two-story mass was standing in 1814 when Clay corresponded with Latrobe about designs for the wings.[11] A sketch enclosed in a letter to Clay indicates that Latrobe's plan for the wings was similar to that in the reconstructed Ashland (*Fig. 75*—compare *Fig. 189*). The void in the center of this diagram may indicate the architect's lack of familiarity

OF THE BLUEGRASS

76. *Poplar Grove.*

forms which has been pointed out in the planning of the Transylvania area—appears during this brief but remarkable stage in the development of Fayette County architecture. In a sense, this consciousness of spatial design foreshadowed the Greek Revival, but it shows here as an indigenous development, unaccompanied by the stylistic innovations which characterized the later movement. This characteristic was apparent not only in large houses like Ashland, Hunt-Morgan, and Pope, but in comparatively small ones as well. Such a one is Poplar Grove.

POPLAR GROVE This little house, four miles from Lexington on the Parkers Mill Road, was built for William Sullivan, who acquired the property on which it stands in 1808-1810.[12] The house has a pedimented entrance pavilion featuring a wide fan doorway and a lunette in the tympanum (*Fig. 76*). The pattern of the leading in the side lights is a half version of that in the wider Hunt-Morgan house doorway (*Fig. 63*). Poplar Grove has a twelve-foot-square entrance hall. Directly across from the frontispiece is an archway opening into the back hall, in which an enclosed stairway rises from the south corner (*Fig. 77*). Two rooms of equal size, with presses flanking the fireplaces in both, are located on the left side of the house. A large parlor and small chamber behind are on the right (*Fig. 78*). In spite of its restricted size, one gets a remarkable feeling of spaciousness inside

with the layout of the existing part of the building, which suggests he had nothing to do with its planning. If—as seems likely—its interior shapes corresponded to those of the later Ashland, they included an elliptical stairhall and three octagonal rooms. One of the latter, *a cabinet,* is in the south wing, and is lighted by a skylight like that intended for the Pope house rotunda. The woodwork of the early Ashland was of indigenous character—as in the Pope house—judging from two mantels and parts of the stairway in the gardener's cottage built by Thomas Lewinski in 1844. The fittings in the cottage are presumed to have come from the original house. Lewinski's reconstruction of Ashland in 1857 will be discussed in Chapter Nine.

A new sense of interior space relationships—the counterpart of that awareness of aesthetic effect in the disposition of large architectural

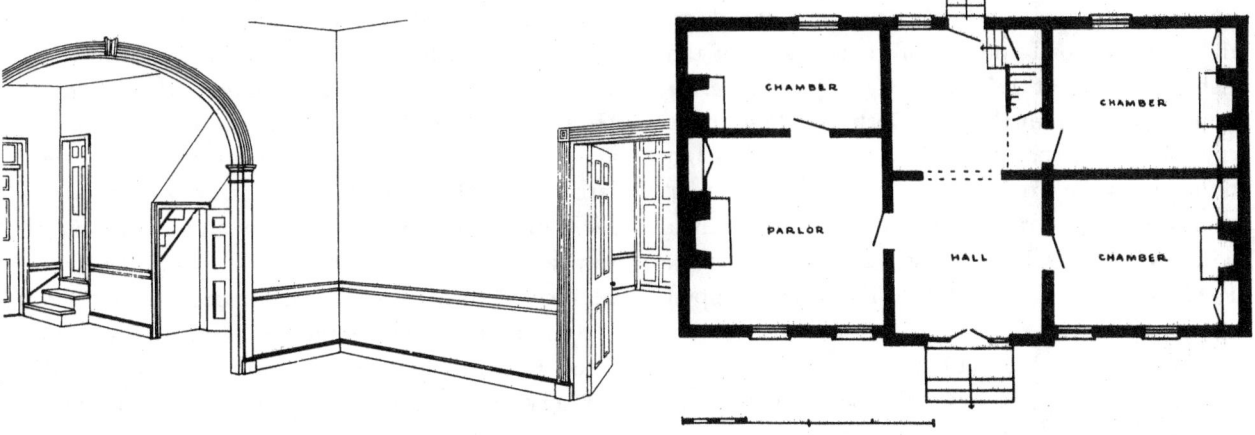

77. *Hall at Poplar Grove.*

78. *First Floor Plan of Poplar Grove.*

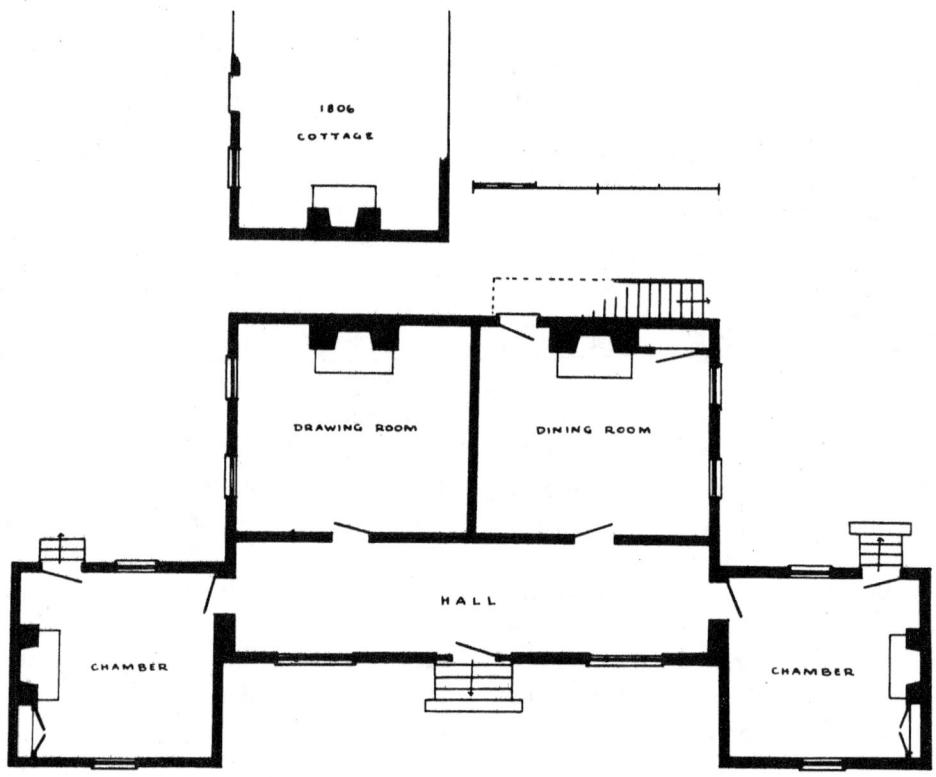

79. Floor Plan of Winton. Restored.

this house. Casual planning contributes to this effect. The hall arch is not centered, nor is the fireplace on the parlor chimneybreast, and the front windows are not placed equidistant from the entrance pavilion. The interior wood trim is simple, some of it reeded, and delicately scaled. Two chambers are on the second floor.

Similar in form to Poplar Grove are the smaller Price residence above Todds Road on the Liberty Road and the original design of the Ashton house, at 145 East High Street in Lexington (now remodeled). Both of these have corresponding rooms off a transverse hall, a fan doorway in the front wall, with pediment (larger than at Poplar Grove) rising above, pierced by a window. The Ashton house was given a Greek Revival facade (*Fig. 112*), which was stripped off in 1941.

WINTON The cluster of late eighteenth-century log houses seven miles north of Lexington, originally composing Winton, was mentioned in the first chapter. A brick cottage was added to the group in 1806, and the main residence, also of brick, was constructed in 1823, for Samuel Meredith. Although virtually single-storied, the new house contained a hall of monumental proportions across the front, entered through a Palladian doorway and lighted by a pair of windows of three parts each. There were a drawing and dining room on one side, and a chamber at each extremity (*Fig. 79*). The crosswise front hall plan recalls the layout of the Bodley house and—to some extent—that of the Hunt-Morgan house. The three attached units at Winton were pedimented in front.[13] The large middle block housed a dormitory or *garçonnière* under the roof, reached by an outside stairway at the back of the house. Cooking was performed in one of the earlier cabins. In 1866 the main house was enlarged. A staircase was fitted into the space of the north chamber and the service rooms were brought under the same roof in this wing, which, like the center block, was made two full stories. At this time the log cabins were moved to the side yard. A decade later the 1806 brick cottage was demolished. About the same time a large stone winehouse was built by the scientist, teacher, and historian, Dr. Robert Peter, who, with his wife, a granddaughter of Major Meredith, occupied Winton. Dr. Peter favored the European custom of winebibbing over the local preference for whisky and some of the fields at Winton were transformed into vineyards. Besides fine antique furnishings, such as are found in other early Bluegrass homes, the house contains many historic treasures, among them mementos of Patrick Henry, the builder's uncle.

The striving for more interesting architectural forms and volumes was coincident with a keener appreciation for horizontality. Man may be impressed by vertical extension, but by nature he moves about on the level surface. Nowhere is this understood better than in the Far East, where even palaces show a tendency to spread outward, maintaining a single story. This trend appears in the following group of Fayette County houses, all of one story. Most of these houses were built low to the ground, with wings practically at ground level. All, save one, have hipped—as opposed to gabled—roofs, so that there are cornices on all sides stressing the horizontal, and the pitch of roof planes is invariably low. The house mass is brought into relationship with the ground it stands on, and the building becomes very much a part of its setting.

GIST-PECK HOUSE   The little house that stood on the southeast corner facing Mill at Maxwell Street in Lexington was the home of John Peck, who purchased the property in 1827 from Levi Gist. Gist had obtained it ten years earlier from the builder Luther Stephens, of Stephens and Winslow, contractors for the 1806

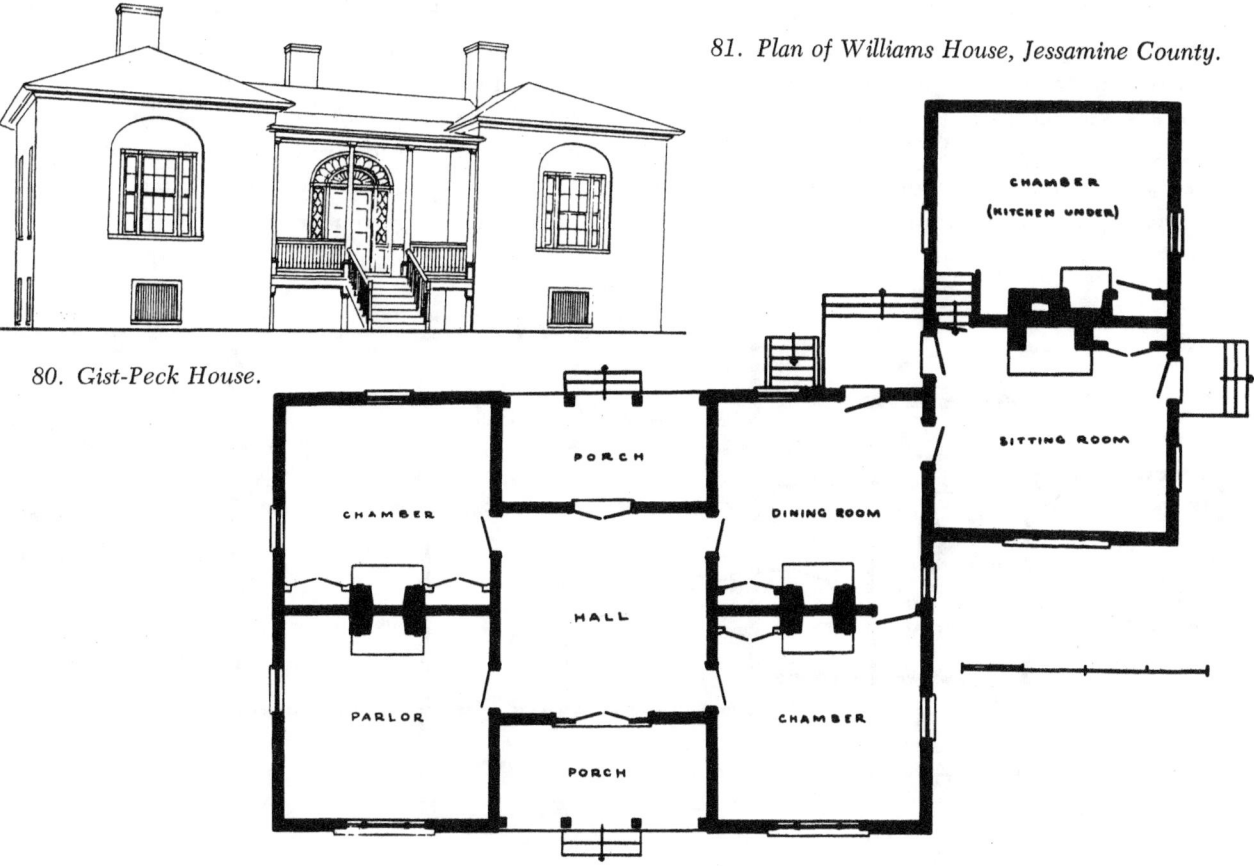

80. *Gist-Peck House.*

81. *Plan of Williams House, Jessamine County.*

82. *Lewis Manor.*

Lexington courthouse planned by David Sutton.[14] The Gist-Peck house had walls of beautifully laid Flemish-bond brickwork, including the high basement, and it was crowned by a shingled hipped roof (*Fig. 80*). Twin projecting pavilions, each with a window of three lights recessed in a blind arch, flanked a porch sheltering a fan doorway. Woodwork about these front openings was reeded. The porch roof came below the main cornice line and was supported on four slender round posts, of which the center pair were placed closer together than the outer ones. The walls within the porch were plastered for texture and color contrast with the brick elsewhere. The cornices were exceptionally thin and deep, casting dark shadows that diminish their tangibility. Throughout, the design shows disregard for classic proprieties: in the way the porch, in its proportions and the spacing of its members, avoids becoming a portico; in its absorption into the building composition; and in the importance given the roof and chimney forms as compared to the walls.

The Gist-Peck house is not unlike another small house, known as the Williams place, on the west side of the Nicholasville Pike in Jessamine County. This house lays more stress upon horizontality: it snuggles close to the ground; its stone foundation makes a line level with the tops of the basement windows and the porch floor; and its arches are flattened. Undoubtedly the ceilings are lower than in the Lexington house. The cornice of the porch is not dropped, and its posts are square instead of round. Some clue to the plan of the demolished Gist-Peck house can be gotten from the layout of the

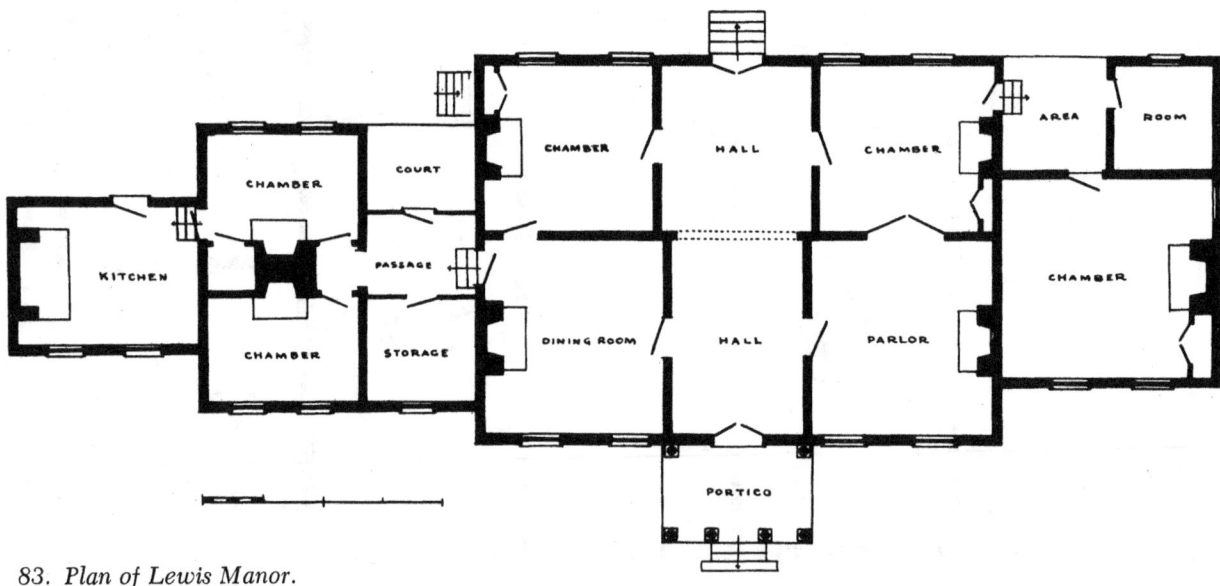

83. *Plan of Lewis Manor.*

OF THE BLUEGRASS

Williams place, which has a square central hall between porches, flanked by four rooms, a chimney between each pair, and a wing to one side (*Fig. 81*). An extra chimney showing on pictures of the Mill Street residence indicates either a fireplace in the hall (not in the Williams house) or a room occupying the area of the rear porch. The plan is a diminutive version of Stratford (*ca.* 1725), the home of the Lees in Westmoreland County, Virginia.[15] On the Hewitt map the house at Mill and Maxwell is shown with indentations at front and back, the southeast arm been better related to the size of the panes in the lunette over the door and the fenestration in the wings. Perhaps a portion of the west wing, composed of two rooms with fireplaces back to back between closet and vestibule, is the earliest section of the house (*Fig. 83*). The kitchen lies beyond. A brick front wall has been filled in between the presumably early unit and the main mass, which are alike in having hipped roofs. The principal pavilion is two rooms deep and has a central transverse hall, divided by a wide arched screen. Light is admitted at both ends

84. Morton House.

of the building longer than the others, rather than with an extra wing attached, like the house on the Nicholasville Pike. The destruction of the Lexington house and neglect of the other (when examined during the early 1940's it was being used for storing grain) constitute major losses to Kentucky's architectural heritage.

LEWIS MANOR   In 1788 Colonel Thomas Lewis acquired land three miles west of Lexington on the Viley Road, where he built a rambling house, or "manor," probably shortly after 1800. The tetrastyle portico on the south front has full round supports against the brick wall, like those on the Cleveland-Rogers house, but in place of being set on pedestals, these have double entases, with fillets at windowsill level (*Fig. 82*). Such disregard for orthodoxy extends to the use of a double abacus and a quarter-round base mold set on a high plinth. The six-paned window sashes in the main block probably replace earlier twelve-paned sashes, which would have through semicircular fan windows over dual-leaf doors, a type of entrance which preceded the elliptical variety with side lights. The east wing is short, containing a single large chamber and a tiny room in the lean-to, both entered from a roofed area open at the back. Free planning of the wings seems to have been prompted by the fulfillment of immediate needs, rather than the desire to impress through adherence to formal balance. The place was renamed Kilmore in 1915.

MORTON HOUSE   Larger and more sophisticated than Lewis Manor is the residence built in 1810 for William Morton, whose grand manners and scale of living prompted the townspeople to address him as "Lord" Morton. The house is situated in what today is called Duncan Park, on the northeast corner of Limestone and Fifth streets. Morton came to Lexington from Baltimore in 1788 and engaged in several commercial enterprises, returns from which made

85. Rose Hill.

possible the building of the spreading house on Limestone. Cassius M. Clay, who purchased it for $18,000 in 1838, two years after the builder's death, spoke of the house as "the most elegant in the city."[16] Here the stormy emancipator resided for a dozen years. The house passed then to Lloyd Warfield. Great Palladian windows and a tall arched doorway pierce the facade of the center block, linked by low, parapeted forms to terminal pavilions (*Fig. 84*). The connectors are but slightly recessed behind the plane established by the first, third, and fifth masses, which have hipped roofs and quoins at the corners. The building is unique among early examples of Bluegrass houses in having stucco covering the brick walls. The largest room in the house, opening at the back of the entrance hall, is the three-bayed drawing room, with a curved recess on the west side, and large, double doors connecting with the parlor on the south.[17] A cross passage separates the parlor from a front chamber, across the entrance hall from which

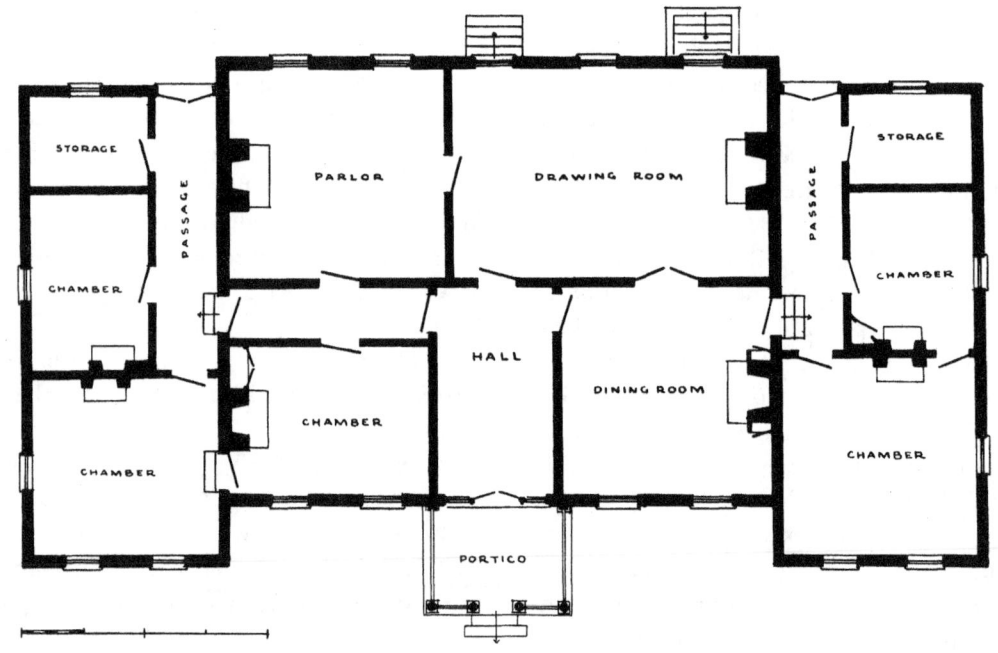

86. Plan of Rose Hill. Restored.

87. Bird's-eye Rear View of Rose Hill with Restored Dependencies.

is the dining room. Each of the end wings seems to have housed three chambers. Certain changes have been made in these areas, including the addition of bay windows.

ROSE HILL   Diagonally across the intersection of Limestone and Fifth streets from the Morton house stands Rose Hill, built for John Brand about 1812.[18] In certain respects the design of Rose Hill is indebted to that of its neighbor, especially the main block. However, the later house is a three- instead of a five-part composition; its end pavilions are lower and advance several feet in front of the adjoining central mass (*Fig. 85*). The fan doorway is wide with leaded side lights, and has clustered colonnettes separating the voids. The Greek Ionic portico dates from at least a quarter of a century later. Although it detracts somewhat from the importance formerly lavished on the doorway itself, the portico adds interest to the entrance and is in perfect harmony with the preexisting forms. Rose Hill has a well-thought-out plan, which is basically an inversion of that of the Morton house (*Fig. 86*). A series of passages facilitates circulation to all the rooms, except that one has to cross the dining room; but this room was used only at mealtime, when servants were passing in and out anyway. The passages in the wings, which function as an insulation for sound between the living rooms and lateral chambers, have walls of unplastered brick. Drawing room and parlor occupy the garden front,

overlooking the brick terrace. The centermost window in this facade has its sill at floor level and is equipped with three sashes and a flight of outside steps, allowing egress directly from the drawing room to the terrace, as in the Hunt-Morgan house. The side passages also open onto the terrace by means of double doors. At the

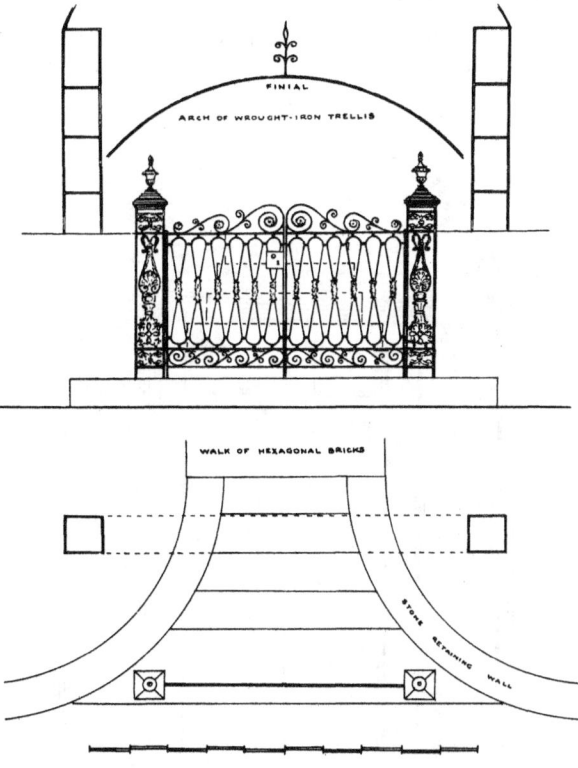

88. Elevation and Plan of Front Gateway and Steps to Rose Hill.

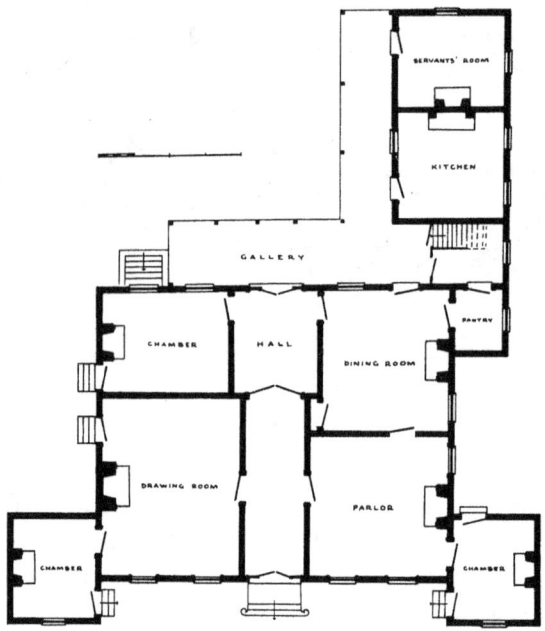

89. Plan of Norton Cottage. Restored.

north side of the brick terrace are the two-storied kitchen and houseservants' quarters, with a smokehouse nearby, opposite the main residence. Once a brick privy and stable were located to the west of the quarters, and an ice-

90. Rear Hall Door of Norton Cottage.

house was to the south of the dwelling proper (*Fig. 87*). Slave cabins were in the southwest corner of the yard. Of exquisite design is the ironwork front gate on Limestone Street, probably contemporary with the portico (*Fig. 88*). The house has been little changed. A kitchen and bathrooms have been installed within its enclosure, a bay window added on the south side, the porch railing removed, and the small-paned windows replaced by plate glass. Excellence of proportions, good disposition of parts, and fine details have earned acclaim for Rose Hill. No house in Kentucky better deserves to be preserved and maintained for its architectural merits.

NORTON COTTAGE   The house once situated on High Street southeast of Limestone was called Norton Cottage in the 1838 city directory. At that time it was the home of John Norton, who had purchased the property twelve years earlier from Levi T. Smith, son of Elijah Smith. The house was low, with protruding end pavilions and an ell on the west rear corner. A central passage, leading to a square hall behind, divided the drawing room and parlor, each opening into a small chamber at the side. Another chamber and the dining room were at the back, looking out upon a gallery that connected with the service rooms (*Fig. 89*). A stairway near the dining room door led from the gallery up to chambers over the kitchen wing. The back hall doorway was enframed by a flattened fan and side lights with oval panes of alternating sizes, its reeded woodwork similar to that of the Hunt-Morgan frontispiece (*Fig. 90*). The Middleton, Wallace & Co. lithographic view of the mid-1850's shows the house to have had end gables, but this source cannot be trusted as absolutely reliable on matters pertaining to architectural details.

John Norton sold the house on June 8, 1859, to Judge George Woolley,[19] whose remodeling of it is discussed in a later chapter. The Norton-Woolley house was razed in 1946, and the Buick garage built on its site.

COOLAVIN   Listed in the 1838 city direc-

91. Coolavin.

tory as "Coolavin, Judge Hickey. East [sic] Sixth st.," the low ranging house west of Broadway had been built for its owner, Thomas Hickey, before 1820. Coolavin resembled Lewis Manor (*Fig. 82*), although more symmetrical and covered by gabled rather than hipped roofs (*Fig. 91*). The pedimented portico was more refined, having slender Tuscan columns set on square pedestals, with railing between. The front door with its fan light was enclosed by pilasters supporting a broken pediment on impost blocks (*Fig. 92*).[20] Narrow windows to either side recall the entrance arrangement at Federal Hill (*ca.* 1795) near Bardstown, or of George Washington's birthplace, Wakefield (early eighteenth century) in Virginia. A transverse hall divided by an arch ran through the middle of the Hickey house, with twin parlors on the east side, a library and office beyond in the wing, and a sitting room opposite. There were two chambers in the west wing, a dining room behind the sitting room, and a smaller eating room, kitchen, and two bedrooms in the north ell, with a gallery skirting its long wall (*Fig. 93*).[21] Early dependences included a brick cabin, icehouse, and privy, to which group later were added a carriagehouse and a barn. Acquired by Charlotte Hart and Daniel Webster Price during the year following the Civil War, the house was renamed Locust Grove.[22] All that remains of the house today is a remnant of the ell, serving as a little house west of Price Avenue. The enframement of the

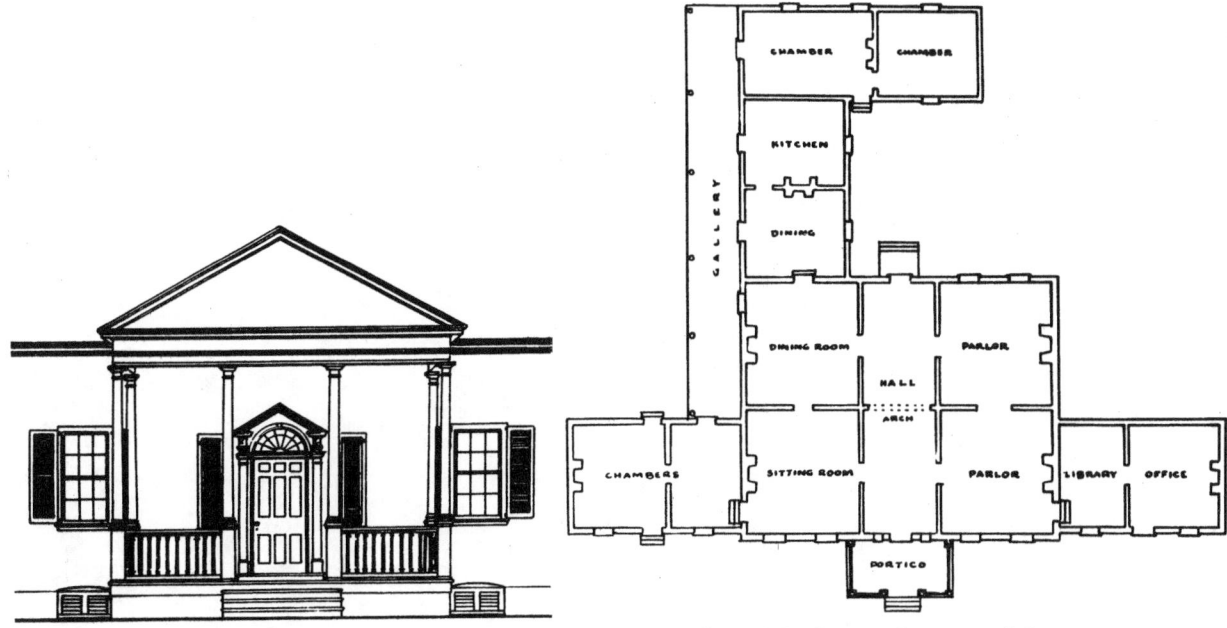

92. Portico Detail of Coolavin.

93. Plan of Coolavin. Conjectural Restoration.

front door graced the entrance to an antique shop on West Short Street across from the Baptist church through the 1940's.

GLENDOWER   Another house that belonged to this group was Glendower, called Wickliffe House after becoming the home of Robert Wickliffe in 1826 (so listed in the 1838 directory), and known as Preston Place during the Reconstruction period. It was located on West Second Street, beyond Jefferson. The Middleton, Wallace & Co. lithograph of Lexington shows Glendower to have been a hipped-roofed formal composition of seven parts, but the Hewitt map of 1861 indicates that the plan was essentially the same as that which persisted into the present century. This consisted of a central mass two rooms deep and five bays across the front, with a slightly projecting pedimented entrance pavilion. Balanced wings of three bays were recessed to either side. An attached rear ell on the west and a detached dependency on a line with the east flank formed a court at the back of the house. This scheme was developed further by William Preston after 1865, with square towers dominating additions made on both sides. The resulting picturesqueness recalled buildings admired during Preston's service as ambassador to the court of Spain several years earlier. Glendower was razed in March of 1942 and Euphrasia Hall (a nurses' home) erected on its site.

PARADISE   A final example of the low-slung house type is Paradise, situated a mile from Lexington on the east side of the Cynthiana (Russell Cave) Pike. It is a compact, hipped-roof brick cottage, two rooms deep, presenting a Palladian doorway set in a tiny, projecting, gabled entrance bay.

Similarities are to be noted between the houses of this group and Ridgeway (1805-1805) at Saint Matthews, near Louisville,[23] the Grange (1818) near Paris, Kentucky,[24] and the Taft House (*ca.* 1820) at Cincinnati.[25] The Grange, which is the closest to the Fayette group geographically, is also closest in type, and like Rose Hill, has a Greek Revival portico. Ridgeway is more on the order of Homewood (1798-1800) at Baltimore,[26] or some of Jefferson's smaller dwellings (such as Farmington near Louisville) but has a plan similar to that of the Morton house. The Taft house is built of wood, and is elaborated with classic details.

CLASSICISM 6

THE ASSERTION of originality—in the stress laid upon abstract elements such as fan doorways, unusual geometric forms, and compact, low masses capped by hipped roofs—manifested in Bluegrass house building during the second decade of the nineteenth century was superseded after 1820 by architectural effects gained through the use of classic orders, pediments, and arcades. This was a regional version of classicism which (unlike the later revivals) was without affectation, yet lacked the freshness and distinction of the brief geometric phase. The obvious limitation of strict classicism was adherence to architectural orders. An order is a conventionalization wherein the elements of the post-and-lintel supporting system follow prescribed forms, the column divided into base, shaft, and capital, the entablature into architrave, frieze, and cornice, each part having predetermined shapes governed by canonical proportions. The ancient world handed down five orders: the stocky Doric from Greece, the graceful voluted Ionic from Asia Minor, the foliated Corinthian, the Roman version of the Doric called Tuscan, and the Roman combination of Ionic and Corinthian into the composite order. Two of them being modifications of the other three, and certain restrictions of detail being common to all, there was not a wide selection. But these five orders became the design scale for architectural styling throughout the entire Renaissance movement, of which a belated but enthusiastic resurgence was known as Classicism.

Classicism reached a climax in English architecture toward the end of the eighteenth century, in the works of such men as the conservative Samuel Pepys Cockerell, the progressive Sir John Soane and the Adam brothers. Robert Adam developed his taste for classic design during a four-year residence in Italy concurrent with the excavations at Herculaneum. After his return to England he applied the motifs he had acquired in the planning of buildings and especially interiors in partnership with his younger brother, James. Their well-integrated—though somewhat dry—manner was publicized in *The Works in Architecture of Robert and James Adam,* printed at London in ten parts from 1773 to 1786. By this means the Adamesque mode reached America, where it enjoyed some measure of popularity, though modified by simplification, the use of baser materials, and limitation to isolated details.

The classic style became known as Federal in the United States, coming to the fore simultaneously with the establishment of the federal government following the American Revolution. The chief protagonists of the style were Thomas Jefferson, Charles Bulfinch, and Benjamin Henry Latrobe. The first notable monument of classicism here was the porticoed Virginia capitol at Richmond, designed by Jefferson in collaboration with Clérisseau in 1785. The Richmond capitol antedated the Madeleine in Paris, which was the first of the great European temple reproductions of modern times, by twenty-two years.[1] Bulfinch traveled abroad during 1785-1787 and returned to implant classic architecture in and around the city of Boston. The Englishman Latrobe had been a pupil of Cockerell and had moved in the circle of Soane and his group.[2] Soon after his arrival in America during the mid-1790's, Latrobe was entrusted with a number of important commissions. In his work on the Capitol in Washington he contributed two "American orders"—inspired by Indian maize and tobacco plants—to the New World architectural vocabulary. Latrobe was primarily an innovator, and distinguished himself by setting up the Greek Revival as a separate style, whereas in England it remained part of the classic idiom.

We have already seen the appearance of classic elements in mantels and doorways in Kentucky houses beginning in the 1790's. Some of these applied features bespeak the far-reaching influence of the brothers Adam. An example is a chimneypiece in the parlor of the Barker house on the Cleveland Road above Athens, which mantel is said to have come from a residence that stood on East Main Street near the present railroad crossing in Lexington.[3] Its design includes festoons in the frieze, classic figures in low relief on the imposts, and garlands in the sunken panels of the pilasters (*Fig. 94*). Background and moldings are of wood, and the sculptured forms are of cast metal. The mantel is similar to one in the Marshall house (1800) near Washington, Kentucky.[4] The refinement of such chimneypieces cannot be said to be typical of the Bluegrass. Craftsmen here had little time, opportunity, or inclination to pursue archeological studies and hence developed no great concern for correctness. As a rule, they adapted motifs according to their individual fancy, and the results sometimes went to the other extreme, illustrated by the mantel in the parlor of Greenwood, on Redd Road, facing Steels Run (*Fig. 95*). The breadth of the mantel exceeds the width of the chimneybreast by about a foot on either side, to compensate for which the ends are boxed in and the front extensions elaborated with two chains of rings in narrow vertical recesses. The breakfront shelf projects over the frieze with a central panel containing an urn and swags, with stiff pinnated flower stalks in the spaces to either side and spread-wing eagles in the end blocks. The supports below are coupled, full-round, flask-shaped colonnettes

94. *Mantel in Barker House Taken from a Residence on East Main Street.*

95. Parlor Mantel at Greenwood.

sharing voluted capitals reminiscent of some proto-Ionic archetype. In these two examples are contrasted the quiet, proper taste of imported standards, and the virile, somewhat primitive interpretation of a provincial individualist.

Classicism in Bluegrass architecture took on two specific forms. The first strove for a grand impression in double-storied houses through use of colossal-order pilasters as strong vertical accents. The second application of the classic was in houses, usually of a single level, the main feature of which was an arched portico.

Use of the colossal order in America predates the Federal style. It was on at least one house of the late seventeenth century, the John Foster (Hutchinson) house (*ca.* 1688—demolished 1833) in Boston. Its three-storied facade was unified by Ionic pilasters and imposts flanking the entrance bay and stationed near the outer corners. By the middle of the eighteenth century, giant pilasters had become an accepted decoration on the fronts of great houses. A residence built before the American Revolution—the Roger Morris house (1765) in New York—had a freestanding colossal-order portico,[5] but this was a premature example. The portico became the hallmark of the architecture of Jefferson and his contemporaries along the Atlantic seaboard, and appeared on the Gulf coast, but it did not yet figure in the architecture of central Kentucky. The colossal order here was reserved for applied work—for pilasters and running moldings built into brick walls.

The initiator of the colossal-order phase of Bluegrass building was a man whose background is still shrouded in mystery, but whose creative endeavors and influence remain very much in evidence. He was the first local man to declare himself an architect, as opposed to any of various designations used for mere builders, such as housewright, housejoiner, or carpenter. On a copper plate, deposited in the cornerstone of the Grand Masonic Hall designed by him and dedicated in Lexington in 1824, was an inscription that ended with the credit, "Matthew Kennedy, Architect."[6]

Matthew Kennedy had been in this region before entering practice in 1812. An advertisement in the *Kentucky Gazette* for that year reads: "THE subscriber informs his friends that he has returned to Lexington, where he intends to co-partnership with *James W.* BRAND, to pursue his profession of *House Carpenter & Joiner* In all its branches, if liberally encouraged. . . . [signed] MATTHEW KENNEDY." Kennedy's address is given as "between Mr. Samuel Long's shop and Mr. John W. Hunt's factory, on the opposite side of the street, in the house formerly occupied by Mr. Atkinson." Samuel Long, it will be recalled, was the builder of the Bodley house. He was listed in the 1818 directory as an Upper Street resident, whereas the address of Benjamin Atkinson, a painter, was given on Main Street. Kennedy began to work independently within two years. During the summer of 1814 he inserted a notice in the *Gazette* stating his need for "TWO or THREE boys as apprentices, to learn the Carpenter's Trade."[7] The following year his former partner, James W. Brand, died.[8]

In 1816, Matthew Kennedy embarked upon his most important commission, which was for Transylvania University. A new building was needed to house the school, which had outgrown the two-story brick building erected in 1792 toward the Third Street extremity of the college lot.[9] On March 2 the Transylvania board of trustees "appointed a committee to inquire into the expediency of erecting buildings," and late in the following month a plan was adopted. Kennedy was asked to make drawings, and an

ANTE BELLUM HOUSES

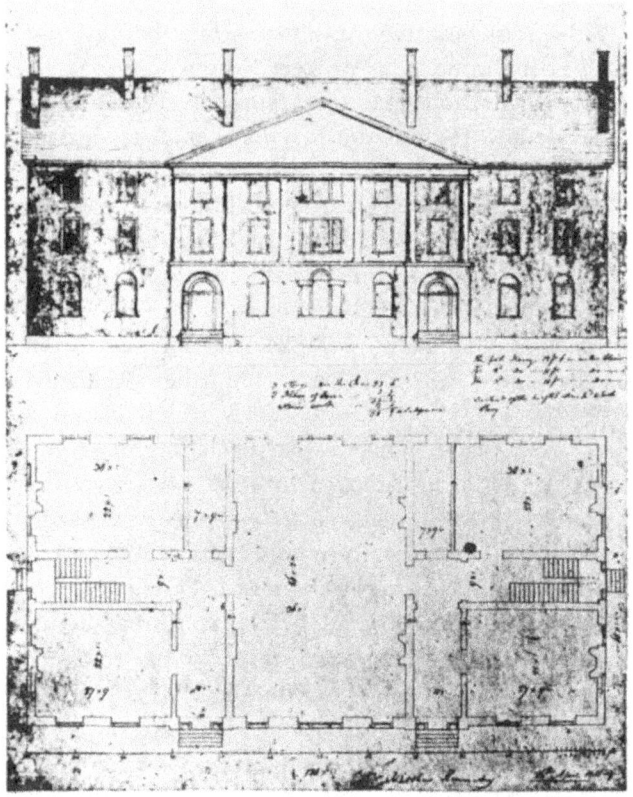

96. *Elevation and First Floor Plan of Building for Transylvania University. Ink and Wash Drawing by Matthew Kennedy.*

elevation and plan of the first floor are preserved in the archives of the college. He conceived a three-storied building nine bays across, with gables at the ends, a central pavilion of five bays, the first story of which was given a basement treatment, with fan doorways in projecting blocks to right and left and a Palladian window on the axis (*Fig. 96*). Two pairs of engaged columns and a pair of pilasters above supported a broad, plain pediment. The first floor provided a large assembly hall between passages, connecting with stairhalls bounded by the classrooms in the four corners of the building. The forest of chimneys shown on the elevation indicates that the upper floors were divided into smaller rooms for instruction and student residence. The room arrangement evidently was carried out faithfully, but the external appearance was modified. Although the portico treatment was eliminated, the pediment was retained, its tympanum pierced by a lunette. A hipped roof was substituted for the long gabled form. A balustrade surmounted the cornice and an octagonal baroque-manner cupola rose from the center of the roof (*End Papers*). One must admit that the effect of the executed building, although more old-fashioned, was bet-

97. *Kennedy House. Restored.*

ter than that of the drawing. If the great portico had been retained, however, it would have given the Kentucky institution a home stylistically abreast of its contemporaries in the East. Bulfinch had completed University Hall for Harvard in 1815, and Jefferson did not lay the cornerstone for the first building of the University of Virginia until October, 1817.

In 1827, Kennedy constructed another building for Transylvania, and this one had pilasters embracing two stories. The new building was the Medical Hall at Market and Church streets.[10] Neither of Kennedy's Transylvania buildings now exists. The academic building burned in 1829, after which the university purchased the present campus beyond Third Street and built Morrison College. The old lot eventually became a public park. A second medical hall was erected to replace Kennedy's edifice in 1839.

KENNEDY HOUSE The house on the southeast corner of Mulberry (North Limestone) and Constitution (Second) streets was built on a lot owned jointly by Matthew Kennedy and James W. Brand, its erection undoubtedly occurring after the latter's death in 1815. Kennedy owned about half the block along Constitution Street, and was living in the corner house at the beginning of 1831.[11] Several years later, the place was sold for $6,000 to John Brand.[12] The design of the building is unlike that of any previous residence we have seen in the Bluegrass. The elements of its facade are powerfully organized by four tall brick pilasters rising to a broken cornice, a pediment placed above with a lunette concentric to a blind arch in the tympanum (*Fig. 97*). The pedimented motif is similar to the entire front of the 1827 medical building a few blocks away. The house is two bays broader than the Medical Hall, and like the earlier academic building, has a hipped roof. The truncated area probably was enclosed by a railing, such as could be seen on a similar house on the Old Frankfort Pike near Midway in Woodford County up to a few years ago. The street facade of the Kennedy house recalls the garden front of the Hammond house (1773-1774) in An-

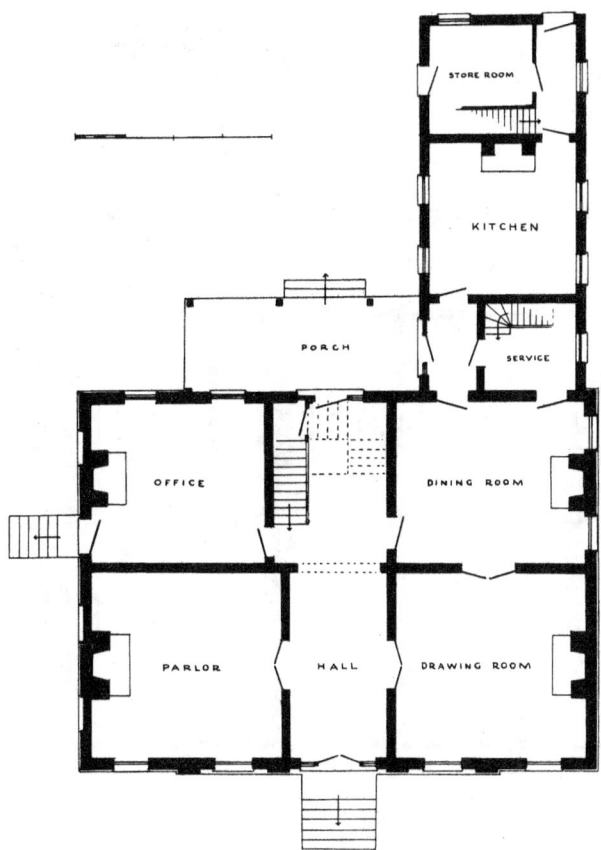

98. *First Floor Plan of Kennedy House. Restored.*

napolis, Maryland, by the architect William Buckland.[13] The Lexington design does not have the belt course of the other, which cuts uneasily across the vertical pilaster shafts. In common with the 1816 Transylvania building, some of the windows in the north sidewall of the Kennedy house were false. The plan is quite normal. A transverse hall is divided by an arched screen, the wider rear portion containing the staircase. The closet under the stairway gets daylight from one of the side lights of the back door (*Fig. 98*). The office adjacent to the stairs has a private entrance toward Constitution Street. Parlor and drawing room, across the hall from one another, form a suite at the front of the house. The dining room is behind the drawing room, with the service wing beyond. The storeroom at the end is a later addition. Chambers on the second floor follow the plan of the rooms below, with the exception that part of the area over the front

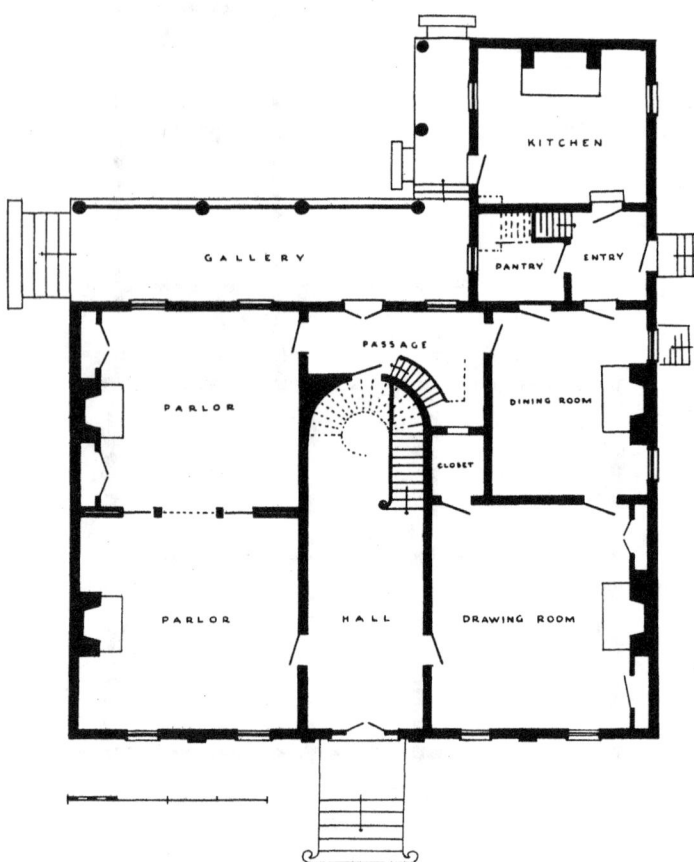

99. Principal Floor Plan of Grassland.

100. Paneled Screen between Parlors in Grassland.

hall becomes a small bedroom lighted by a triple window. Alterations dating from a few years before the Civil War include the installation of great sliding doors between each pair of rooms flanking the hall, the addition of a recessed entrance and a Corinthian portico, hoodmolds over the front fenestration, plate glass in the sashes, and bricking up the blind windows on the north end of the house. Recently, the building has served as an antique shop, roominghouse, and rummage center.

GRASSLAND   Among the most gracious and best preserved domestic establishments in Fayette County is Grassland, located between the Walnut Hill and Jacks Creek roads, now connected by Shelby Lane, which the house faces. It was built for Major Thomas Hart Shelby in 1823, which date is incised in the cornerstone on the east side of the building. Grassland resembles the Kennedy house, but has gabled ends, larger windowpanes, and a main block greater than the one on Limestone by about six feet in breadth and depth. Grassland also has finer interior fittings. Its long central hall features a staircase that curves gracefully around an open well, the passage with service stairs behind allowing for sequestered cross-circulation (*Fig. 99*). The rooms to the east of the hall can be thrown together by means of a thirteen-foot screen composed of side doors that slide back into wall pockets, and a double central leaf that disappears upward into the partition separating the chambers above, a wide carved archivolt on pilasters spanning a series of panels with re-entrant corners over the doors (*Fig. 100*). Across the hall in the drawing room the breakfront mantel is plain, having an elliptical panel in the centermost frieze block, and paneled pilasters enframing the fireplace. The latter is unusual in having stone instead of brick facing. Built-in presses are to either side, and another large closet serves this room, which may have been used for banquets on special occasions. The family dining room behind is considerably smaller; it has the same relative position as the dining room in the Kennedy house, also opening into a rear entry, with the kitchen beyond. Round brick posts to the rear gallery are like those at the Woolfolk house. A hollowed-out log, nineteen feet long and a little over a yard in diameter, for salting meats in the basement, must have been installed before the laying of the first floor.

The principal dependencies of the house are mostly intact, and constitute a noteworthy collection (*Fig. 101*). Included are a washhouse (perhaps a summer kitchen) with cook's room over (reached by an outside stairway), on a line with the service wing; a square smokehouse and octagonal icehouse to the west of the residence itself; and a coachhouse with attached tackroom and two privies southeast of the other buildings. The ensemble is spread over a 250-foot layout (*Fig. 102*).

THE MEADOWS   A mate to Grassland was The Meadows, located a mile east of old Lexington, north of the Winchester Pike. It was built for Dr. Elisha Warfield during the early 1830's. The facade originally was identical to the front of Grassland—including the extension of the cornice across the middle bay—yet the hipped roof and divided stairhall related it to the Kennedy house. The rear wing, which was considerably longer than those on either of the other two houses, went back from the righthand side of the main block. The Meadows suffered considerably from *fin-de-siècle* modernization: the staircase and mantels were replaced, pressed tin ceilings installed, and an ugly eclectic porch fixed before the front door. About 1950 a subdivision mushroomed along the wide street laid on the site of the driveway leading off Loudon Avenue up to the Warfield house, and in 1960 The Meadows was razed.

In surrounding counties are several houses close in appearance to the Kennedy house. The one on the Old Frankfort Pike in Woodford has been mentioned. It is said to have been built in 1825 by Samuel Wallace.[14] This house has rather heavy details, such as three upright oval sunbursts carved in the apron paneling of each of the windows in the living rooms. The Greek Doric portico would have been added later. A square smokehouse has a carved urn set on the apex of its pyramidal roof. The removal of the balustrade from the roof of the main house detracts considerably. Another house that is similar and not far distant faces the Leestown Pike and nearby Midway. A late nineteenth-century gingerbread porch spoils its facade. The two examples have 12- and 15-paned windows respectively. A third country house outside of Fayette is Buknore in Bourbon County, which bears the inscription "W. Buckner 1841" on the keystone over the entrance. Like Grassland, this one has a gabled roof. However, it has wings to either side, rather than at the back. A hallway arch springs from entablature imposts set on single Greek Doric columns surmounting

101. Main House and Dependencies at Grassland.

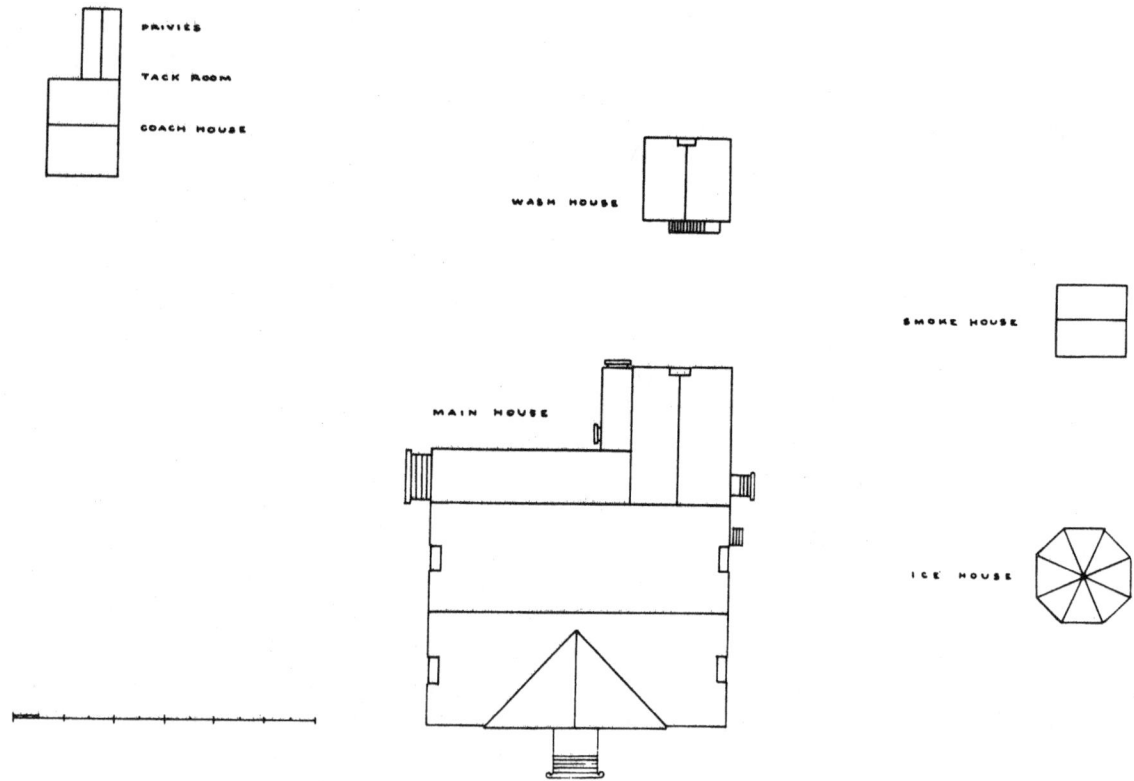

102. Roof Plan of Buildings, Grassland.

cubic plinths against the walls. Sliding doors recede into the walls between pairs of columns, resembling the corresponding feature in the much later house, Cedar Hall, on the Bowmans Mill Road (*Fig. 140*). Auvergne, built in 1837, also in Bourbon County, is practically a duplicate of Buknore.[15] Windows in both are 24-paned. A local tradition assigns the pair to an "English architect," who remains nameless. One more house that should be cited specifically stands on Lancaster Avenue in Richmond. It has a hipped roof and 15-paned windows. The wood members of its doorway have been adopted for our reconstruction drawing of the Kennedy house. (*Fig. 97*). Lunette and side lights in the Richmond house have been filled with later colored glass. Designs related to these buildings are to be found in houses at Frankfort, Bardstown, and Lebanon, although these have not the remarkable parallelisms that link the buildings named above. The construction of these houses ranges over a period of about two decades, and it seems significant that Matthew Kennedy was living—and presumably practicing—in Lexington throughout this score of years.

The Kennedy-house type—reproduced faithfully at least six times in Fayette and adjoining counties—although indebted to classicism for the basic design of its front elevation, was in no wise accountable to classic architecture for its individual parts. Pilasters were composed of shaft, necking, and a topmost molding that could answer for an echinus (*Fig. 97*), but there was no base and no abacus. Above, there was no full entablature, but only a simple cornice. The cornice responded to the pilasters by jutting forward over each of them. Despite archeological imperfections, as pure design the form is complete. Raking cornices identical with the horizontal one describe a pediment embracing the range of pilasters, and with a blind arch encircling a lunette pushing up into the tympanum, the superimposed triangle and supporting rectangular shapes are successfully coordinated into a unified design. Satisfactory effect justifies the abbreviation of parts.

Pediments, used occasionally among early brick Kentucky houses—as in small porticoes, and the entrance pavilions of Poplar Grove and Winton—appeared consistently in the last group of houses with which we have dealt. We now turn to the smaller division of houses of the 1820's that come under the heading of classicism, and here we find the pediment given greater prominence in the total scheme.

The first building to be discussed here is somewhat related to the one-story houses described in the preceding chapter, but the low, spreading form it might have had is transformed by high gabled roofs containing bedrooms on the second floor, and by a conspicious display of the portico. In the earlier group, the portico was missing, or unassuming (as at Lewis Manor), but certainly not so well integrated into the masonry fabric.

WHITE COTTAGE   Listed in the 1838 city directory as the home of Farmer Dewees, the house which faced the head of Rose Street in Lexington was built for Dewees *ca.* 1824, or for his predecessor a few years earlier. Dewees was a partner of the firm of Dewees and Grant, tobacco and oil manufacturers. In honor of its early owner, the street bounding the west side of the property was changed from Back to Deweese (spelled incorrectly with a final vowel).

A tradition persists that there were gardens on the rise of ground around White Cottage laid out by the famous and eccentric botanist Constantine Samuel Rafinesque,[16] who concluded his central Kentucky sojourn in 1826. Quite apart from its fine natural or implanted surroundings, the Dewees house compelled notice. Its most striking feature was the 35-foot recessed portico composed of a five-bayed arcade sustaining a steeply pitched brick pediment pierced by a Palladian window (*Fig. 103*). Arched windows and arched transoms over doors lighted the drawing room and halls beyond the portico, and single arched windows, disguised as Palladians, let light and air into the terminal rooms. The external walls were covered with stucco, like those of the Morton house, and the corners were finished with a similar dentate. Here the comparisons end, White Cottage being a bold eccentric. The inspiration for the Dewees house is a puzzle, especially with regard to the sunken portico. It may have come from a published diagram of some sixteenth-century villa in the vicinity of Venice or Vicenza, or from some interpretation of the Italian designs in the British Isles, just as the arcades at Washington's Mount Vernon evidently were taken from the hemicycles at Haddo House, Aberdeenshire, Scotland, illustrated in William Adam's *Vitruvius Scoticus* (Edinburgh, 1750).[17] The portico arcade of White Cottage may have been suggested by

103. White Cottage. Restored.

one of Jefferson's buildings, such as the basement treatment of Pavilion VII or the students' ranges at the University of Virginia in Charlottesville, the latter probably derived from a Robert Morris design.[18] The clear-cut quality of White Cottage suggests the severity of the architectural compositions of the French designer Claude-Nicolas Ledoux (1736-1806), which, however, are difficult to relate inasmuch as Ledoux's works were not published until two decades after the building of the Lexington house.[19] The arches of the portico spring from a square abacus set directly on the cylindrical shaft, a uniquely Ledoux motif. The intermediary may have been some French house of the lower Mississippi River region, where encircling *galeries* supported on round brick pillars date from the middle of the eighteenth century, as at Parlange (1750) at New Roads, Louisiana.[20] The elevated main floor of White Cottage simulates the raised-basement type of house of the Deep South, and the tall, round-headed voids opening onto the portico indicate high southern ceilings. The plan of White Cottage, with twin transverse halls flanking the central drawing room (*Fig. 104*), is similar to the arrangement of Gloucester (*ca.* 1800), a house a few miles below Natchez.[21] A small stairway in the east hall ascends to the upper floor, where there is a chamber over each of the three original rooms and the front portico. A hipped-roof extension was added on the left end, which made the house exceedingly broad. There was a lean-to at the back, probably a gallery originally.[22] During the early 1870's the house became the residence of H. Howard Gratz, publisher of the *Kentucky Gazette*. In 1888 members of the Christ Church Women's Guild opened the Protestant Infirmary in the Dewees house, and eleven years later it went under interdenominational Protestant management, with the name changed to the Good Samaritan Hospital. Other buildings were erected and occupied until the middle of the first decade of the present century, when the hospital was moved to its present site on South Limestone Street. White Cottage deteriorated rapidly and was finally demolished in June, 1940.

Below the Old Frankfort Pike in Woodford County, near Versailles, is a house called Pleasant Lawn, built in 1829 for Daniel Jackson Williams.

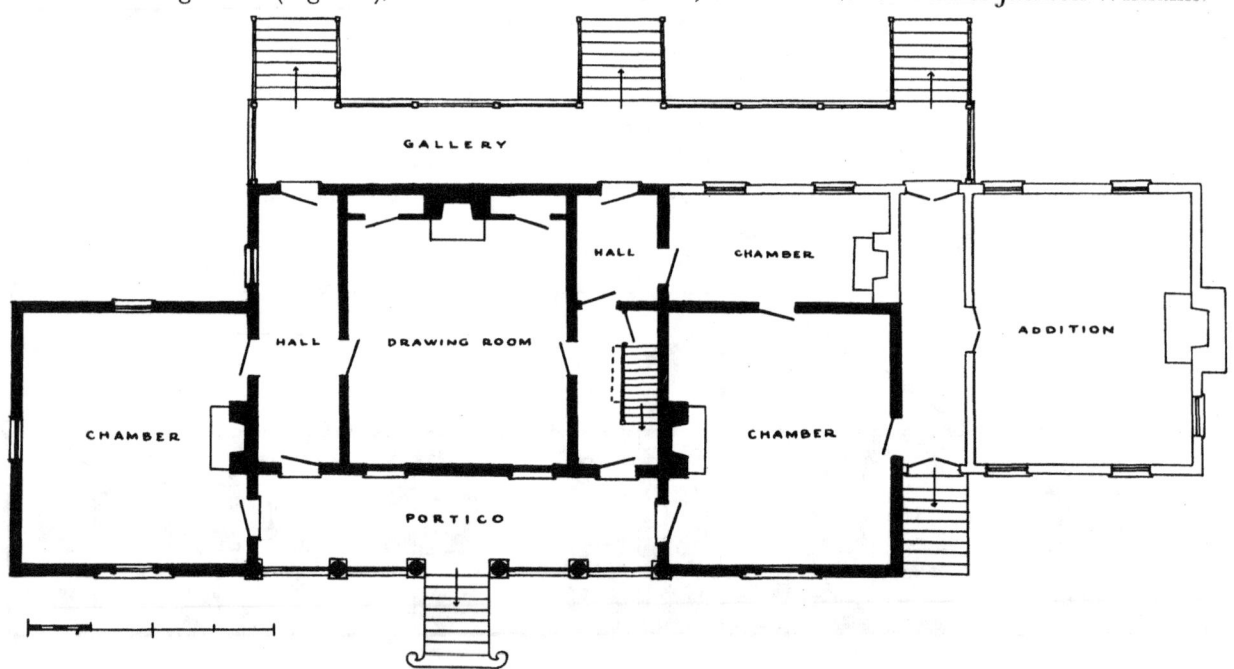

104. *Plan of White Cottage. Unshaded Portions Conjectural Restoration.*

105. Doland House.

106. Classic Cottage. Restored.

It bears an affinity to White Cottage in its general impression and in its two indented porticoes. The rear one—six bays across—is about equal in size to that of the Dewees house, and the front arcade—of nine bays—is forty-eight feet in breadth. The porticoes are placed at opposite halves of the long house form.[23] The pediment over neither conforms to the arcade: the front one, although on axis with it, spans only five bays, and the rear one is centered between the fourth and fifth bays. A Palladian window is in each brick tympanum. The similarity ends with the vertical structure. In plan the two sections of Pleasant Lawn contain a stairhall between a pair of rooms of about equal size. The outside walls of this house were not stuccoed and probably never painted. Special recognition is claimed by the primitive landscape murals, painted by Alfred Cohen, in its drawing room.[24]

DOLAND HOUSE   An abridgment of the White Cottage design materialized in the front addition to the Doland house on what was then the Harriets Mill Road (corner of Bethel Road and Dolan Lane) in the northwest corner of Fayette County. The recessed portico is only three bays wide, turned wooden posts holding up the brick pediment, into which is crowded a small Palladian window *(Fig. 105)*. Only the walls inside the portico are plastered and painted, in which respect, as well as in the spacing of the supports, the Doland house is reminiscent of the Gist-Peck house *(Fig. 80)*. Passages eliminated, the three rooms open directly onto the portico. Ceilings of the main story are quite high, the cornice continuing level with that of the earlier house at the rear, which is two-storied, the first floor somewhat below that of the front mass. Corbie steps of medieval type are on the back gable.

A CLASSIC COTTAGE   In Lexington, a block away from White Cottage, where the Esplanade now meets Main Street, stood a diminutive house of pure classic taste. The wooden portico, of low, elliptical arches springing from six Tuscan columns, spanned the entire front, giving the building a temple form. A Palladian window adorned the pediment, and a leaded fanlight was superimposed over the front door, compared earlier to a plate in Asher Benjamin's *The Builder's Assistant (Fig. 106*—see also *Fig. 36)*. Steps at the center of the portico rose between pedestals thrust forward at the base of the third and fourth columns. The columns are complete in all their parts, and the architect seems to have been conversant with classic elements. The design as a whole shows sensitive planning. However, one wonders over the lack of window height in the main story. This could be remedied by an additional row of panes or an arch to the upper sashes, which would make the windows more in keeping with the airy quality of the arcade itself, and at the same time provide better lighting for the rooms. The chimneys indicate that the house was two rooms wide and two deep, and the dormers (one restored) indicate some use was made of the upper floor. The elevation of the house *(Fig. 106)* was made from a photograph in the collection of the late Charles R.

Staples, whose label identifies the house as belonging to Mrs. Susan Bell. Susan Bell is listed in the 1859 city directory as living on Short Street between Walnut and Back (Deweese) streets.[25] It is possible that she owned a strip of land extending through the entire block from Main, but if so, it was intersected by an alley midway between the two streets. The name is marked with an asterisk, denoting that she was a colored person.

THE GREEK REVIVAL 7

THE GREEK REVIVAL movement literally came into being in America with Benjamin Henry Latrobe's Bank of Pennsylvania, designed in the spring of 1798 and brought to completion during the summer of 1800.[1] The popularity of the Greek Revival in this country was inevitable for several reasons: it was the logical conclusion of the classic idiom that had been gaining momentum since before the Revolution; it had a bigness and simplicity compatible with American ambition and directness, and in line with new machinery developments; and it struck a chord responsive to New World ideals, the ancient Greeks maintaining the freedom of small city states and the contemporary Greeks rebelling against the tyranny of the Turks in an attempt to regain their independence. The Greek Revival was more widely and enthusiastically accepted in the United States than in any European country, becoming virtually the national mode of the first six decades of the nineteenth century.

An Englishman, James Stuart, who carried on extensive archeological research in the Aegean area during the middle of the eighteenth century, designed the first Greek monument of modern times, the Garden Temple built at Hagley, England, for Lord Lyttelton in 1758.[2] James Stuart and Nicholas Revett published four volumes of plates depicting *The Antiquities of Athens* between 1762 and 1816, with a supplement in 1830. These London publications provided the design sources for the forthcoming movement in the United States.

Benjamin Henry Latrobe (1764-1820) was thoroughly imbued with the latest British fashion at the time he landed at Norfolk in 1796. The need for buildings in the young republic provided a greater opportunity for application of Greek Revival concepts than had been offered in England. It was a timely moment for a change of style in America, and Latrobe's innovation was found wholly suitable.

The American protagonists of the Greek Revival came to constitute a numerous band, of which only two need be mentioned here. They were the foremost disciples of Latrobe, Robert Mills (1781-1855) and William Strickland (1787-1854). Mills' work showed a tendency toward simplification, his completed buildings often achieving an austerity far excelling even that of his original designs, as in the case of the Washington Monument, which emerged a cleancut obelisk devoid of the Doric peristyle surrounding its base that figured in the early renderings.[3] Strickland was a brilliant designer, combining literal elements into new and daring compositions. During his later period he worked just south of Kentucky, around Nashville, but his influence in the Bluegrass was largely indirect. He tutored the son of Matthias Shryock, the youthful Gideon Shryock (1802-1880), who introduced the Greek Revival into Kentucky in the statehouse built at Frankfort during the period 1827-29.[4]

As the culmination of the classic trend, the Greek Revival style made conspicuous use of the orders, with the portico, often of colossal size, being its most striking feature. Complete entablatures, or at least architrave and cornice, were used internally, in conjunction with flat pilasters and full-round columns. The use of steampowered tools supplanted carving by hand.[5] Designing of details was taken over by the architect, which, theoretically at least, made for greater consistency throughout. The Greek Revival architect concentrated more upon paperwork, often with a builder to perform the physical task of constructing the structure from his drawings. With the turning toward Greek inspiration, the arch fell into disuse, particularly in domestic buildings, but with the heavy post-and-lintel system, new effects were explored with deliberation. An awareness of space led to the opening up of interiors. Double parlors were separated by tall sliding doors that rose to the entablature, or by a screen of free-standing columns, so that two rooms virtually became one. Greek triglyphs and anthemions appeared on friezes, replacing the earlier Adam sunbursts, rosettes, and stars. Egg-and-dart and bead-and-reel took the place of modillions, which, however, returned to join the later motifs toward the end of the Greek period; dentils increased in size. Floral forms were modeled in plaster for centerpieces or cast in iron for window grilles and other external decoration. These were produced locally or imported from the eastern states.[6] Interior wallpaneling went out of fashion. Panels in doors became fewer and larger, a single pair of tall panels becoming as much of a hallmark for the Greek Revival as the six-panel door had been for the previous periods. Mantels often now were of marble, some manufactured in Louisville, Philadelphia, or New York from Egyptian, Italian, or Vermont stone, and costing but little more than the wood equivalents.[7] Chairrailing was eliminated and the baseboard became heavier, attaining a height of eighteen inches. Windows and windowpanes expanded in size,[8] but the frames became narrower, differing from the earlier flat, pegged variety in being splayed, and mitered at the corners. Window sills—now frequently of stone—and outside stone steps became square-cornered blocks, devoid of nosing. Characteristic tooling consisted of a one-inch outer margin of ribbing perpendicular to the edge, enframing an area of chiseled indentations. Stone lintels sometimes replaced brick voussoirs over voids. Front doorways became recessed, the portal flanked by columns, antae or pilasters. Flemish- and common-bond brickwork continued in use, and also an all-stretcher, unbonded type came into being, as in the pilastered front wall of the former Hunt house on Barr Street. The average room and average dwelling grew larger and more monumental.

The landscape setting began to be brought more into accord with the architecture, but not the architecture in accord with nature. A brick terrace was laid around houses, often measuring six or more feet across, thus creating an artificial mat for the building, and at the same time making planting impossible in the immediate vicinity. Under the influence of Greek Revival formality, tall, straight trees were spaced uniformly along the driveway leading to the "big house," reflecting the regimentation established by the great cylindrical columns of the portico. Earlier houses had been placed on prominent rises of ground to obtain a view, but mansions of the Greek Revival period were set on hills in order that they might *be* viewed. Such was their ostentation.

Greek Revival architecture was no more bound to the exclusive use of Greek forms than the Classic Revival had been to Roman. Roman elements, in fact, continued to be employed, although in a more masculine vein. The Egyptian also figured in the style—as in Mills' Washington Monument in the nation's capital, Strickland's First Presbyterian Church in Nashville, and the 1857 receiving vault in the Lexington Cemetery—but seldom outside of public buildings and memorials.[9] Incorporating geometric forms for pure effect, heedless of historical precedent, was one of the delightful diversions of the Greek Revival, distinguishable from the abstraction of the decade prior to 1820 in that here the geometry was applied to uprights rather than to horizontals, that is, to elevations rather than to plans, to solids instead of to voids. Circular, oval, or polygonal rooms no longer were considered so desirable in themselves. Yet there was greater awareness of the relationship of rooms in suites, and of opening up one room into the next.

The Greek Revival traversed the Alleghenies with the return of Gideon Shryock, making its debut, as has been said, in the Frankfort statehouse, which played a role in Kentucky analogous to that of Latrobe's Philadelphia bank in America. In 1830, the year after the completion of the statehouse, Shryock undertook the erection of a new edifice in Lexington for Transylvania University, to replace the Kennedy building that had burned. The foundations were under construction on the old lot (site of Gratz Park) when the board of trustees acted upon the purchase of a larger campus on the north side of Third Street. On this was to be built a building half again as large as the one begun.[10] The result was Morrison College, completed in 1834, a majestic pile of rigid forms, with a proud Doric portico of six columns elevated on a high basement and broad stairs between cubic antapodia. The facade is reminiscent of William Strickland's United States Naval Home in Philadelphia, built in 1826.[11] Horizontal parapets concealed the sloping roof lines of Morrison College. The style seemed particularly well suited to public buildings, but its elegance was too desirable to be barred from residential design.

The Greek Revival entailed the greatest stylistic change in American architecture up to this time. Formerly—especially inland—people had not much bothered with the identity of sources. It mattered little that parapets and crowstepped gables, prominent chimneys, leaded glass, and chamfered posts were medieval, whereas pediments and porticoes, quoins and columned enframements were classic. But in the Greek Revival period, attention was paid to such details. Things had to be done *à la mode,* and if neglectful, one ran the risk of being unfashionable. The guides to correct taste were the architectural books that superseded the earlier builder's guides, the newer ones usually of larger format and more refined engraved plates than their predecessors. Yet it is not to be suggested that the later books presented only illustrations of correct specimens of Greek architecture, like the Stuart and Revett volumes published in England. Far from it: after the initial appearance of a few plates of orders, books advocating the Greek Revival stressed the modern adaptability of antique elements.

The first American architectural book to offer the Greek orders was John Haviland's *The Builder's Assistant,* published in Philadelphia in three volumes from 1818 to 1821. Foliated rosettes in the Haviland book may have served as

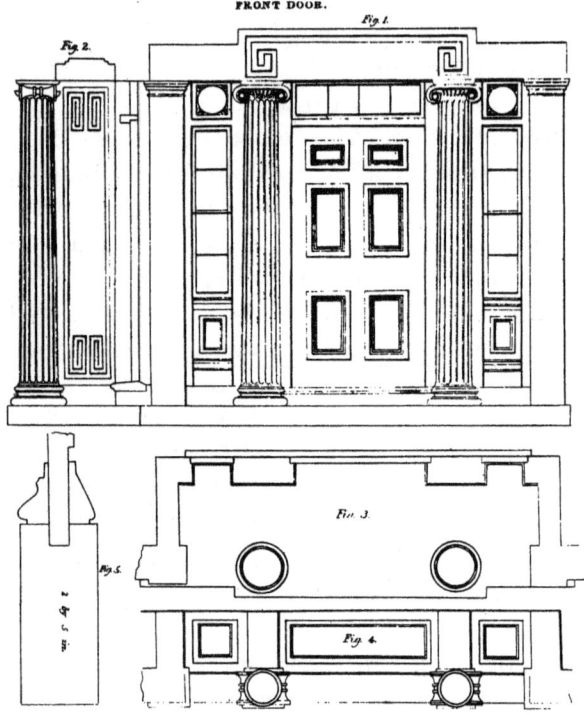

107. *Design for a Front Door. Edward Shaw, Civil Architecture (Boston, 1836), 78.*

models for the plaster motifs in the coffered ceiling of the senate chamber in the Shryock statehouse at Frankfort, and in particular the centerpiece from which the chandelier is suspended.[12] The sixth enlarged edition of Asher Benjamin's second book, *The American Builder's Companion* (1827), was the next containing Grecian motifs, although confined to the orders of two Greek temples, the Parthenon and the temple on the Ilissus. The majority of the architectural books devoted primarily or exclusively to the Greek Revival were published during the 1830's. Besides Haviland and Benjamin, the principal authors were Minard Lafever, William Brown, Chester Hills, and Edward Shaw. The design for a recessed front door in Shaw's *Civil Architecture* (Boston, 1836) was the obvious prototype for the main doorway of a former house near Lexington called The Elms. Fluted Ionic columns *in antis* support a flat architrave raised a few inches in the center, forming a broad panel in which is a sunken fascia whorled in angular helices at either end, directly above the

columns (*Fig. 107*). The door itself behind is encompassed by side lights and a transom. As interpreted in The Elms, built by John McMurtry on the Harrodsburg Pike during the later 1840's, the doorway is more shallow and, although the elements are all accounted for, the proportions have been changed. Dual-leaf doors, in a wider opening, replace the single door; the side lights continue up to lintel level, the five-pane height corresponding to the balance of the first-floor windows in the facade (*Fig. 108*). The columns are more slender, their shafts without fluting. A copy of the Shaw book was owned by the architect Thomas Lewinski, who was associated with McMurtry on several projects, as well as related to him through marriage.[13]

The author and designer whose books were most influential upon Kentucky architecture was Minard Lafever (1797-1854). Strangely enough, this architect's principal executed buildings were Gothic Revival churches in Brooklyn, New York.[14] The Greek mode was reserved for secular architecture, and Lafever achieved, through his borrowings from the antique, designs that often showed great sensitivity and beauty. His five

108. *Front Doorway of The Elms.*

OF THE BLUEGRASS

109. *Design for a Front Door. Minard Lafever, The Modern Builder's Guide (New York, 1833), plate 63.*

books went into fourteen or more editions between the appearance of the first one, *The Young Builder's General Instructor,* in 1829, and the last, *The Architectural Instructor,* published posthumously in 1856. Illustrations in the earliest have to do mostly with minor embellishments, and alternative versions of each item are given. Design 50 inspired Ionic columns with anthemion appliqué in the porticoes of the Cochran house and Lemon Hill. Plates in Lafever's second book, *The Modern Builder's Guide* (New York, 1833), were finer in every respect than those in the first. The high standard of quality can be seen in Plate 63, inscribed "Designed and Drawn by J. H. Dakin for Lafever" (*Fig. 109*).

This frontispiece by the New York–New Orleans architect was adapted for the entrance to the Holloway house in Richmond, Kentucky.[15] The entablature, with its frieze taken from the doorway on the north side of the Erechtheum on the Athenian Acropolis, was duplicated twice in Fayette County doorways—at Waveland off the Nicholasville Pike, and at the McCann house on the Richmond Pike. In these frontispieces, decorated pilaster shafts and freestanding fluted Ionic columns *in antis* uphold the entablature (*Fig. 110*). The transom design in the Dakin rendering may have inspired the oft-repeated cast-iron grille inserted in Lexington attic windows, as in the Butler house (*Fig. 151*) and others, and including downtown commercial houses. The door design in Plate 81 in *The Modern Builder's Guide* suggests the entranceway of the late Greek Revival house at Kirklevington (*Fig. 125*), three miles below Lexington.

Lafever's third, finest, and most popular volume was *The Beauties of Modern Architecture,* issued at New York in 1835. As indicated by the title, stress was laid upon original concepts, although derived from antique sources. *The Beauties of Modern Architecture* presented the ceiling centerpiece from which hung the

110. *Front Doorway of Waveland.*

chandelier in the living rooms of a goodly number of the better Greek Revival residences in Kentucky. In Fayette, such centerpieces appeared in the Gibson house, the McCann house, the McCauley house, and the Johnson house. This centerpiece was a radical pattern in high relief, composed of petals and tongues, ovoids, rinceau, anthemions, and rosettes (*Fig. 111*). The rosettes were omitted in the Fayette examples, but were enlarged in the hall centerpiece of the Holloway house at Richmond.[16] Round recessed panels encircle the center flowers in the Gibson and McCauley houses in Lexington. The centerpieces were cast in plaster in mass production, and perhaps offered for sale by catalog.[17] Gideon Shryock recognized the merits of the plates in the 1835 Lafever book. The architrave inside his Southern National Bank (1837) in Louisville was supported on screens of colossal Corinthian columns based on the order of the Monument of Lysicrates at Athens, shown in Plate 43 of this volume. The 40-foot tall facade of the Louisville bank is an adaptation of a "Sliding Door Design" delineated in the *Beauties* (Plate 25).[18] A doorway similar to that shown in the book separates the double parlors at Cedar Hall, with Ionic columns on both sides of the sliding doors. (*Fig. 140*). Another is in the McCauley house,

111. *Centerpiece Design. Minard Lafever, The Beauties of Modern Architecture (New York, 1835), plate 21.*

112. *South and East Views of Ashton House. Restored.*

but here the entablature encircles the rooms. A heading resembling that of the "Sliding Door Design" figures on the enframement to a single door, shown on Plate 1 in the third Lafever book. This was actualized in unpainted walnut in the hall doorways of the Ward mansion near Georgetown. The jutting outer molding near the top, called "Greek ears," and battered sidepieces constitute the salient features of the common type of door of the Greek Revival period, as in Waveland and the Butler and McCauley houses. Sometimes a crowning cornice was used, as in the front hall of the McCann house on the Richmond Pike.

The boldness and high-styled quality of the Greek Revival made earlier houses look obsolete. Additions to existing buildings now invariably were carried out in the latest vogue, whereas formerly new wings had exhibited no special stylistic distinction from the buildings to which they were attached. In some cases the original structure was remodeled in order to be made consistent with the later part, as in Higgins

Mansion and the Gibson house in Lexington. In others the application of the new style was superficial, as in the example to be considered next, which did not benefit in either enlargement or internal improvement.

ASHTON HOUSE   The Jacob Ashton house, built on East High Street (at present facing Rodes Avenue) in 1834, was a story-and-a-half Federal cottage, with a Palladian window in the pediment over the front door, and an open gallery on piers at the back, where the ground slopes down to Town Fork. A decade later it was enhanced by a wood distyle Doric portico at the entrance. A sympathetic treatment across the balance of the facade included pilasters and a heavy entablature rising above the original cornice level (*Fig. 112*). The gable facing the street was masked by a rectangular parapet with paneled projections at the ends, the top of the Palladian window left showing above the pedimented roof of the portico. Decorative scrolls to either side probably were suggested by similar motifs on the Cochran house two doors away (*Fig. 145*). The heaviness of the Ashton house facade in comparison to the slight proportions of the original gallery across the rear illustrates the difference between the Greek Revival and Federal styles. The front was stripped off, the gallery replaced by a new brick addition, and the inside staircase reversed during alterations for conversion into a business house in 1941.

During the decades prior to the Civil War, one means of bringing a house up to date was the addition of a Greek portico. The size varied in accordance with the magnitude of the house to which the new porch was attached. The most sensitively designed addendum of this kind was the Ionic portico affixed to Rose Hill on North Limestone in Lexington. It is admirably suited to the character of the whole house, in spite of the fact that it overshadows the colonnetted fan doorway (*Fig. 85*). On the Bodley house at Market and Second streets a small portico became the frontispiece, copied after the tetrastyle Doric entrance porch of the Woolley house (*ca.* 1841) on the opposite corner. A two-storied portico along the north end of the Bodley house, presumably added at the same time, forms a pleasant link between house and garden. A colossal-order entrance portico was centered on the facade of Mount Brilliant (1792) on the Cynthiana (Russell Cave) Pike, which makes the exterior out of scale with the delicacy of its late eighteenth-century interiors.

HIGGINS MANSION   The residence between High and Maxwell streets (now skirted by Lexington Avenue) acquired by Joel Higgins in 1834 was a squarish, two-storied brick building, two rooms deep, with a central hall. The staircase ascending in the southeast corner of the hall had low and easy steps, its railing plain but delicate. A wide rear door under the landing was nine-paneled outside and batten with diagonal boards inside, reinforcement against sav-

113. Higgins Mansion. Restored.

age attacks of pioneer days. Higgins remodeled and enlarged this primitive house, giving it a grandiose front composed of a great portico of six rectangular brick piers supporting a full entablature and low-pitched pediment spanning the entire breadth of the building, an upper balcony having a delicate railing of wrought iron (*Fig. 113*). The portico motif was carried out on the single-storied flanking pavilions through the use of pilasters. The ends of these forms were gabled, the roof line finished with a simple raking board, the base and capitals of the pilasters turning the corner, but not the shaft itself. The main entablature extends only over the portico, in which respect the building resembles Morrison College. Large panes of glass in the windows of the main block replace sashes that probably contained twenty or twenty-four panes. The alterations achieved their purpose: in the MacCabe Directory for 1838-1839 the house was listed as Higgins *Mansion,* the only house in the directory honored by such an ennobling designation.

GIBSON HOUSE   The big house on the north side of West Second Street, about midway between Broadway and Jefferson Street, has seen many changes during its long existence. Built for Thomas January in the early 1800's, it was acquired by the Bank of the United States in 1820, and then became the home of the Episcopal Theological Seminary in 1834.[19] At this time the building consisted of a two-storied central mass three bays wide and two rooms deep with the chimney between, a narrow stairhall to the east, and a low porch across the front. Wings extended to the side and back, embracing a rear court (*Fig. 114*). There were several large dependencies behind the main house. Tobias Gibson of Louisiana became the purchaser in 1846, and called in the architect Thomas Lewinski to make "proposed alterations and improvements." Lewinski devised the monumental tetrastyle portico of fluted Ionic columns, and very likely combined the front room and passage into a single large reception hall. Two years later Gibson engaged John McMurtry to demolish the west rear (former chapel) wing, and to heighten the flanking wings and service ell into two full stories, a gallery of equal height to be built across the rear of the house and along the ell.[20] The front wall was carried up above the cornice height of the shallow portico, which gave the house an impressive appearance (*Fig. 115*). Clusters of octagonal chimneystacks rose atop the masked roof. The windows were enframed by cast-iron moldings with Greek ears. Besides the additional rooms on the second floor, the principal internal improvement carried out by Mc-

114. *Episcopal Theological Seminary, 1834-1846. From a Contemporary Lithograph.*

Murtry was removing the partition between the two parlors in the right wing and substituting "an Entablature supported by handsome Ionic Columns fluted also Pilasters against the wall." The architect likewise was "to run around said Parlor Ceilings A Handsome & appropriate cornice in Plaster and Put up in each ceiling an appropriate Center Piece in Plaster furnished in Good style & Taste." The centerpieces were modeled on the Lafever design we have seen (*Fig. 111*). The effect of the screen was similar to that in the Weir house (*Fig. 144*), except that the columns were Ionic. Egg-and-dart took the place of the cornice modillions. Twin marble mantels were brought from Louisiana by the owner to be installed in the parlors. Access to the gallery could be had through the tall rear windows. Now a large house, the building contained a library back of the reception hall, a pair of rooms for dining opposite the parlors, and an entry, pantry, kitchen, and scullery in the ell (*Fig. 116*). Chambers on the upper floor corresponded roughly to the rooms below. A narrow passage extended from the stairhall to the southwest bedroom, and a dressing room was inserted between the chambers over the dining rooms (*Fig. 117*). Space for a bathroom was provided over the pantry. Later changes to the Gibson house included plate glass in the windows and terracotta hood molds over the front openings. More recently, concrete disks have replaced the column bases. Early in the present century the house became the Campbell-Hagerman College for girls, and later part of the Lexington Conservatory of Music. Still later it was divided into apartments.

ALBERTI PLACE   Nine miles east of Lexington on the Winchester Pike stood a rambling building combining log, frame, and brick construction, resembling an inn more than a private residence (*Fig. 118*). Part of the building has recently been destroyed. The earliest section of the house was the front, built of logs, to which a frame structure was attached, the two parts separated by a long crosswise corridor containing a stairway, with shorter passages leading off at right angles, the halls terminating on various galleries (*Fig. 119*). One can only guess at how much of this house was in existence when it was purchased with thirty acres of land by John Charles Alberti for $900 in 1821.[21] In 1853, John Leer Bledson Alberti enlarged the landholdings,[22] and probably the house as well. The brick pavilion on the northwest corner is said to postdate the Civil War slightly.[23] The effect of the house is both impressive and casual, the various segments unified by side galleries. One's eye is brought to focus upon the front portico,

115. *Gibson House after the Remodeling of 1848.*

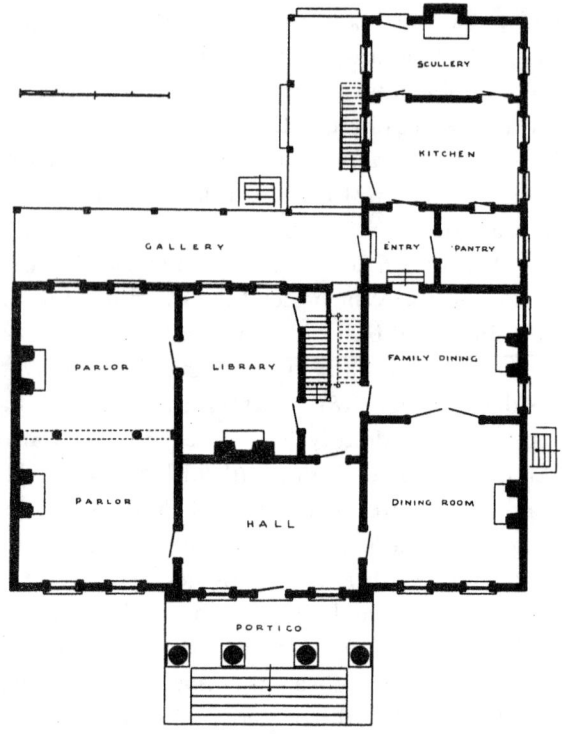

116. First Floor Plan of Gibson House.

where tall, square piers support interpenetrating roofs with pedimented ends. Twin doors occupy the center span of the wall, and benches stand beneath false windows to either side, with a projecting balcony above at the level of the paneled parapet over the east gallery. The supports here also are square wood piers, shorter than those in front, whereas the west and rear porch roofs are set on rustic round posts. The latter lacking parapets, the house seems rather squat seen from these sides. Rooms are dimly lit because of the encircling galleries and the scarcity of windows. The kitchen is the exception, being surprisingly well lighted and ventilated. The largest room is the dining room, as in many southern plantation homes. The upper chambers in the main part of the house are reached by the straight flight of steps in the crosscorridor, or the stairway ascending from the back porch.

The characteristic Greek Revival residential type in the Bluegrass is a symmetrical two-storied house, with the entrance sheltered by a pedimented tetrastyle portico the height of the house itself, and corresponding pilasters incorporated in the brick walls. Columns are arranged in pairs and the pilasters coupled at the corners. The column shafts are usually unfluted. Like the earlier round piers, they are constructed of wedge-shaped bricks, but are covered with stucco and painted. Bases and capitals are normally of wood, although acanthus leaves of the Corinthian are of cast iron. The front windows have triple lights, the shutters of the wider central void, when open, obstructing the narrow side lights. A transverse hall crosses the main block of the house, which may be either one or two rooms in depth, and a service ell extends behind. This species of house remained in fashion from the late 1830's until the mid-1860's, appearing in several distinct versions and undergoing slight modifications, with a tendency toward ornateness and a heightening of proportions during the later phase. The prototype of this group perhaps may be found in Virginia Federal architecture, in a house such as Horn Quarter in King William County, built for

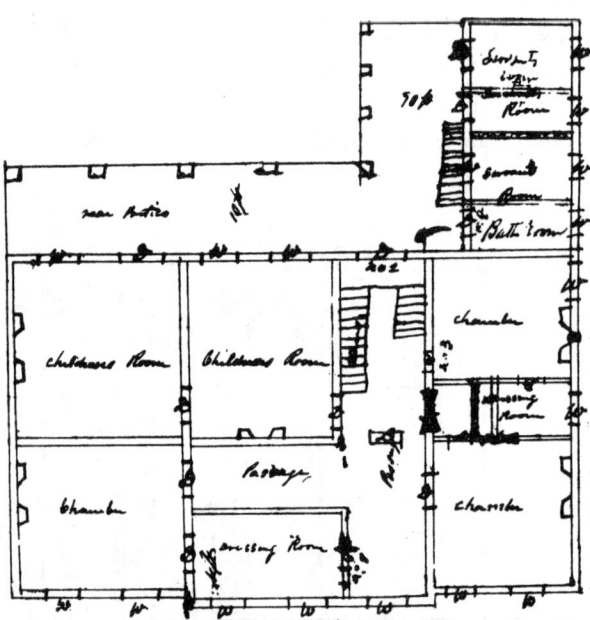

117. McMurtry's Sketch for the "Chamber floor—upper Story" of Gibson House. Letter to Gibson, July 11, 1848.

OF THE BLUEGRASS 89

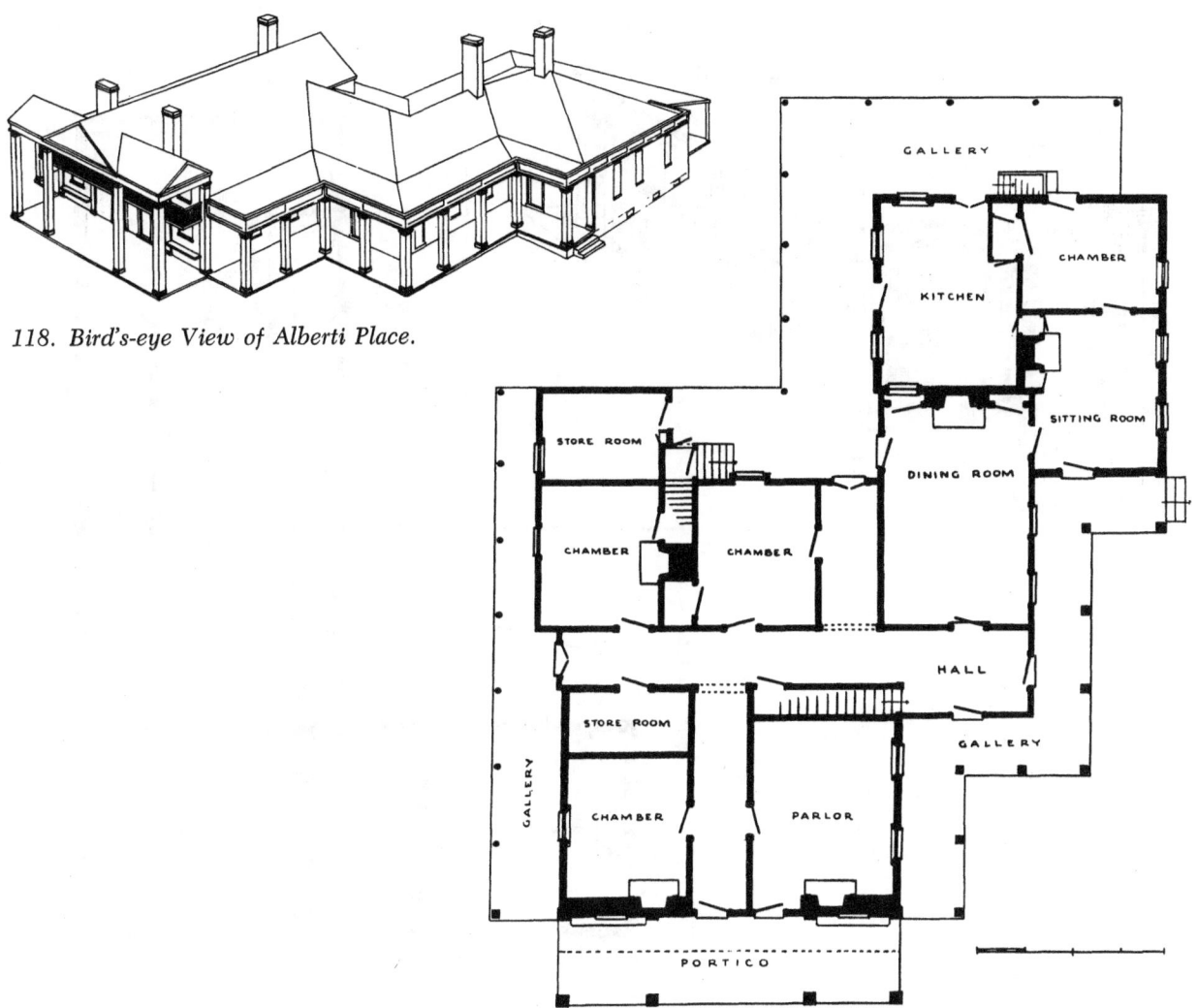

118. Bird's-eye View of Alberti Place.

119. Plan of Alberti Place.

George Taylor about 1800.[24] Resemblance lies in the portico and triple windows piercing a form of similar proportions, but there are no pilasters at the corners of the building, and the doorway has a fanlight typical of its period. Closer in style and period, although farther away geographically, is Sachem's Wood at New Haven, Connecticut, the Greek Revival house by which the New York architect Alexander J. Davis inaugurated his professional career in 1828.[25] The New Haven house does not have triple windows, and the outer supports to the portico are square antae instead of round columns. The Fayette County examples are divided into several groups according to the order of the portico, of which the first, and most pleasing, is—like Sachem's Wood—Ionic. The earliest is Shady Side, located about five miles from Lexington on the Paris Pike. The structure referred to is a front addition dating from about 1838, attached to the house built for Clifford Thompson in the 1790's.

WAVELAND Typical of Greek Revival design in Kentucky is Waveland (now the Kentucky Life Museum), on the Higbee Mill Road near the Nicholasville Pike. Waveland was constructed for Joseph Bryan about 1847. The builder is said to have been Washington Allen.[26]

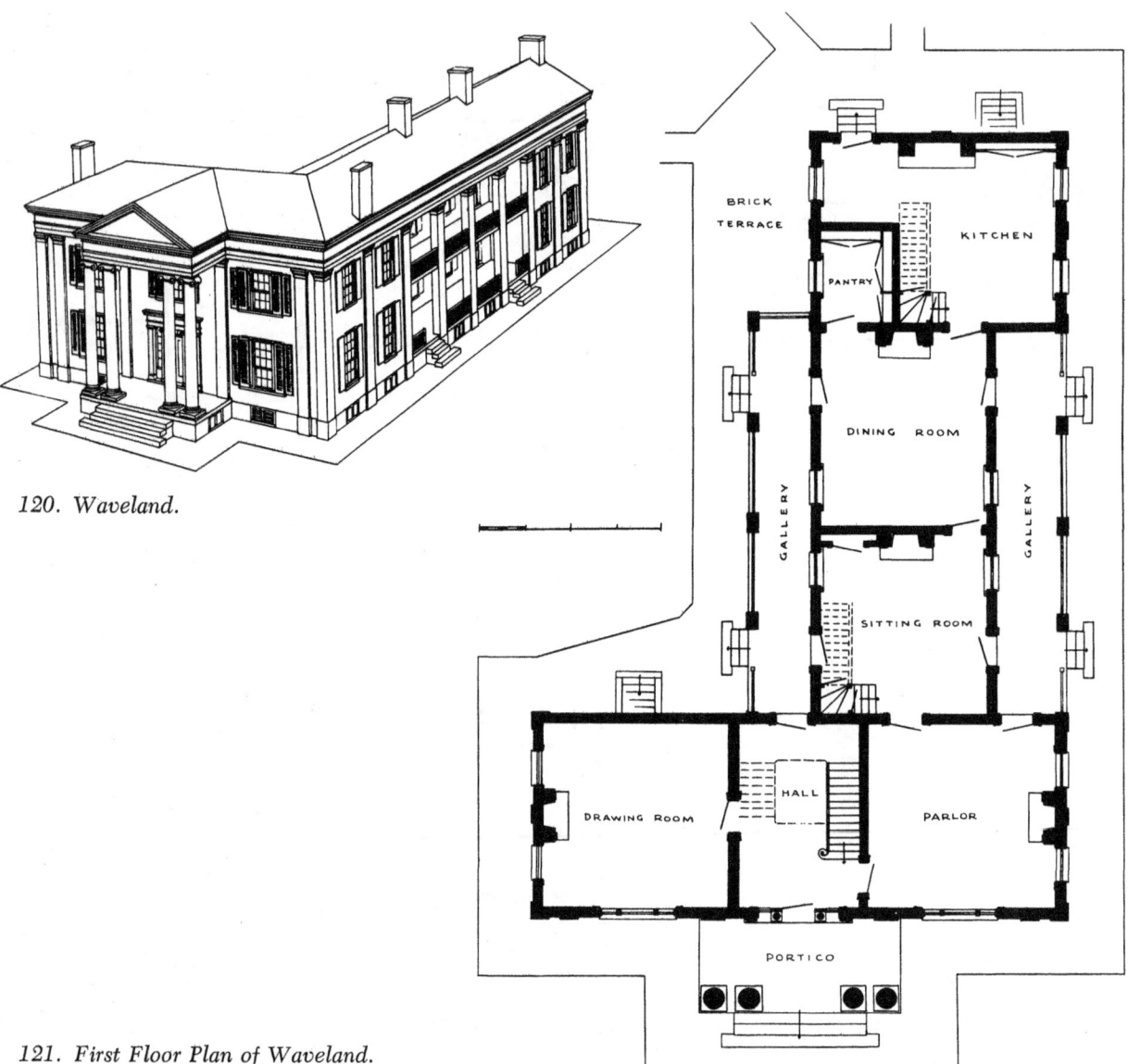

120. Waveland.

121. First Floor Plan of Waveland.

The paired portico columns are so close together that the volutes of the Ionic capitals almost touch. Broad stone steps rise to the wide center intercolumniation (*Fig. 120*). A range of nine pilasters or piers extends along the east flank of the inverted L form, recessed galleries on two levels occupying the four middle bays. The main doorway, with frieze taken from the Erechtheum, probably by way of Lafever's *Modern Builder's Guide,* has been illustrated (*Fig. 110*). It opens directly into the stairhall, with the drawing room and parlor of equal size to either side. An open gallery beyond the hall connects with the sitting room and dining room, and a pantry and kitchen are beyond (*Fig. 121*). A subsidiary stairway is in a corner of the sitting room, and a similar one is in the kitchen. The centering of windows between pilasters on the flanks places openings close to the chimneybreasts in the drawing room and parlor. The principal windows have fifteen panes in the first story and twelve in the second. Brick-built dependencies close to the house include an icehouse, a smokehouse, and a two-storied dwelling —originally houseservants' quarters—with a low porch on the east side. These buildings are reached by brick walks of herringbone design, extending from the terrace which encircles the residence proper at ground level (*Fig. 122*).

A house with a front mass resembling Waveland is that built (or rather rebuilt) for Sam Holley in 1852 at Payne's Depot in Scott County, only a short distance from the Fayette line.[27] A more pretentious example is Lynnwood in Mercer County.[28]

McCann House   Six miles southeast of Lexington on the Richmond Pike, is a house built for Benjamin McCann in 1847 at a cost of $40,000. At the time of the Civil War it was the home of Alexander Bush, and now is called Castlelawn. The McCann house (*Fig. 123*) has a facade similar to that of Waveland, but by actual measurement it is five feet narrower across the front. The end columns stand not quite so close together, and the windows are not so evenly spaced between the pilasters, but in other respects the houses are alike; the doorways are identical. The Richmond Pike house is a more compact form. The main mass is two rooms deep, with a short service ell attached. The front door opens into a reception hall, and a narrower enclosed stairhall is behind. The two pairs of rooms on each side are interconnected by large double doors. The door moldings form Greek ears at the top and support an overdoor frieze and cornice. The back gallery can be reached through the triple window in the rear parlor on the right, and a stairway in the dining room—corresponding to the subsidiary stairways in Waveland—is the only means of attaining the chamber above this room (*Fig. 124*). The centerpiece in the front hall is like those in the Gibson house parlors. The service room opens onto a dogtrot. The kitchen is beyond. The open dogtrot is a retarded feature for a house dating from the mid-1840's. The McCann house has undergone a few minor changes. The wall between the front hall and stair section has been removed, and the isolated upper chamber made to connect with the other rooms on this floor. The house has been attributed to the architect-builder John McMurtry.

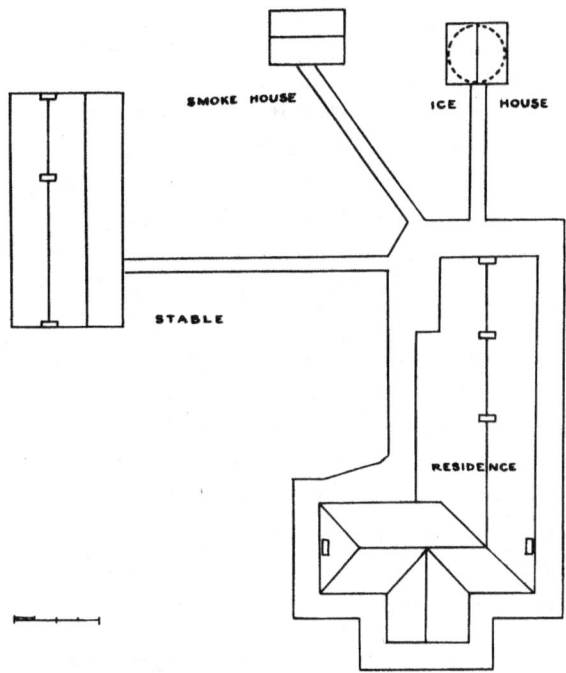

122. *Roof Plan of Main House and Dependencies, Waveland.*

Kirklevington   Hamilton A. Headley purchased 415 acres on the Tates Creek Pike three miles from Lexington in 1853, and added over 250 more during the next few years. On this estate he built one of the more imposing, and one of the last, of the Greek Revival mansions in Kentucky. Although actually postdating the war, the house belongs to the ante bellum tradition. The front and long left flank have much in common with Waveland. The flank, however, is one bay shorter, the gallery being three instead

123. *Benjamin McCann House.*

of four bays long. Conspicuous are the deeper cornices and rows of brackets spaced along the frieze, looking wholly out of place on an otherwise classic mass. Acroteria of debased form are at the summit of the pediment and ends of the front cornices. The portico columns have fluted shafts, and their bases and capitals are of stone, a unique material for these parts in Bluegrass residential building. The proportions are somewhat tall, which is especially noticeable in the fenestration, and windows in the two stories are of equal size (four panes high). The front doorway may be compared to Plate 81 in Minard Lafever's *The Modern Builder's Guide,* the first edition of which was over thirty years old when the house was built, but a seventh printing had come out only a little over a decade before, in 1855. The Headley doorway shows more fastidiousness of detail; it has colored glass—divided into small squares and long rectangles in the Eastlake manner—in the transom and side lights, fluting in recessed panels in the pilasters, more elaborate consoles, and lacelike scallops edging the narrow door paneling *(Fig. 125).* An extension at the back is of the same length as the front mass, so that the plan of the house is a great H, the initial letter of the builder's first and last names. Similar stairhalls are centered in both front and back wings. The property passed to Joseph Clark in 1878, and four years later was acquired by Archival Logan Hamilton, who gave it the name of Kirklevington, after a breed of cattle. The nearby Negro settlement—originally called Frog Town—later adopted this title, but

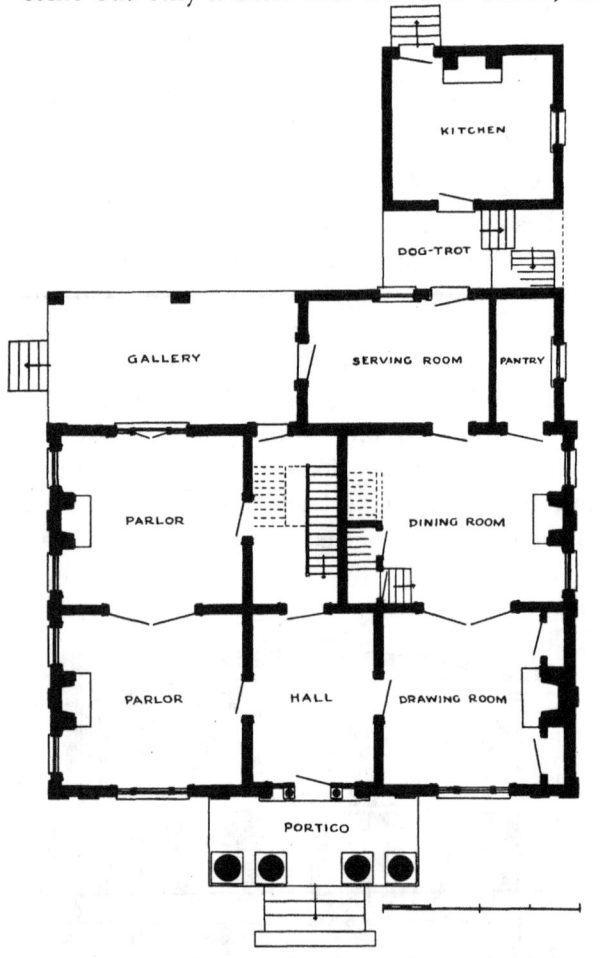
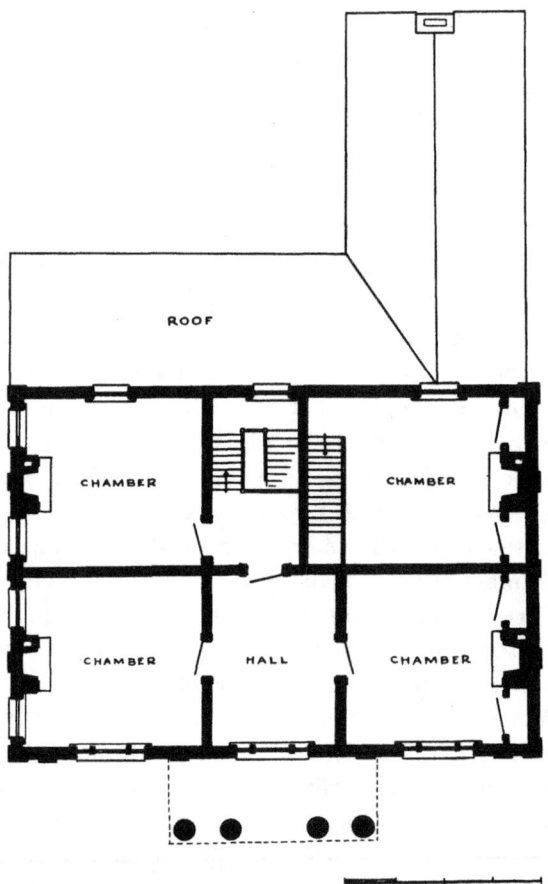

124. First and Second Floor Plans of McCann House.

125. Front Doorway of Kirklevington.

by 1900 the inhabitants were pronouncing it "Kirklivingston," and so it has remained.

A house that resembled Waveland and Kirklevington is Elmwood, on the northeast corner of Fourth and Walnut streets in Lexington, built by William Moses Brand during the 1840's or 1850's. It differed from the two country houses by having pairs of single windows to either side of the portico, which, according to an old photograph, appears to have had voluted column capitals.[29] The portico was removed after a fire, the superstructure changed, and the house remodeled extensively in 1905. A frame house following the same main lines is Science Hall on the Hornsback Mill (Briar Hill) Road, a front addition to an early brick dwelling.

A second group of Greek Revival houses is distinguished by a Roman Doric rather than an Ionic portico, with the end columns not so closely spaced, and with the dentils beneath the cornice usually omitted.

BUENNA HILL   A house appealing for its simplicity is Buenna Hill, built for Robert Innes by John McMurtry during the late 1840's. It is nine miles out the Cynthiana (Russell Cave) Pike. The building looks heavier than the Ionic examples lately seen; the proportions of the portico are more square, with stone steps across the entire breadth (*Fig. 126*). Triple windows are limited to the first story. The ends of the front block are pedimented, and the left flank of the inverted L shape is only six bays long, three devoted to a recessed gallery, over which the cornice drops to the architrave. The architect's good sense of planning has relegated the stairway to a hall back of the front foyer, an arrangement repeated a few years later in the larger house for Charles Innes across the pike (*Fig. 129*).

THOMAS-MOORE HOUSE   A sister house to Buenna Hill was built, presumably by the same

126. Buenna Hill.

ANTE BELLUM HOUSES

The house now called Colonial Home at Bethel also belongs to this class. Except for the column spacing, which is like that of the Thomas-Moore portico—with the bases restricted to a plinth, and with steps only at the central intercolumniation—its facade repeats that of Buenna Hill. The residence at Bethel has a hipped roof. The principal block is two rooms deep, with a single-storied kitchen ell off center at the back, between a gallery and a porch. A pair of square dependencies beyond are placed symmetrically in relation to the two-storied mass, in disregard of the upset of formal balance occasioned by the ell (*Fig. 127*). A portico similar to that of Colonial Home is on the plain house above Johnston's Mill in Scott County.

Two other residences related to this group, in adjoining counties, merit our attention. The first is the Noah Spears house (1854) on Pleasant Street in Paris, which, like Davis' Sachem's Wood, has square piers for end portico supports. The pair *in antis* have polygonal shafts that give the effect of fluting.[30] The second is the Allen house on Cane Run Road, below the Frankfort Pike near Georgetown. Finer in proportions and details than any of the others, this house has channeled Greek Doric columns to the portico, and triglyphs and other details in the entablature.[31] A compact rectangular block two rooms deep, it contains a circular staircase at the end of a transverse hall.

The third group of Fayette County houses is characterized by Corinthian columns. The acanthus-leaf capital usually denotes a later building in central Kentucky, belonging to the decade of the 1850's. The leaves cast in iron usually have a fine sculpturesque quality.

CORINTHIA Corinthia, designed and built by John McMurtry, and completed in September of 1854,[32] was the home of Charles Webb Innes. The building was an enlarged version of Buenna Hill, facing it across the Cynthiana (Russell Cave) Pike; the massing, however, follows a T rather than an L shape. The proportions are more upright, especially those of the windows and doors (*Fig. 128*). Triple lights were used for

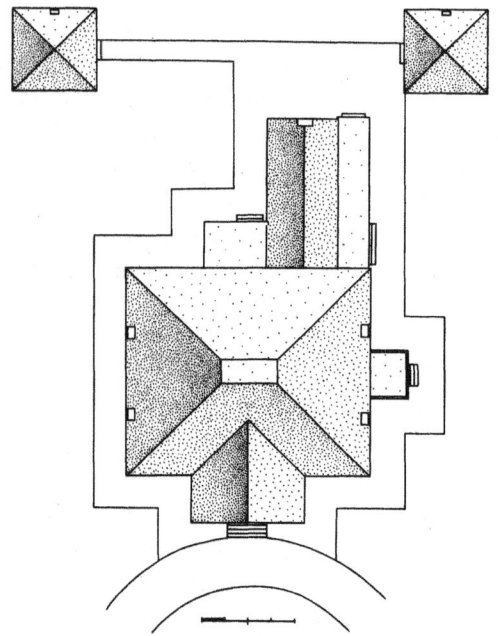

127. Roof Plan of Residence and Outbuildings, Colonial Home.

architect, three miles nearer town, across from Mount Brilliant, either for Major Barak G. Thomas during the mid-1840's, or a little afterward for William Grant Moore. There are several minor changes: the front doorway enframement has Greek ears rather than pilasters, the center window above is composed of three parts, and the portico columns are more closely paired. The house has been altered, and the brick walls painted white.

128. Corinthia.

OF THE BLUEGRASS

all of the front fenestration. Column bases are without plinths. The greater size of the house makes the chimneys seem insignificant. The plan is such that the front suite of hall and parlors can be isolated from the rest of the rooms. Sliding doors permit the opening up of this area into an interior fifty-eight feet long (*Fig. 129*). The main stairhall is directly behind, accessible to each of the side galleries and to the dining room between them. A secondary stairhall is behind the latter, with a pantry at one end. The kitchen is in the basement. Two chambers are at the base of the T plan; one, presumably for

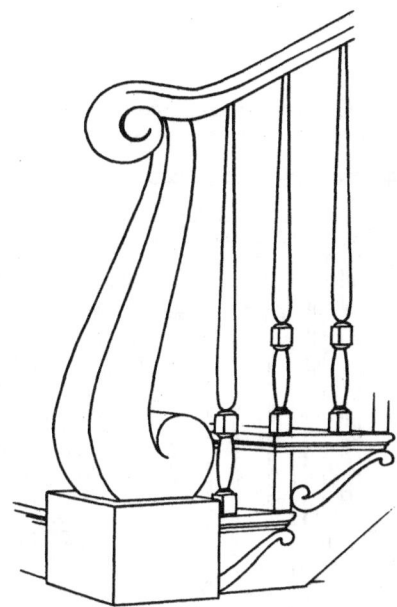

130. Newel Post of Main Staircase, Corinthia.

vagrants, opens off the south gallery. The arrangement of the second floor is similar. Flowered centerpieces in the parlor ceilings are of trivial design, and the woodwork throughout is rather thin and out of scale with the size of the building. A detail acceptable in design is the voluted newel post of the main staircase, like an element from a piece of Empire furniture (*Fig. 130*).

PETTIT HOUSE The house on the Nicholasville Pike just north of Stone Road was built for William B. Pettit about 1857. It is to Corinthia as the McCann house is to Waveland —that is, a deeper, compact mass, with a portico of the same order (*Fig. 131*). The proportions of the Pettit house—especially of the windows—

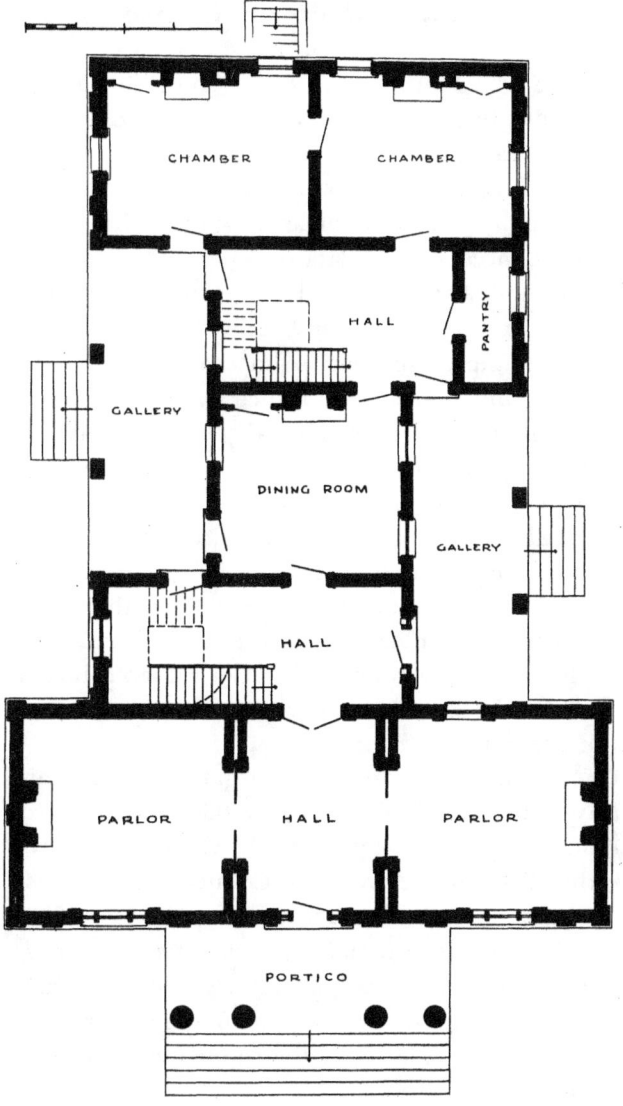

129. Principal Floor Plan of Corinthia.

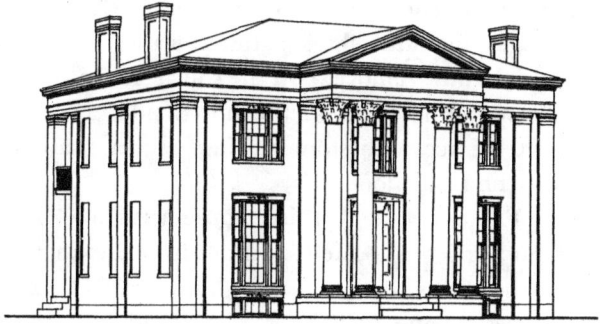

131. Pettit House.

132. Front Doorway of Hartland.

are more agreeable than those of Corinthia. The front steps are retracted into the podium of the portico, and the portal is recessed, with small Corinthian columns engaged to the doorway. Pilasters are applied sparingly along the flanks, where most of the windows are blind. The disposition of rooms is similar to that in the McCann house. The present designation, Alleghan Hall, comes from the building's having been a boy's school from 1887 to 1900, operating under the name of Alleghan Academy. The stone fence that borders the Nicholasville Pike was constructed from materials salvaged from the Lexington courthouse, burned in 1897. Later changes include white painted walls, a porte-cochère (now removed) on the south side, a porch corresponding to it on the north side, a raised front terrace with stone railing, and a fanlight over the front door.

FAIRLAWN   A third house with a Corinthian portico is located six miles from Lexington on the Paris Pike. It was built for Thomas Hughes during the 1850's. The land had been called Elkton by Edward C. Payne, who acquired it in 1816, but Hughes renamed it Fairlawn, or "Farelawn"—according to the spelling on the 1861 Hewitt map. The windows here are the same height on both stories, those upstairs single rather than of three lights. The plan is practically an inversion of that of the Pettit house, the double parlors being on the left side of the transverse hall, the sitting room and dining room on the right. The ell, however, is to the side of the dining room and not at the back. The railing on the roof is modern. Fairlawn retains its lovely rose-colored brick walls and maintains a well-kept look. After its purchase in 1926 by Payne Whitney, it was called Greentree.

SAYRE HOUSE   Another house in Fayette County that should be mentioned here is Bell Place, in Lexington on East Main Street. Originally built in 1845 for David A. Sayre, after a design by Major Thomas Lewinski, the house experienced several catastrophies. The last disaster was a fire in the 1890's, which prompted considerable remodeling. Painted white, it gives a first impression similar to that of the Pettit house, but upon closer inspection one notices a discordance in architectural detailing that is typically Victorian: the window divisions are gross, the Corinthian capitals lack plasticity, the dentils between frieze and cornice are too large, the porte-cochère on the side is insignificant, and, like the bay window dangling over the front door, out of context on a Greek Revival building. The house may not have had Corinthian columns before the fire. It is now owned by the city of Lexington.

The largest and most elegant house of this type in central Kentucky is the Junius Ward mansion on the Georgetown-Frankfort Pike, near the Allen house in Scott County. It is a rectangular mass, three rooms deep built in 1856, and retains its original silver and crystal fixtures, wall colors, and wallpapers. Its elliptical staircase is a noteworthy construction. The building was once considered by the commonwealth for a statehouse.[33]

The fourth group of houses differs from the

first three in having square piers in place of round columns in the porticoes. The obvious reason for this difference is economy. As this might suggest, other elaborations increasing construction costs usually were dispensed with also. Thus we find no full entablature encircling the building, but a simple cornice, pilasters only at the junction of the portico with the wall, and interior woodwork of the plainest type. Despite these cost cuts, the quality of workmanship remained at a high level. The Spurr house on the Athens-Boonesboro Road is typical of the group. The majority of the others are within a few miles' radius south and west of this house.

HARTLAND The residence built for John Hart during the 1840's, five miles below Lexington on the Armstrong Mill Road, combines dignity with simplicity. Coupled rectangular brick piers to the portico set the pattern for five triple windows in the facade, surrounding the chaste frontispiece, with Greek Doric columns *in antis* (*Fig. 132*). As at Waveland, a parlor and drawing room open off the central stairhall. The house is L-shaped; dining room, gallery and kitchen are located in the two-storied wing.

Delta, on the adjoining farm, is a house much like Hartland. The doorway also boasts Greek Doric columns, but it has two single windows instead of a compound window to each of the main rooms. Even more similar to the Hart house is Belair, on the Walnut Hill Road about three miles south-southeast of Hartland. It was built for Thomas Hart Shelby, Jr., in 1852. Continuing a mile or so farther in the same direction, one comes upon Highland Hall, facing the Richmond Pike. This house is a late example, built either on the eve of the war or soon afterward, as indicated by the looseness of the design and the use of double windows (*Fig. 133*). A photograph of Highland Hall went to the Philadelphia Centennial of 1876, illustrating "a typical Kentucky home" that cost $20,000 to build.[34] The windows in the wing are single and very narrow. Another kindred house is at the extreme west end of the county, the Carter place on the Military Road. It repeats the double windows and four-piered portico, but the pediment and roof of this house are more steeply pitched. Interior fittings in the Carter house are of Gothic Revival design; the doorframe in the

133. Highland Hall.

parlor, for instance, is colonnetted and battlemented.

A frame version of Hartland is the Bowman house, four miles from Lexington on the Harrodsburg Pike. The use of short timbers, perhaps, has prompted dividing the portico into two levels, with superimposed slender piers and two abbreviated entablatures. This portico was remodeled about 1959. Springhurst, halfway back to town, also was a frame house, having a portico resembling that of the Bowman house, but, like Delta, having two single windows to the main rooms. Springhurst burned in the spring of 1950. A similar survivor is Liberty Hall near Avon.

Of the numerous brick houses having rectangular portico piers in surrounding counties, only one seems worthy of our attention. It is the Baker house at the end of Baker's Lane, a short distance out of Nicholasville on the Lexington Pike. The size and general disposition of the house is like Waveland, with even the Erechtheum frieze appearing on the front doorway, though over Doric columns *in antis*. The portico is considerably broader than those we have been considering, embracing three bays of a five-bayed facade, much like the pillared portico that was added to Mount Brilliant. True to the tradition of houses with piers instead of columns, there are pilasters on the Baker house only where the portico abuts the front wall.

The broader portico brings us to the second important division of Greek Revival residences in the Bluegrass, those that follow the general scheme of the earlier Kennedy house type, carrying the classic form to its logical conclusion with a freestanding portico.

WALNUT HALL Walnut Hall, off the Newtown Pike north of the Iron Works Road, was built after 1842 for Victor Flournoy, a scion of a French Huguenot family, whose name was an anglicization of *Fleur Noir*. The facade of the main body of the house consists of five equal bays raised on a high podium, with full entablature, and a tetrastyle Doric portico reached by a straight flight of steps on axis with the front door, which was recessed behind slender Ionic colonettes *in antis* (*Fig. 134*). The main columns are attenuated and without channels. The architrave and frieze are separated by a fillet with pendant guttae, and a Greek meander occupies the upper half of the frieze. Brick pilasters, evenly spaced along the flanks, as across the south front, give an air of regularity to the building. As is normal in Greek Revival houses two rooms deep, there is a truncated hipped roof, this one with a railing around the flat summit. Dividing the two pairs of rooms in the principal

134. *Walnut Hall. Restored.*

OF THE BLUEGRASS 99

block is a central transverse hall, at the far end of which ascends an elliptical staircase, more narrow and steep than might be expected. The twin parlors on the right side are separated only by a screen of Corinthian columns. The entablature in these two rooms repeats the meander featured on the outside.

Walnut Hall became the property of Major John S. Clark in 1879. In 1892 one of the world's foremost horsebreeding establishments was founded here, and continues as such to the present day. Two-story wings were later thrown up on both sides of the original house, a banister and belvedere were set on top, a couple of cast-iron female lantern bearers on pedestals were placed at the base of the front steps, and a wrought-iron railing of poor design was added around the portico and stairway, with a matching balcony over the front door.[35]

MCCAULEY HOUSE Resembling Walnut Hall is the house built by John McMurtry for John McCauley in Lexington on a five-acre lot on Maxwell Street, acquired in 1850.[36] However, the Doric columns of the portico are of wood with channeled shafts, and the house does not have such a high basement, but includes a third floor (Fig. 135). Grilled windows in front beneath the plain entablature light the rooms of the third story (at floor level); the entablature turns the corners of the house only for the depth of a pilaster, thus permitting full fenestration in the upper ends of the house, which have parapets above the roofline between the chimneys. Deeply indented is the front doorway in the wider central bay, its Ionic columns having thick shafts. Inside, matching supports coupled with antae flank both sides of the sliding doors in the double parlors. The other openings are enframed by pilasters and the entablature encircling these rooms, resulting in awkward, leftover spaces above the doors. Ceiling centerflowers are after the Lafever design. Marble chimneypieces are geometrically severe, with a suggestion of pilasters. A long staircase occupies the rear of the central hall, which is lighted by a skylight (Fig. 136). The heavy newel post has volutes at

135. *McCauley House.*

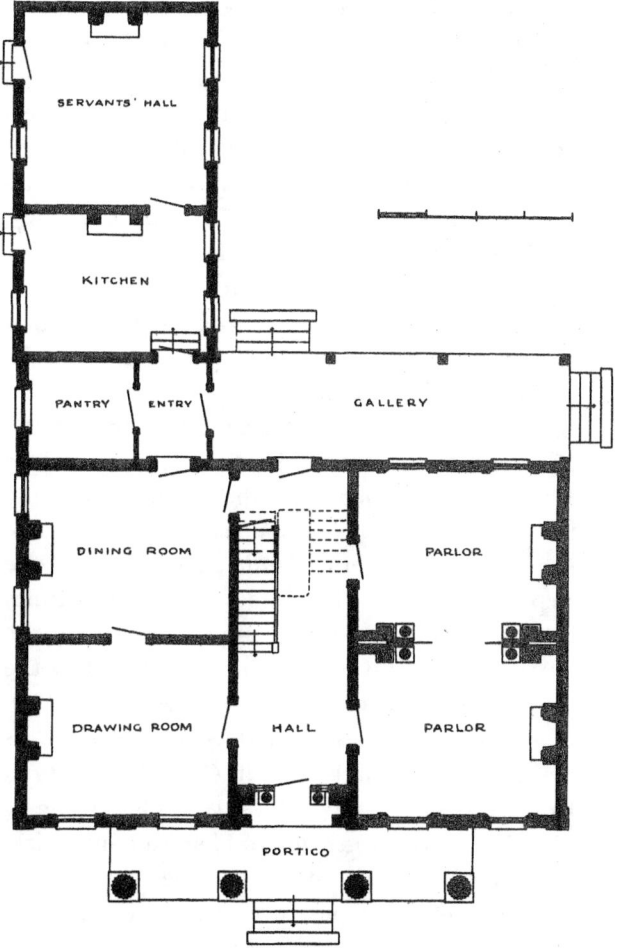

136. *First Floor Plan of McCauley House.*

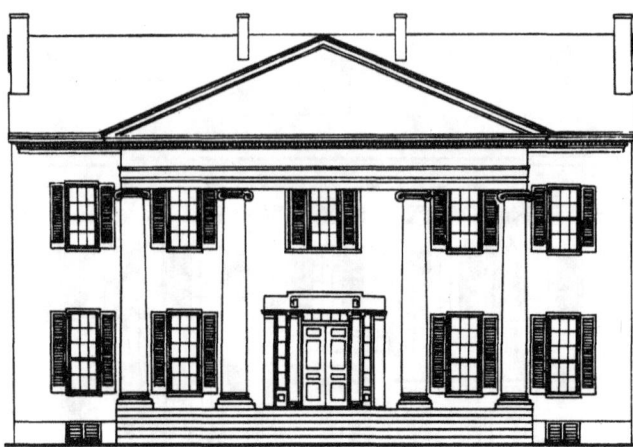

137. The Elms. Restored.

top and bottom, somewhat like that at Corinthia. The service ell of the McCauley house is an earlier two-storied dwelling converted to this purpose. The appurtenances once included a stable, smokehouse and a two-storied servants' house.[37] The grounds have dwindled to a fraction of their former size, with a church interposed between the house and Maxwell Street. Now reached from Lexington Avenue, the McCauley place has served as an Episcopal seminary, Professor A. I. Totten's School for Boys, a sorority house, and a university residence hall.

THE ELMS   A house greater in size than the two houses with Doric porticoes just described was The Elms. Another McMurtry design, it was built a mile below Lexington on the Harrodsburg Pike for William Leavy, before 1854, during which year the architect became the owner. The conspicuous feature of The Elms was its ponderous Ionic portico, with stone steps running the full breadth, as in the Innes houses. A full entablature appeared only on the portico, the architrave coming slightly below the lintels of the second-story windows (*Fig. 137*). The front door has been illustrated earlier, as being derived from a plate in *Civil Architecture*, by Edward Shaw (*Figs. 107-108*). The facade of The Elms was constructed of Flemish bond brickwork, which Shaw said was "deemed the neatest, and most elegant; but in execution is attended with great inconvenience."[38] The window pattern resembles that of the McCauley house, minus the attic openings. Pilasters were limited to the ends of the portico. The centermost bay of the house is about twice that of the other intercolumniations, which permits a very wide central hall, fifteen by forty feet, with an open-newel staircase at the back curving around a six-foot circular well to the third floor (*Fig. 138*). Niches for life-size pieces of statuary protrude midway in the hall, with pairs of rooms opening to either side, and a 62-foot gallery on axis at the back. The gallery is alongside the rear wing containing dining room, secondary stairhall, kitchen, and other service rooms, over which was a full second story containing a similar arrangement of chambers. On the McMurtry estate of about 250 acres were brick servants' quarters, a large carriagehouse, stables, barn, and a gristmill, according to the specifications billed in the

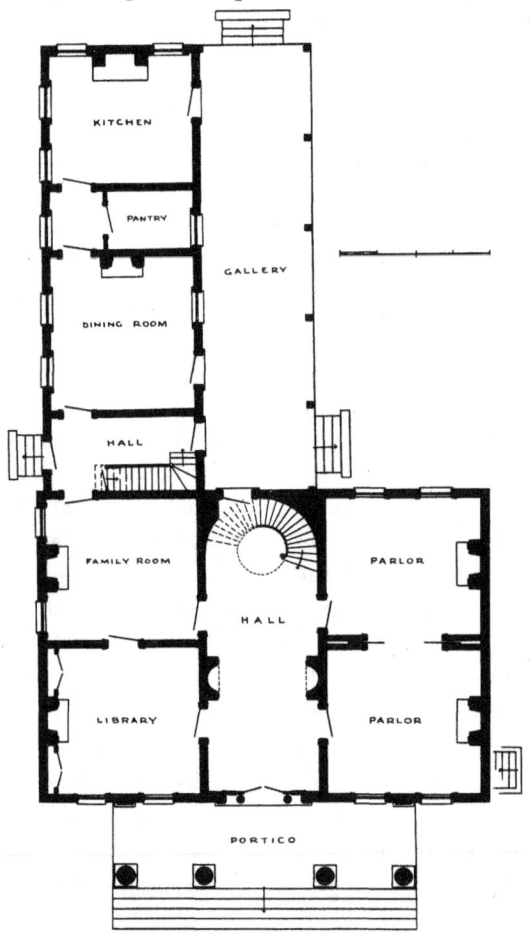

138. Main Floor Plan of The Elms. Restored.

139. *Cedar Hall.*

140. *Parlor Detail, Cedar Hall.*

newspaper at the time the property was auctioned in the autumn of 1856. McMurtry had gotten into financial difficulties in building the School for the Deaf in Danville, and The Elms was counted among security losses. The house became an orphanage and then part of the Lafayette High School before it burned in the spring of 1940. The remains of its charred brick walls were pulled down and a new building erected on the site.

CEDAR HALL   A mate to The Elms is the existing house called Cedar Hall—or Helm Place, after recent owners—on the Bowmans Mill Road a short distance off the Harrodsburg Pike. Said to have been built, like The Elms, for William Leavy, it was taken over by George H. Bowman, who offered it for sale at the end of 1858, advertising it as being "recently built." The front steps do not span the entire portico, the windows are the same size in both stories, and the doorway is more conventional than that of The Elms (*Fig. 139*). The staircase in the central hall ascends in straight flights. Woodwork throughout is more refined than in The Elms, the pattern for the enframements in the living rooms taken perhaps from Plate 49 in Minard Lafever's *Modern Builder's Guide* (New York, 1833). The columned doorway between parlors is a pleasant design (*Fig. 140*). Its entablature does not encompass the rooms, as in the McCauley house. The rear ell is not so large as that of The Elms.

A frame house in Fayette County, following the form and order of The Elms and Cedar Hall, is Clifton, north of the Iron Works Road and west of the Paris Pike. It was the home of Carter Henry Harrison, who sold it in 1855, going to Chicago, where he served several terms as mayor of that city. Clifton is smaller than the two houses just discussed, and the portico architrave comes down to a level with the division between the sashes of the upper windows.

There are several fine brick houses of similar facade throughout central Kentucky, such as Aspen Hall in Harrodsburg,[39] the Holloway house near the Richmond cemetery, and the Showalter home in Georgetown. All of these have full entablatures to the house proper. The first two are two rooms deep, the last two of only a single-room depth. Clay Hill, a Federal

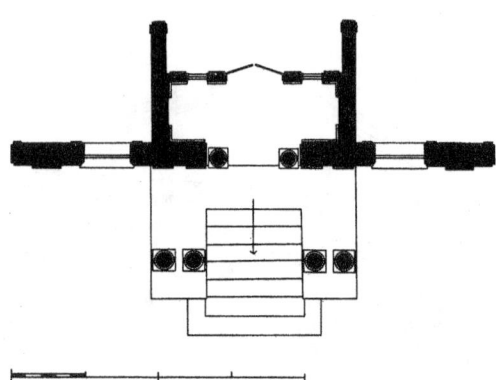

142. Detail Plan of Entry, Peck House.

141. Peck House. Restored.

house in Harrodsburg, acquired the same form after midcentury remodeling.[40] A house east of the Harrodsburg Pike, near Danville, is more of a provincial type, like The Elms. Nearby Arcadia, the Isaac Shelby house, bears a strong resemblance to these though it has a Doric portico.[41] Apparently no houses of this type in the Bluegrass made use of the Corinthian order.

If the five-bayed Greek Revival house with colossal tetrastyle portico is to be accepted as a further development of the Kennedy classic house, a literal descendant is a house with an incomplete pediment embracing three bays of the facade, having a small portico at the entrance, which was recessed, the total effect resembling the Kennedy house after alterations.

PECK HOUSE   On High Street, facing present-day Stone Avenue, the house built by Henry J. Peck on a lot purchased from William Boyce on October 1, 1854, exhibits several design traits that set it apart from other Greek Revival houses in America. Although its form follows that of the two-storied Kennedy house or Grassland (*Fig. 101*), there is a different treatment of details (*Fig. 141*). A single pilaster, with full base at ground level, separates each of the outer pairs of windows, merging with the horizontal cornice. A raking cornice carries up the front gable, and the garret is lighted by a small triple window, centered over the large one which opens onto the balustraded flat roof of the portico.

Ionic posts are coupled (as originally must have been the pedestallike posts of the balustrade), with advanced end blocks to the entablature. The portico steps rise between cubic antapodia with paneled fronts. Pilasters against the wall respond to the coupled columns, and a single pair of similar columns stand *in antis* in the opening to the deeply recessed doorway (*Fig. 142*). Facade unity is achieved through use of warm-colored red brick for the entire wall surface from ground line to cornice, supplemented by chimneystacks of the same material rising above. The basement story is fairly high, its windows entering into the overall fenestration pattern. End gables are finished with narrow raking boards. The transverse hall, containing the staircase in straight flights, separates twin rooms to right and left, and a gallery is at the back overlooking Town Fork of Elkhorn. Hood molds have been placed over all of the front windows, jigsaw panels inserted in the angles of the cornice, dormers set on the roof and recently the house was painted white.

BELL HOUSE   Comparable to the Peck house in most of its features is the Dr. David Bell residence, sometimes called Red House, on the west side of Broadway south of High Street. The differences are that the portico here is more plain, the colossal pilasters are without bases, the first- and second-story windows are alike in size, and pediments terminate the ends of the

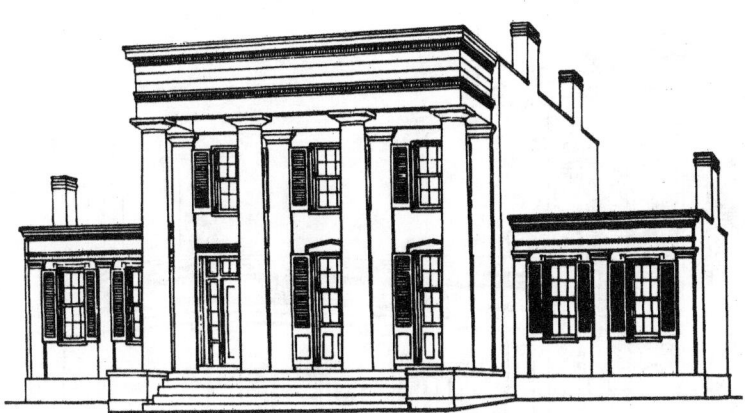

143. Weir House. Restored.

144. Parlor Screen and Fireplace in Weir House.

roof. The Bell house was built on a terrace high above street level, and there are ashlar retaining walls of exquisite curvilinear profile to either side of the flight of stone steps leading up from the front gate, and an iron fence set in a low stone wall along Broadway.

The temple-type house, given a portico across its entire two-storied block, is, perhaps, the most characteristic form in Greek Revival architecture. The classic cottage on Main Street in Lexington was a small, premature version of the same. The first Greek Revival building west of the Alleghenies was Shryock's Kentucky statehouse, a prostyle temple scheme. Few Greek Revival residences in central Kentucky have a colossal-order portico spanning the entire front, the exceptions being Diamond Point in Harrodsburg,[42] and the Bryan house (1856) on the Lexington-Nicholasville Pike, just over the Fayette line in Jessamine County. The former is remembered for its elaborate Lafever doorway, the latter for its plainness and awkward proportions. Fayette County offers several fine specimens with porticoes spanning a two-storied, three-bayed mass, to which are attached low pilastered wings. Throughout the United States, this species of Greek Revival house possibly equals or exceeds in actual numbers those of the strict temple form.

WEIR HOUSE The house some distance back from the street, facing Limestone at the northeast corner of Third Street, may have been begun by James Weir before his death in 1832. It took shape during the regime of a nephew of the same name, a decade or more later, and attained final form in the early 1850's, either for John H. Woolfolk (1851-1852) or Chief Justice Thomas A. Marshall (after 1852). The house exhibits some of the heavy, cubic quality of Morrison College (1833), two blocks away, for which reason it has been attributed to Gideon Shryock. Like Morrison, the house has baseless Doric columns, only with smooth shafts (*Fig. 143*). Broad steps rise between antapodia. The entablature is quite boxlike, with the placing of the plain frieze and triple-banded architrave reversed, separated by a row of guttae, and a course of dentils between the misplaced architrave and shallow cornice. Surely Shryock's training under Strickland would eliminate him as a possible author of such an unorthodoxy. The feeling of this facade relates it to that of Walnut Hall, and one suspects the same unknown builder of having been responsible for both houses. The main doorway is off center, opening into a stair-hall running alongside the double parlors in the main block. These rooms—again as in Walnut Hall—are separated by a screen of Corinthian columns and an entablature with a bracketed cornice, the last continuing around the entire interior (*Fig. 144*). The chimneyfronts have

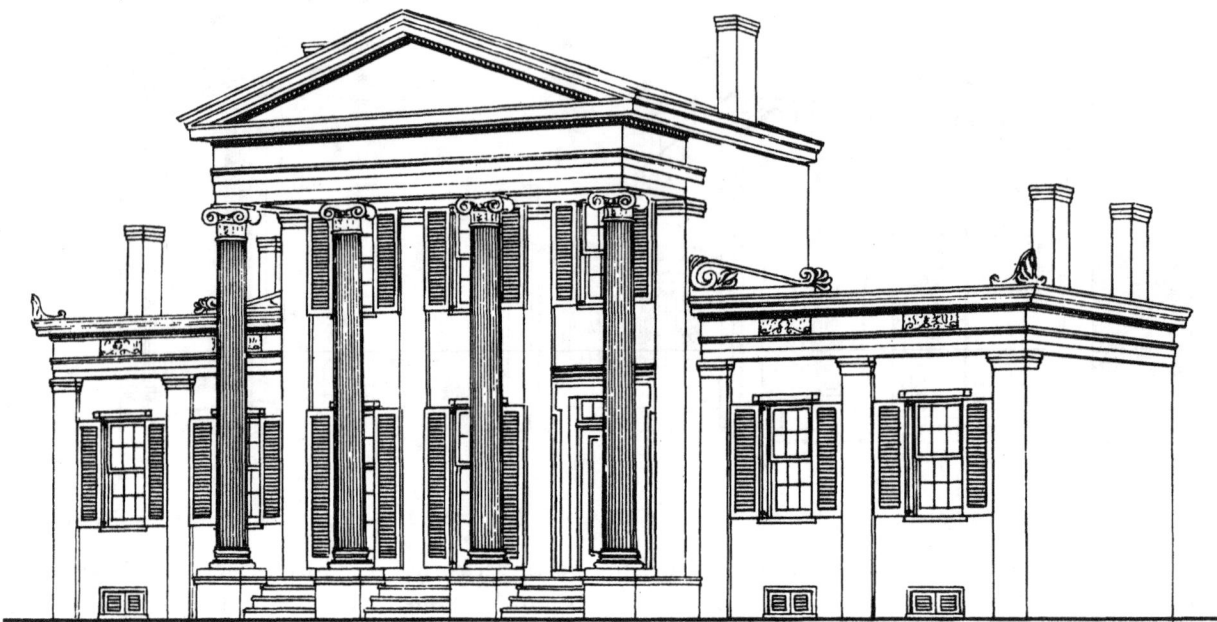

145. Cochran House. Restored.

matching marble mantels, in the spandrels of which are carved *nikes* and *putti* in low relief, with a female bust in high relief on the cartouche keystone over the round arched fireplace. The service ell was destroyed around 1910, and a new, two-storied wing was built on its site, joining the south wing, which, with its mate opposite, also acquired a second story. Plate glass replaces the original small windowpanes.

A duplicate of this house was built on the adjoining lot after the burning of a hemp factory here in 1846. The neighboring residence, which was altered into an Italianate villa, will be discussed in a later chapter.

COCHRAN HOUSE An architectural composition of fine proportions and unusual details was built on High Street, where the Kentuckian Hotel now stands, for James W. Cochran, probably soon after his purchase of the lot in 1840.[43] The Ionic portico was inspired by the order of the north porch of the Erechtheum. Its columns were set on pedestals, with steps between (*Fig. 145*). The doorway in the east bay was without colonnettes and was not recessed. Pilasters on the side pavilions rose from the ground, and the entablatures continued along the flanks of these blocks. Unique were the grilles in the parapet frieze aligned with the front windows, the antefixes at the corners, and the scrolled forms abutting the main cella. Pilaster shafts were not indicated on the sidewalls, though corner capitals were complete, as in the nearby Higgins Mansion (*Fig. 113*). The central mass of the Cochran house was only one room in depth. The columns, which were fitted onto the McConathy house next door, now part of the Kentuckian Hotel, are all that now remains of the Cochran house.

LEMON HILL Related to the Cochran house is Lemon Hill, built for Abraham Lunsford Ferguson on the estate inherited from his father in 1840. It is on the Cleveland Road two miles north of the Winchester Pike. One finds here similar columns, with shafts of wood and bases and railings of iron, but the portico is wider, the architrave abbreviated, the pediment more steeply pitched, the tympanum filled with rustication, and pilasters are stationed only at the outer corners of the main block and of each wing (*Fig. 146*). Upstairs rooms are under the hipped roofs of the wings, the windows close to floor level. The effect, quite different from that of the High Street house, is reminiscent of the

146. Lemon Hill.

Redwood Library (1748-1750) in Newport, Rhode Island.[44] Lemon Hill also suggests an early Jefferson design for Monticello, adapted from one by Robert Morris.[45] A recessed doorway on the right flank has simplified Doric pillars and an entablature similar to that of the portico. For symmetry, a blind window is inserted on this end, and another on the far side of the house. An elliptical centerpiece in the ceiling of the portico is unusual, as is the rustication in the pediment. The front doorway of Lemon Hill, which is centered and has Ionic colonnettes *in antis*, seems to have been derived from Lafever's *Young Builder's General Instructor* (1829), Plate 50. Through it one enters the thirty-foot drawing room, behind which are the dining room and stairhall, with a gallery beyond (*Fig. 147*). A false door in the drawing room balances the real one to the hall. The rectangular centerpiece in this room has an inner motif identical to that in the hall of the Elley villa (*Fig. 179*), plus a whorled outer border containing chrysanthemums, or similar flowers, in molded frames. The south wing houses two chambers with passage between them. The longer wing to the north contains the master's room and anteroom, the side entry and stairway to the upper floor, and pantry and kitchen. This part of the house alone has a basement. The L-shaped gallery functions as a means of circulation from the service quarters to the main hall. Over the drawing and dining rooms are chambers of full height, from which steps lead down to the upper rooms of the wings, which have sloping ceilings. Despite its superficial dressiness, Lemon Hill is a genuine country house. In some respects it is more satisfying from the rear view,

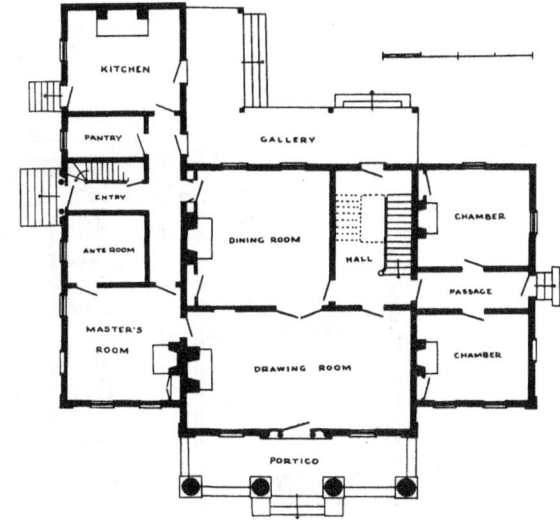

147. First Floor Plan of Lemon Hill.

where the formal elements are not in evidence. Here, one would hardly suspect the house of belonging to the Greek Revival era, and might place it two decades earlier.

A building with affinities to Lemon Hill is the Betty Bryan house on the Harrodsburg Pike beyond the Wilmore Road in Jessamine County. Its columns are a little more stocky, the portico more contracted, and the parapet-entablature on the wings is raised, with an extra pilaster between the windows. The house is virtually only one room in depth, with a low service ell at the back accessible across an open porch. The portal is off center and leads into a stairhall, by means of which one reaches three of the four front rooms (one an upstairs bedroom), the fourth located in the wing beyond the parlor.

Along the stretch of the Winchester Pike below Lemon Hill are to be found several houses of midcentury vintage whose common features may be referred to as the Winchester Pike style. Each is composed of a heavy two-storied mass crowned by a low-pitched hipped roof, the facade pierced by three triple openings of rather narrow proportions, the center doorway sheltered by a small portico having square piers. Shorter wings of one or two stories are variously attached to the sides. All excepting the Darnaby house—the one closest to town, on the south side of the pike, between the Chilesburg and Cleveland roads—have broad pilasters with deep entablatures; in this exception there is substituted a sunken-panel effect in brickwork.

LEAFLAND   The second of the houses in the Winchester Pike group out from Lexington is Leafland, the Jacob Hughes residence on the north side of the road, a short distance past Alberti Place. It has a wing on each side, that on the east being of two stories (*Fig. 148*). The breadth of its forms and narrowness of the voids give the building a look of great solidity. The entablatures of house proper and portico are reduced to a flat architrave and flat frieze, separated by a single fillet. The portico is of wood. A wide transverse hall, entered through a recessed portal, connects the four rooms on each floor of this block. In the northeast corner ascends a staircase similar to that in Grassland, but the banisters are heavier and the side and back walls come together in a normal right-angle corner, instead of following the curve of the stairs. The ceiling downstairs is fourteen feet and that upstairs fifteen, the latter taking advantage of the entablature height.

Across from Leafland, beyond the Combs Ferry Road, stands the Graves house, Edgewood, the largest of the group, with two-storied wings on both sides. Above the Winchester Pike at the county line is the John Howard Sheffer house, completed in 1854, which resembles Leafland, except it lacks the low western wing. It is called Dunreath, Scottish for Wooded Hill.

148. *Leafland.*

One notes that trees figure in the names of all the houses of this group.

A dwelling called Maple Grove, on the Briar Hill Road beyond Avon—about two miles from Lemon Hill and three north of Dunreath—may be considered midway between the Waveland and Innes house type and the Winchester Pike style. Although it has end pediments and a pilaster arrangement similar to that of Buenna Hill (*Fig. 126*), its portico is like that of Leafland (*Fig. 148*).

HAYES HOUSE   The Samuel T. Hayes house, on the Sulphur Well Road at the corner of the Cleveland Road, also bears some affinity to the Winchester Pike group by reason of its hipped roof and the vertical bands on the facade. The small portico has octagonal stone piers incorporated with traceried Tudor arches and railing around the upper deck, a central doorway upstairs as well as down. A stone, high in the wall at the end of the extended left flank, is inscribed with the date 1854 and the initials of the builder.

CASTLETON   The rest of the rural Greek Revival houses of any consequence in Fayette County are, like the square-pillared houses discussed (Hartland, etc.), without pilasters. A handsome example is Castleton, completed for David Castleman on the Iron Works Road, east of the Mount Horeb, in 1841. The Castleman house has a small front porch and a recessed doorway upstairs as well as down. All of the columns are of the Ionic order. Those sustaining the portico itself are cut from stone, probably a late nineteenth-century replacement contemporary with the terraces on either side. The smaller Dedman house on the Military Road exhibits a comparable facade, substituting Doric for Ionic columns. A house severe in design is Forkland, so named because of its situation, at the apex of Hickman Creek and Town Fork of Elkhorn, on the Winchester Pike. It was probably built by Benjamin Warfield after 1847. It is a five-bayed building, two rooms in depth, a parapet masking the roof, and a distyle Doric portico sheltering the entrance.

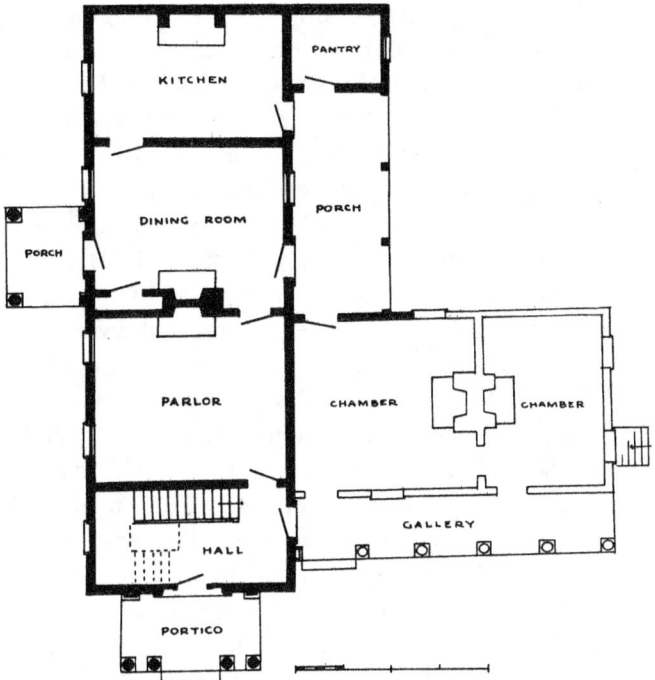

149. First Floor Plan of Laird House. Unshaded Portion of Wing Conjectural Restoration.

Auvergne, a mile and a half south of Lexington on the Tates Creek Pike, is a large L-shaped house, built during the mid-1850's by John Clark. It has a small portico with coupled Ionic columns. The facade has double windows, except over the central entrance, where the opening has the usual three lights. A range of five square piers supporting a full entablature distinguish a deep, two-storied gallery along the south side of the rear wing.

A structure unusual both in form and plan is the Laird house, three miles from Lexington on the Leestown Pike. It is made up of a long, narrow two-storied block, containing stairhall, parlor, dining room, and kitchen in a row on the main floor, with three chambers above, and having a low extension to one side, a gallery at the front, and a porch at the back (*Fig. 149*). Doric columns are in the main portico, and one assumes similar ones to have been in the gallery; most of the wing has been destroyed. A pediment crowned the narrow end of the house, facing the road.

Among lesser country houses belonging to this period is Oakwood, the Richard Allen residence of the late 1840's. It has become famous as the home of the builder's literary grandson, James Lane Allen, after whom the road that runs past the place has been named. The author changed the title of the house to Scarlet Gate. In recent times it has been altered and enlarged considerably.

JOHNSON HOUSE   A house for Edward P. Johnson was designed by Major Thomas Lewinski in 1846, and presumably was built the following year on North Limestone facing the east end of Second Street. It was a two-storied house raised on a high basement, the front windows all of three lights, and those on the main floor given emphasis by pilasters, frieze, and cornice (*Fig. 150*). A dozen wide stone steps between antapodia ascend to the main entrance, which is recessed behind two pairs of Ionic columns. The banks of windows to either side are set in vertical planes slightly indented, as in the Samuel T. Hayes house. Twin parlors on the north side of the hall are divided by large sliding doors between flat pilasters. Round centerflowers similar to the Lafever design (*Fig. 111*) are in each of these rooms. The back parlor opened on a gallery. Two corresponding rooms and a rear ell of two stories were to the south of the transverse hall. Becoming Sayre Female Institute in 1855, the house was transformed into a fashionable girls' school by the addition of two stories, with a rectangular brick belvedere at the apex of the roof, and a cast-iron porch at the entrance. The alterations were carried out by John McMurtry for David A. Sayre.[46]

The Johnson house, as well as the other Greek Revival examples within the city limits, would have been as much at home in the country as in town. Most of them were surrounded by ample grounds, but even where such was not the case—as with the Ashton and neighboring Cochran houses—there was little evidence of concession to the urban encroachment upon human privacy. A house easily accessible to a much-traveled street is expected at least to have a somewhat different arrangement of the entrance than the house in a more remote location, but few nineteenth-century American residences indicate that their builders gave any special attention to the problem. The Hunt-Morgan house has been pointed out as a praiseworthy exception of the early period, and now our attention is turned toward another example, three decades later, that meets the situation with equal success, although in a different manner.

BUTLER HOUSE   The architect John McMurtry built the house for James C. Butler on a

150. Johnson House. Restored.

151. Butler House.

lot purchased in February, 1846, fronting the west side of Broadway between High and Maxwell streets.[47] McMurtry's own residence in the pointed style was on the property to the south. The Butler house has a restrained facade, three bays across, with a wing of two bays far back on the right side. The plainness of these forms is relieved by cast-iron anthemion grilles in the attic windows and a small distyle Ionic portico placed before the columned entrance (*Fig. 151*). The front ends of the architrave and cornice are advanced above the columns, and steps rise between pedestal bases, somewhat after the fashion of the porch to the Peck house (*Fig. 141*). The plan of the front block superficially resembles those of early Lexington houses, such as that of the Lake house (*Fig. 47*), or McMurtry's first home on North Broadway near Second Street, built about 1837, where a stairhall extends the depth of double parlors. However, in the Butler house one enters a separate vestibule, with a fireplace, and passes through this room into the front parlor to the right, or into the stairhall behind. The staircase faces the rear gallery and the garden; the door to the dining room is at its foot, and that to the back parlor opposite (*Fig. 152*). The orientation of the house away from the street is further indicated by the hinged panels beneath the windows of the back parlor, joining it to the gallery. A pair of cleanly cut black marble mantels with Greek ears adorn the chimneybreasts in the twin parlors. Beyond the dining room are a pantry, service stairs, and the kitchen.

A number of contemporary townhouses, approximately the size of the Butler house, were built either closer to or on the streets of Lexington, some of them by McMurtry. The George A. Bowyer house at 324 South Upper Street is one, with similar grilled attic windows, here separated by carved consoles supporting the cornice. Two adjacent to the street are opposite the architect's former residence on North Broadway. The one nearer Second Street had a fancy wrought-iron railing on each side of the stone steps, and two matching decorative screens about five feet high set into the ends of the longer first step. The screens have been removed. The entrance motif to the house next door consists of a curved flight of steps leading to a large flat slab supported on miniature round Doric columns, all of gray limestone, with a railing containing patterns like those on the neighboring front steps, following the contours of the stone-

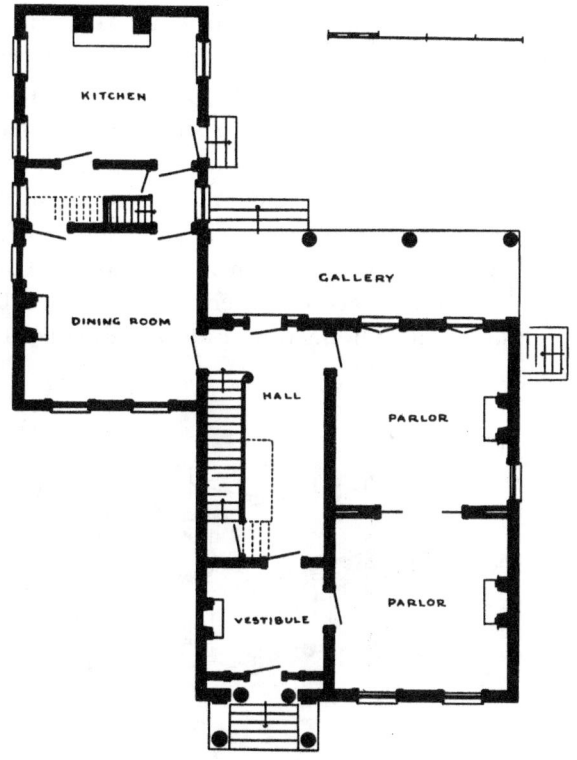

152. Principal Floor Plan of Butler House.

153. Detail of Stoop to House on North Broadway below Second Street.

work (*Fig. 153*). The sidewalk has been lowered about half a foot, leaving the stoop looking rather stranded. Other dwellings display simple rectangular versions, such as the entrance platform with iron railing to the house on the northwest corner of Short and Jefferson streets.

Many five-bayed Greek Revival houses near or adjacent to the streets also abounded in the city, most of them having recessed entrances with small columns *in antis,* like the house long used for Saint Peter's Catholic School on Barr Street (now demolished), or the McConathy house that inherited the portico from the Cochran house on High Street. Another stood on Main at Ayres Alley, on the site of the present Lafayette Hotel. This one had a parapet creating an interesting skyline, and a mate to it was at the southwest corner of Maxwell and Mill streets. An odd house at the north intersection of Barr and Walnut streets has an entrance bounded by pilasters, with colonnettes inside, standing by the front door. Its present fenestration, probably not original, seems to belong more to the Federal than to the Greek Revival period. The five windows upstairs are evenly spaced, but the facade is enframed by thick pilasters at the corners, supporting a carpenter's entablature. Across Walnut, facing the end of Barr Street, stood the Augustus Hall house by Lewinski, having a portico similar to that on the Butler house. The Hall portico was converted to fit onto the house at 471 West Second Street. Another example in this class is the Woolley house at Second and Market streets, the portico of which has been mentioned as having been copied for the Bodley house diagonally opposite. The columns of the Woolley portico are of stone.

Not all Greek Revival houses were two-storied. Though the rambling type enjoyed little of the popularity it had known during the first quarter of the nineteenth century, it reappeared occasionally, and in the 1840's America produced such a distinctive house as Gaineswood at Demopolis, Alabama.[48] The Bluegrass made its contribution in the Hunt house.

HUNT HOUSE   On the 90- by 290-foot lot on Barr Street that Mrs. Hunt acquired from her father in 1843, the young barrister Francis Hunt built a rambling twelve-room house. Six brick pilasters spaced along the facade of the central block rose from ground level to entablature, and flanking wings had parapets in front masking their shed roofs (*Fig. 154*). The Hunt house was placed against the west division line,

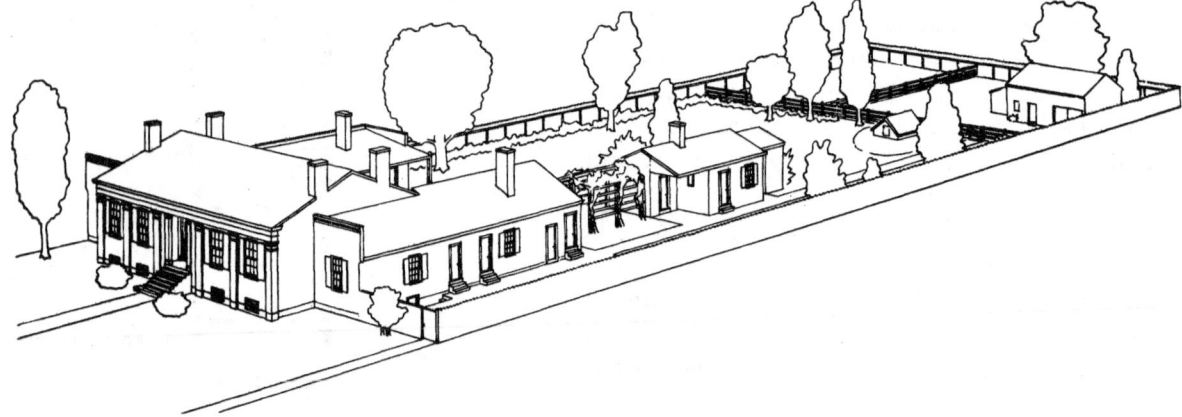

154. Hunt House and Property Restored.

and space for a walled service court was provided on the east side of the house. The wings formed a living court at the rear, opening off an L-shaped gallery (*Fig. 155*). On a line with the service ell were an arbor, a small building housing a smokeroom, quarters, and privies, an icehouse, and a combined stable, carriage house, and cowshed, the last in its own yard adjoining

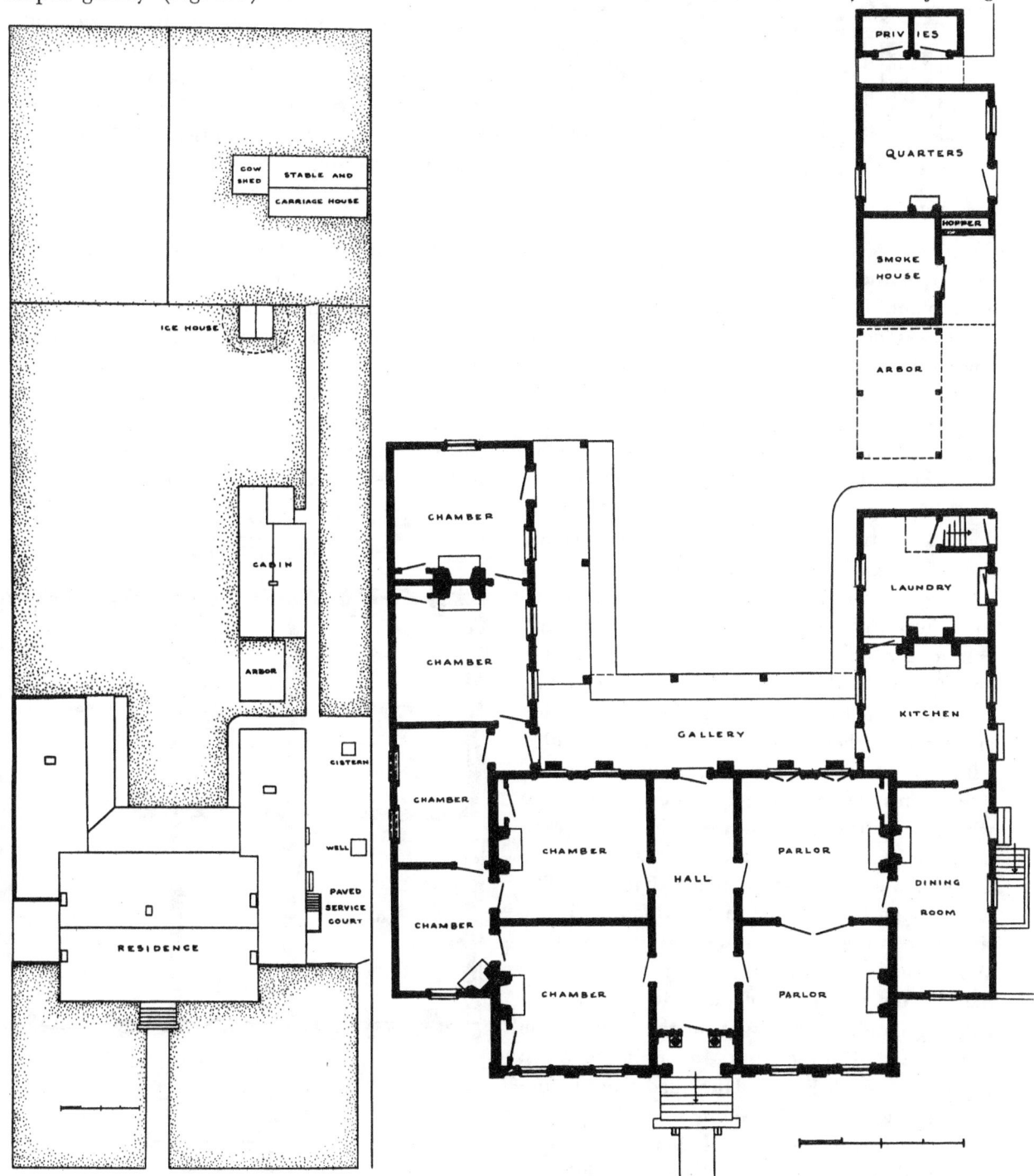

155. *Roof Plan of Hunt House.*

156. *Floor Plan of Hunt House.*

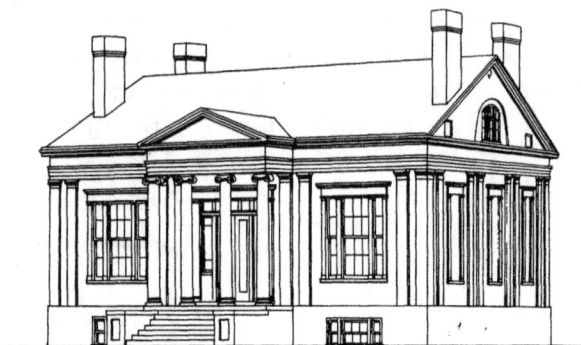

157. Mansfield. Restored.

the alley. A vegetable garden shared the rear section of the lot, which was surrounded by a high plank fence. The lawn adjacent to the house was neatly trimmed and gardened, with flowers bordering the fence.[49] A recessed entrance with Ionic colonnettes at the front door opened into the transverse hall, connecting the four principal rooms and the gallery (*Fig. 156*). An oval centerpiece was on the hall ceiling. Double parlors were on the left side, with a wide doorway between them, the back one having hinged panels beneath the windows, through which one walked onto the gallery. Beyond this room was the long, narrow dining room, and behind the latter, in the ell, a kitchen and a laundry with a servant's room over it. The kitchen opened to the inner gallery on one side and on the other to the service court, provided with cistern, well, and steps to the basement. The rooms west of the hall were chambers, of which only the three nearest the front were original. A corner fireplace, a rarity in Fayette County, was in the small outer chamber. The later room behind had high windows, necessitated because the wall was on the lot line. Woodwork inside the Hunt house was rather delicate for a building of the 1840's, the reeded running moldings having about the same profile as those found in the Hunt-Morgan house (*Figs. 63, 66*), in which Francis Hunt had lived before his marriage in 1841. Mantels in the parlors and main bedrooms were of marble, a simple pilastered version recalling Plate 73 of Edward Shaw's *Civil Architecture*, revised and enlarged in 1834. Though the details lacked distinction, the Hunt house displayed real design value in its planning, the various activity areas being well defined and circulation carefully considered. It was a house in which the accent was on living. The outbuildings disappeared many years before the residence itself, which served as a parish house in connection with St. Peter's Church and School prior to its demolition in June, 1953. During the razing, a copy of the *Lexington Observer and Reporter* for August 5, 1843, was found in a doorcasing.

MANSFIELD A small and compact Greek Revival house, called Mansfield, is located beyond Ashland on the Richmond Pike. It was designed in 1845 by Major Thomas Lewinski for Henry Clay as a residence for his son, Thomas Hart Clay. The original form of this story-and-a-half house consisted of a square block with pedimented ends, the walls divided by pilasters, elevated on a basement and supporting a full

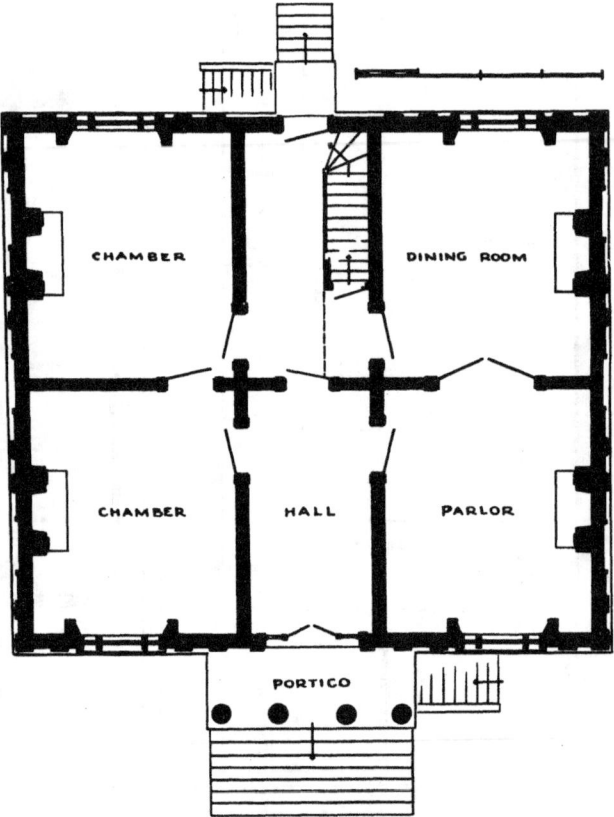

158. Principal Floor Plan of Mansfield.

entablature encircling the structure (*Fig. 157*). A tetrastyle Greek Ionic portico is the chief facade feature. It is small but shallow like the Lewinski portico on the Gibson house (*Fig. 115*), and has antapodia at the extremities of the front steps. Windows to either side are pilastered somewhat in the manner of the first-story fenestration on the Johnson house (*Fig. 150*). Shuttered blind windows filled the spaces between the brick pilasters along the flanks. Applied arches in the tympanums above are concentric with the curved headings of chamber windows. The plan is plain to the point of dullness, having four similar rooms on the main floor, a divided transverse hall, and a straight staircase in the rear half leading up to the two chambers above and down to the kitchen and service rooms in the full basement below (*Fig. 158*). Additions to Mansfield in modern times have made the house the center of a five-part composition that is quite Federal in feeling, like Homewood at Baltimore, or the Morton house on North Limestone in Lexington, the low wings cutting rather awkwardly through the pilasters on the original end walls.

ROGERS HOUSE   Mansfield inspired a house commissioned by Dr. Elisha Warfield for his daughter, Mrs. C. C. Rogers, and built on the east side of South Broadway near Maxwell Street

159. *Rogers House.*

between 1845 and 1848. McMurtry is said to have been the architect. The Rogers house has a high basement and an Ionic portico set before a story-and-a-half mass (*Fig. 159*). The design, however, lacks the formality of details that characterizes the Clay house. The front pediment, on the house rather than on the portico, reminds one of the larger Peck (*Fig. 141*) and Bell houses, the latter located in the block opposite. Also, a single unadorned vertical shaft between each pair of windows omits the frieze and comes in contact with the large voussoirs of the openings. The gabled end walls have parapets between the chimneys, like those on the McCauley house (*Fig. 135*), a single window to each upper chamber. The house has a small wing at the back, but the cooking was done in the basement, as in Mansfield.

THE GOTHIC REVIVAL 8

THE CLASSIC tradition of the Renaissance, which culminated in America in the Greek Revival, flourished with increasing intensity up to the time of the Civil War, yet during the last two decades of this era a rival appeared on the scene as a serious challenge to its supremacy. The rival was romanticism, which found its first full expression in the Gothic Revival. Whereas the Greek Revival marked the end of one movement, the Gothic Revival was the beginning of another. Romanticism gained and maintained primary position over classicism throughout the postwar period, at least up to the resurgence of the latter in the neoclassic vogue brought on by the Chicago World's Columbian Exposition of 1892-1893.

The Gothic Revival originated in England. It was given its name by those who opposed it most strongly, the connotation of the term "Gothic" being "barbarian." But, despite opposition, the Gothic Revival prospered for several reasons. The first, in a land where writing always has been more important than the visual arts, was the rise of the romantic movement in literature. The Gothic motif was taken up by the so-called graveyard poets of the eighteenth century, such as Thomas Gray, and by the composers of the Gothic romances of the nineteenth century, most famous among whom was Sir Walter Scott. Scott built his mock medieval castle, Abbotsford, in 1812, and lived in it while writing the Waverly Novels. A second factor for the popularity of the Gothic Revival in England was nationalism. The original Gothic was regarded as the high-water level of indigenous culture, before it was corrupted by the Renaissance enthusiasm over Mediterranean antiquities. A third motivation was religion. Gothic was the

Christian style. The liturgy and the church building, creating the proper background for the drama of the mass, were inseparable, and many Englishmen returned to orthodoxy out of sentiment for the traditions of the established church. The religious motive was strengthened by the Church Building Act of 1818, inaugurated as a means of improving the morals of the expanding middle class through the construction of churches. Out of 214 new buildings erected, 177 imitated the Gothic style.[1] The religious factor had a sobering effect upon the Gothic Revival. In the early days, the use of the style was superficial and fanciful, as on Horace Walpole's Strawberry Hill (1753-1778). The plea for a better understanding of Gothic architecture through more careful observation of medieval monuments was voiced by the devout Augustus Welby Pugin (1812-1852), who showed the superiority of buildings of the Middle Ages over those of his own times in his *Contrasts; or, a Parallel between the Noble Edifices of the Fourteenth and Fifteenth Centuries, and Similar Buildings of the Present Day*, published in London in 1836 and illustrated by the author's engravings. Pugin himself built over 65 churches in the United Kingdom and many in the colonies, and was responsible for much of the visible design of the London Houses of Parliament.

As has been seen in Chapter Four, surviving medieval elements—such as belt courses, brick cornices and parapets, crowstep gables, steep roofs, complicated chimney forms, exposed rainwater conduits, chamfered posts, clustered colonnettes on doorways, and leaded glass windows—were in use in America before the introduction of the Gothic Revival. These archaic features had been employed as natural components, almost unconsciously. The later Gothic Revival, on the other hand, was quite conscious—one might even say self-conscious—of the forms that it used. Strangely enough, it did not draw upon the medieval elements of earlier building in the United States, but arrived here as though a total stranger, as an importation. The first Gothic Revival building in America was Sedgeley, the country villa of William Crammond, designed by Benjamin Henry Latrobe in 1799 and built in what is now Fairmount Park, Philadelphia (*Fig. 184*). The house itself no longer stands, but the remains of an existing dependency suggest that it was a caricature of the Latrobe drawings. Within the next decade Latrobe made a design in Gothic for the Baltimore Cathedral, not executed, and another for the Bank of Philadelphia. Latrobe's pupil, William Strickland, who is also mostly thought of in connection with the Greek movement, designed and built the Philadelphia Masonic Hall in Gothic during 1808-1810.[2] Also in 1810 the first Gothic Revival townhouse was erected on Chestnut Street in Philadelphia.[3] Thus the Gothic Revival, like the Greek Revival, got its start in Philadelphia, at about the same time, and the initial examples of both were conceived by the same architect.

Our immediate interest in the Gothic Revival takes us to the use of the style in country houses subsequent to Sedgeley. The next important one was Glenellen, built outside Baltimore for Robert Gilmore in 1832.[4] This small, yet distinctive, country seat was designed by the firm of (Ithiel) Town and (Alexander Jackson) Davis, of New York. Davis later planned Loudoun at Lexington. He created numerous houses in this style in the valley of the Hudson River, after the vogue for picturesque residences had been established in the area by Washington Irving. Irving engaged the artist George Harvey to enlarge into a complex composition the tiny cottage which stood on the land he purchased in 1835. The result, which was called Sunnyside, was patterned after Dutch colonial houses and so was not strictly Gothic Revival, but it partook of the same spirit.[5] Davis' designs were circulated in a portfolio of 1837, called *Rural Residences . . . Cottages, Farmhouses, Villas, and Village Churches . . . Published . . . with a View to the Improvement of American Country Architecture*. The plates, of uncertain number, consisted mostly of lithographs in color. Davis also conceived many of the illustrations used in books written by A. J. Downing, the Hudson

River author whose work was most influential in formulating and disseminating Gothic Revival ideals throughout the United States.

Andrew Jackson Downing (1815-1852) was primarily a landscape gardener and horticulturist who in 1838 had built a Gothic Revival house after his own design at Newburgh, New York. Downing's first book appeared in 1841, entitled, *A Treatise on the Theory and Practice of Landscape Gardening Adapted to North America* (New York, London, and Boston). A chapter on "Landscape or Rural Architecture" stressed the integration of country houses with their environment. Later books, dealing more exclusively with architecture, were *Cottage Residences* (1842) and *The Architecture of Country Houses* (1850). Downing's sphere of influence was not limited to the printed page. He also appeared on the lecture platform, and in this capacity he may have visited Lexington, where he was elected an honorary member of the Maxwell Springs Fair Association on October 5, 1850.[6]

Downing characterized the Gothic Revival style as the picturesque, in contradistinction to the classic or Greek, which was designated the beautiful. By these terms he signified that the latter produced symmetrical, compact forms, with simple contours, whereas the former tended toward the asymmetrical, having broken outlines. The Gothic Revival house snuggled into its environment, instead of remaining aloof from it, like the Greek Revival; it sat low upon the ground, its lacework of chimneystacks, pinnacles, towers, turrets, battlements, gables, etc., blending into the tapestry of surrounding nature. Gothic Revival house schemes were presented in a new way in the Downing books. Whereas Greek Revival designs were shown consistently in elevation drawings, Gothic Revival appeared in perspective sketches that included the landscape. This meant that vertical dimensions were left up to the discretion of the builder. Effect was more important than proportions. One notes also the use of a different set of moldings, generally with thinner edges and higher profiles, replacing the Greek cymas, and more naturalistic leaf and flower shapes used instead of the stylized anthemion, egg-and-dart, bead-and-reel, etc. Openings once more were bridged by the arch, after several decades of restriction to horizontal lintels during the Greek regime, and windows took on new interest through varied shapes, the bay window or oriel being conspicuous, its diamond-shaped panes sometimes filled with stained glass.

Unlike the Greek Revival, Gothic Revival houses gathered inspiration from domestic types, mostly belonging to the Tudor, Elizabethan, and Jacobean periods, when brick building was prevalent throughout England. For such houses Downing popularized the term "villa," applied to a "home in the country which is something beyond a cottage or a farm-house," pointing out that this was an international word, "the same in Latin, Italian, Spanish, and English." It signified "the country-house of a person of competence or wealth sufficient to build and maintain it with some taste and elegance . . . the most refined home of America."[7] The word was taken over for rural residences in the Greek Revival and Italianate styles as well, perhaps best suited to the last. Gothic Revival villas are divided into two types: one, in America called the Castellated Style, is modeled on the late castles of British aristocracy; the other was patterned after the cottages of people of lower station, and was referred to here as the Pointed Style. The first is distinguishable by its towers, turrets, and parapets, the second by its overhanging eaves and the carved bargeboards of its steeply pitched gables. In Kentucky there was not such a divergence in size between examples belonging to the two types as one might expect, considering their respective sources.

The popularity of the Gothic Revival in the Bluegrass was due to the activities of the architect-builder John McMurtry (1812-1890). Like Gideon Shryock, who introduced the Greek Revival beyond the Alleghenies, McMurtry was a native. In 1833, at the age of twenty-one, he became an apprentice to Shryock, and a year later subleased a contract from him for completing part of the work on Morrison College.[8] McMurtry remained in this area, working constantly, until the time of his death fifty-six years later. He produced over two hundred buildings, most of them residences. Already we have looked at some of his houses in the Greek style: Buenna Hill, Corinthia, the McCauley house, The Elms, the Butler house, and enlargement of the Gibson house. McMurtry's first essay using Gothic motifs in Fayette County was the Roman Catholic Church of St. Peter on North Limestone in Lexington, dedicated December 3, 1837,[9] a building hybrid in style, three-quarters Greek Revival, with lancet door and windows and a conic spire.[10] It was not a very appealing building, and the Gothic Revival awaited another decade for representatives in central Kentucky that were a credit to the movement. Meanwhile, in 1841, John McMurtry broadened his concept of architecture by a trip to Europe, visiting England and France, and possibly other countries.[11]

McMURTRY HOUSE During the 1840's McMurtry became the purchaser of several pieces of property on the west side of Broadway between High and Maxwell streets, the largest of which was a six-acre tract. He built on and sold some as lots, reserving for himself one acquired in 1845.[12] It adjoined the land purchased the following year by James C. Butler, for whom McMurtry erected a Greek Revival townhouse. John McMurtry's own house was fashioned in the Pointed Style. It was a three-part composition of slightly advanced central pavilion, with the front fenestration consistently of three lights. An ample garret was provided under the steeply pitched roof, with bracketed and bargeboarded gables at front and sides, and a pair of chimneys articulated into prismatic stacks rising above the roof. A bay window on each end lighted the first-floor rooms (*Fig. 160*). The porch across the front was supported on octagonal piers, linked by wide Tudor arches with pierced trefoil spandrels. This graceful stock motif became something of a McMurtry signature and appeared even on the classic exterior of Botherum and the Italianate villa Lyndhurst, as well as on

160. McMurtry House. Restored.

all of his Gothic Revival houses. Hoodmolds over the windows were identical to those used by McMurtry on the gateway (1849, demolished 1890) to the Lexington Cemetery. The McMurtry house had a long two-storied ell at the back toward the north end of the house, according to the Middleton, Wallace & Co. view of Lexington of the mid-1850's, and a small separate dependency to the rear on a line with the south flank. The long ell seems to have had superimposed galleries. Inside, a transverse hall accommodated a long straight flight of steps, which confronted the visitor upon entering. Diagonal ribs crisscrossed the ceiling of the parlor on the right side of the house, a chimneypiece in this room having colonnettes and trefoil spandrels beneath the mantel shelf, above which a tall mirror was enframed by pilasters. To convert the building into a rooming house, the rear portion was rebuilt, unattractive dormers were added on either side of the front gable, and the bay windows on the flanks removed. The house, long known as The Britling, was razed in 1961.

The window pattern of the front of the McMurtry house on South Broadway was so much like that of Hartland, the Johnson house, and others, that if there had been a lower roof pitch, the house could easier have been completed in Greek Revival style. Rectangular glass panes in sash windows are not Gothic Revival fenestration. One concludes from this that John

161. Bayles-Beck House. Restored.

McMurtry was not a thoroughgoing Gothic Revivalist, a point of view that is further borne out by the following two houses.

BAYLES-BECK HOUSE   The cubic house on East High Street, facing Lexington Avenue, was built or remodeled by McMurtry for Jessee Bayles in or after 1845, or for James Burnie Beck, who acquired it in 1848.[13] The front wall was divided into five shallow planes. A small portico, with steps between antapodia advanced before coupled Roman Doric columns, sheltered the entrance (*Fig. 161*). A transverse central stairhall separated two pairs of rooms, and a single window in front or back wall lighted each interior. These elements are Greek Revival, but the castellated parapet masking the low shed roof is Gothic Revival. It is composed of brick panels in the frieze, resembling triglyphs, on which were superimposed roundheaded merlons. The topmost curves have been flattened, and a long front porch with Ionic columns replaces the original portico. There were no openings in the end walls, on which grapevines were trained. The Bayles-Beck house had the severity of an eleventh-century Anglo-Saxon keep.

BOTHERUM   At first glance the stone cottage built in 1851[14] on West High Street (Madison Place) facing Town Fork for Major Madison Conyers Johnson looks Greek Revival. Corinthian columns support pedimented porticoes at the entrance and at both extremities of the front mass, with pilasters spaced at regular intervals

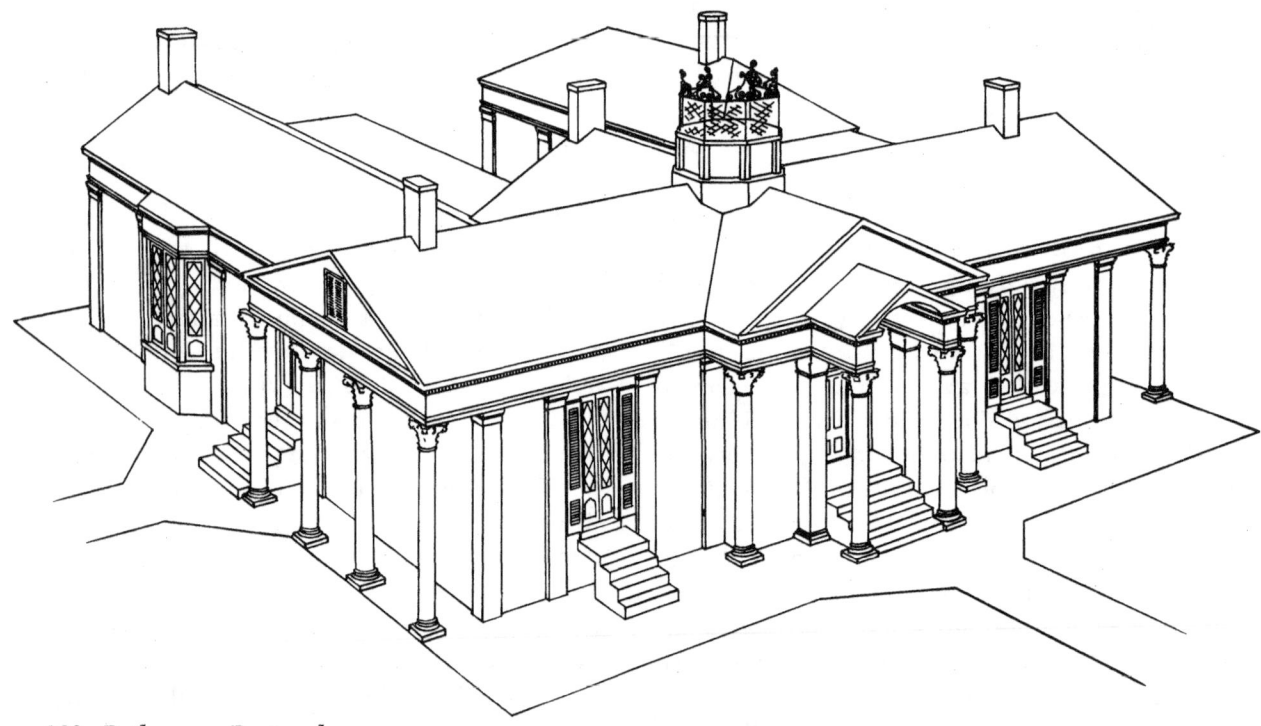

162. Botherum. Restored.

along the wall (*Fig. 162*). But the arch over the entrance steps, the concealed high basement, and the plinths of the columns set on the brick terrace at ground level are features proper to romantic architecture. Upon closer observation one notices the lozenge-shaped panes in the french doors, the oriel on the right flank, the Tudor arch before the west entry, and the octagonal chimney and lookout on the roof, all unquestionably Gothic Revival elements. Except for the recessed door in the library, in which Ionic columns sustain horizontal moldings constituting little more than a cornice, the interior of the house is wholly Gothic Revival. The admixture of styles may have been stipulated by the client, Major Johnson, an extraordinary man who received highest honors in a class of thirty-two upon graduation from Transylvania University in 1823 at the age of fifteen. He was, incidentally, the model for Colonel Romulus Fields, one of the principal characters in James Lane Allen's story, "Two Gentlemen of Kentucky." Notwithstanding, credit for the form of the house must go to the architect. The combination of Corinthian and Gothic was a perfectly natural thing for McMurtry, who once wrote: "All styles may be divided into two classes. One derived from the post and lintel and the other from the arch; the Grecian being the type of the first and the Roman or Gothic of the second."[15] McMurtry was fundamentally a builder, and for him, style followed system of construction rather than historical precedent. In the Johnson cottage the two modes are combined more happily than one would expect. The overall effect is not discordant.

Mounting the front steps one enters a tiny vestibule and passes through double doors into the reception hall, lighted by a skylight at the apex of its vaulted ceiling (*Fig. 163*). This hall must have served as dining room when the major entertained. Niches are in the fireplace wall, and doors in the sidewalls open into the library, bedroom and crosscorridors. Inside walls average 24 inches in thickness, and the double doors —some containing stained glass—swing back into splayed recesses. The octagonal drawing room

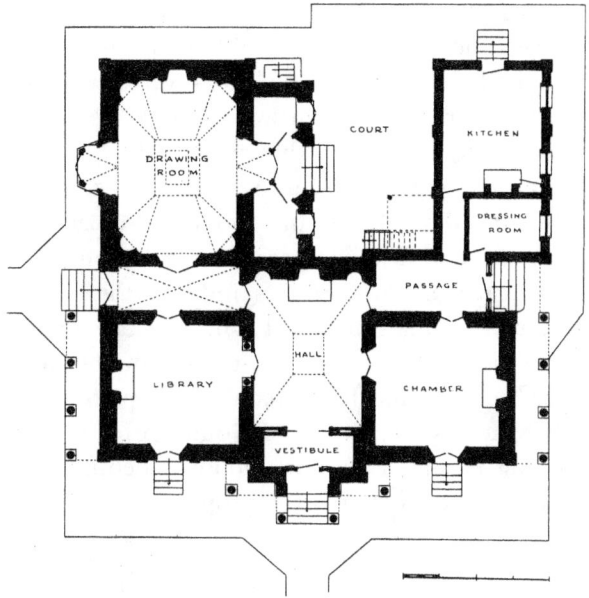

163. Plan of Botherum. Restored.

in the east wing has a coved ceiling enhanced by ribs, bosses, and a centerpiece of vines and gamopetalous flowers modeled in plaster, a similar motif enframing the arch over the mirror above the fireplace (*Fig. 164*). The inner panel of the centerpiece is like that in the drawing room of Lemon Hill. The octagon of Madison Johnson's cottage is lighted by deep bay windows of semihexagonal shape, the west one giving access to a pair of little anterooms, as well as a

164. Cutaway View into the Drawing Room of Botherum.

recessed entry leading into the court. An iron stairway here ascended to the cupola-lookout over the hall. Although the stairs were removed when a later dining room was filled in the space occupied by the court, the cupola still has the delicate wrought-iron railing around seven of its eight sides. A dressing room, with passage alongside, and a kitchen are housed in the west ell, which is brick. The remainder of the house is stone, originally covered with stucco. Additional windows have been cut through the fireplace walls of the front rooms, and plate-glass sash windows installed in the outer oriel of the drawing room. A servant's house is behind the kitchen wing, now over the property line of the diminished lot. The entrance of the drive at one time had iron gates, reputed to have been opened and shut automatically by a mechanism that was tripped by the wheels of a carriage passing over it.[16] Nobody seems to know where this charming, romantic cottage got its name, "Botherum."

Although John McMurtry is to be credited with bringing into being most of the Gothic Revival buildings in Fayette County, he was not the designer of all of them. The pure Gothic Revival designs originated on the boards of architects who were not natives. During the mid-1840's, Major Thomas Lewinski, the Polish émigré, drew plans for two Lexington churches, Christ Episcopal and McChord Presbyterian,

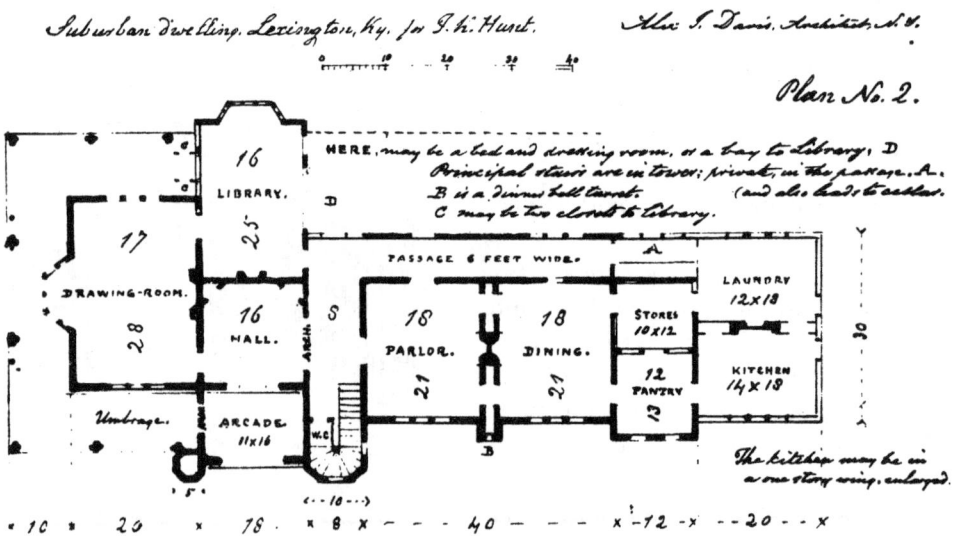

165. "Plan No. 2" for F. K. Hunt. Elevation and Plan by A. J. Davis. Metropolitan Museum of Art, New York City.

166. Loudoun. Restored.

both of which were built in the same block on Market Street, with McMurtry as the contractor.[17] Another project which McMurtry built after the designs of someone else was a residence, Loudoun, the largest and finest of its kind in Kentucky if not in the South. The designer was Alexander Jackson Davis, the architect of Sachem's Wood at New Haven and Glenellen near Baltimore, the author of *Rural Residences,* and the designer of many of the plans in the Downing volumes. Davis began his architectural career in 1827 by making drawings and later prints of outstanding buildings in our coastal cities, and doing renderings for such architects as Josiah R. Brady, Martin Euclid Thompson, and Ithiel Town. Soon afterward he became a full-fledged partner to Town, whose extensive architectural library thus was put at his disposal. Important buildings by the firm include the United States Customhouse (later the Subtreasury Building) on Wall Street in New York, the former House of Mansions that stood on Fifth Avenue across from the reservoir on the site of the New York Library, capitols for Connecticut, North Carolina, Indiana, Illinois, and Ohio, and the Virginia Military Institute.[18] Upon the death of Town in 1844, Davis became sole legatee to the practice. His approach to architecture was pictorial, which led him naturally into romantic eclecticism, and he liked to refer to himself as an "Architectural Composer." The reputation of Davis as one of the finest American architects of his day was well established when he was given the commission for a villa to be built in Fayette County for Francis Hunt, then residing in the rambling Greek Revival house on Barr Street.

LOUDOUN Francis Key Hunt received a sizable patrimony in 1849 and decided to build an impressive residence upon a 56-acre tract on the northern outskirts of Lexington, a gift from his wife's parents.[19] His selection of A. J. Davis of New York as architect was not only a tribute to his reputation, but an indication of Hunt's approval of the Gothic style. Davis submitted several designs. One of these, labeled "Plan No. 2," bears certain relationships to the house that was built (*Fig. 165*). The right end of the house is similar; the remainder lacks interest because of the sameness of window treatment and wall height, and the staircase is cramped inside the tower. The building executed is more attractive (*Fig. 166*). The entrance motif, in which a gabled pavilion is flanked by a tower and a turret, was a favorite of the architect.[20] Davis called the project a "Design in Early English, or collegiate Style." His records show that he furnished a "Set of ten drawings and specification, after much correspondence and sending sketches," for which he was paid $150. Letters and detail drawings (*Fig. 167*) followed, costing an additional $153, the final payment made in per-

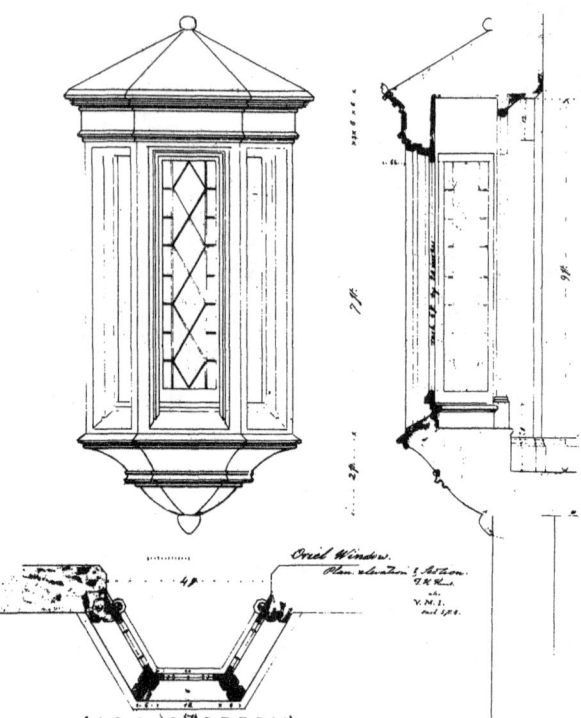

167. Plan, Elevation, and Section Drawings for an Oriel Window for Loudoun, by A. J. Davis. Metropolitan Museum of Art.

son by Hunt in New York on December 13, 1850.[21] John McMurtry constructed the house at a cost of $30,000, which was a large sum in those days.[22] The walls were of hollow brick construction, making use of an air space for insulation, a device introduced into this country in the villas of New Haven, Connecticut, by Ithiel Town.[23] The brick pattern repeated four stretchers and one header, and the walls were covered with successive layers of sand and paint to simulate stone. Details, such as copings, hood molds, and sills, are of cut stone, and the galleries of wood with iron crestings. A half tunnel encircles the main foundations of the house, to eliminate moisture from the footings of the walls and give them added stability. The castellated house is long and rather shallow, the forms building up irregularly to the principal tower to one side of the entrance pavilion. The arcuated front doors, banks of windows, and oriels have lozenge panes; those of the drawing room and hall are filled with enameled glass in grape designs. Groups of chimneystacks, crenelated tops to the tower and turret, parapet walls rising above the roof, and pinnacles on the important gables give interest to the skyline. A comparison of the Loudoun gallery with the front porch on the McMurtry house (*Fig. 160*) illustrates the refinement of conception achieved by the New York architect.

The entrance to Loudoun is through what Davis called the "arcade," a level-crown vaulted porch, on one side opening onto the umbrage, paved with a gray and white tessellation of marble. The first feature one meets inside is the massive staircase of dark wood ascending halfway up one wall and across the back of the main hall. A cutout apron is pendant from the outer edge of the soffit of the staircase. The hall ceiling is crisscrossed with ribs, and the beam spanning the stair well springs from grotesque protomes modeled in plaster. The twenty- by thirty-foot drawing room at the west end of the villa is lighted by a great curved oriel and twin openings at front and back, the windows and louvred shutters of which slide back into pockets in the wall (*Fig. 168*). Shutters elsewhere fold into special recesses. The walls of the drawing room were stenciled *al fresco* in a large floral pattern of fourteenth-century Italian inspiration, and the squares between the crossed ceiling beams painted in geometric designs. The gilded lambrequin that fitted over the arch to the oriel, a pair of matching mirrors in perpendicular style, and the marble mantel originally in the drawing room at Loudoun are now in the residence north of the Hunt-Morgan house on Mill Street, built by Mrs. Hunt after the death of her husband. Behind the hall in Loudoun is the library, lighted by a bay window in the far wall, with full-length bookcases to either side and also next to the red-brown stone chimneypiece and over the door opposite. Glass doors are diamond-paned. The ceiling in this room is divided into sections by ribs connected to attenuated colonnettes along the walls. The parlor, across from the drawing room, has an alcove in the base of

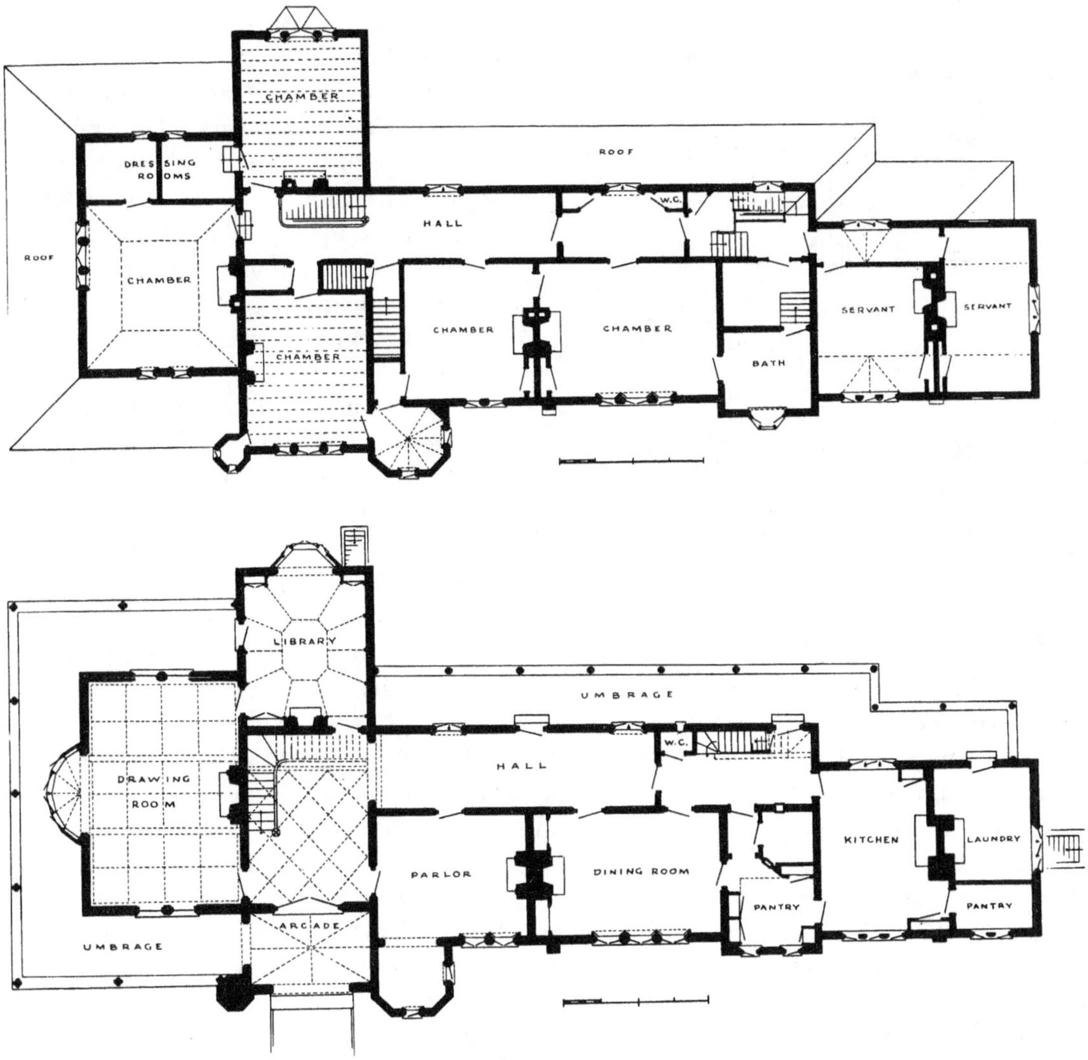

168. First and Second Floor Plans for Loudoun.

the tower. The Davis drawing for its white marble mantel is preserved in the Print Room of the Metropolitan Museum of Art in New York City. Engaged polygonal piers stand to right and left of a Tudor arched fireplace, with spandrels carved in a leaf design similar to that used in the wood doorframes throughout the living area of the house. The centerpiece in the parlor is an acanthus and flower motif (*Fig. 169*). In the dining room is a flat mantel of the same polished stone as that in the library, with recesses for china and silver to either side. The parlor and dining room are mutually accessible to a rear hall, outside of which is the long back

169. Centerpiece in Parlor Ceiling, Loudoun.

170. Front and Rear Views of Gatehouse at Ingelside.

gallery. Pantries, kitchen, laundry, and service stairhall complete the first-floor plan. A water closet is at the foot of the service stairs on the first floor, and another is directly above it. Ceiling heights downstairs are normally fourteen feet, two feet more in the drawing room, and somewhat less in the east wing; the ceilings of the chamber floor average twelve feet. The principal bedrooms have adjoining dressing rooms. Servants' chambers are over the service rooms. Stairs ascend to garret and tower. Loudoun was named from a favorite song of Mrs. Hunt, "The Bells of Loudoun."

The remaining land around Loudoun has become Castlewood Park. The empty villa itself is used by the Lexington Department of Recreation. The galleries have been removed, minor changes have been effected about the parapets, and a gymnasium has been built at the back. However, many of the big trees still survive at Loudoun, giving the place an atmosphere of lingering grandeur.

INGELSIDE   The sister house to Loudoun is Ingelside, designed and built by John McMurtry for Henry Boone Ingels in 1852; the date is incised in a stone escutcheon high up on the principal tower. The entrance to the original 300-acre Ingels estate—a short distance beyond the city limits southwest of Lexington on the Harrodsburg Pike—was through a brick gatehouse. Its road front was a severe, crenelated block of two stories but the front was largely false. Its shed roof sloped down to the first-story level at the back. The corner merlons functioned as chimneys (*Fig. 170*). The carriageway through the center was equipped with a wrought-iron gate. The drive wound through a park to the picturesque villa (*Fig. 171*). The principal facade of Ingelside is a symmetrical composition in which the architect borrowed window, turret, chimney, and parapet details from the Loudoun

171. South Side of Ingelside.

172. North View of Ingelside.

design, cast-iron pinnacles (now removed) from Lewinski's Christ Church, and a tracery porch, perhaps from Downing. The dripmolds over windows and doorways were of the same metal as the pinnacles, rather than of stone as at Loudoun. The casting was undoubtedly carried out at the Bruen Foundry in Lexington, which had been under the supervision of Ingels since the fall of 1848.[24] The three divisions of the Ingelside facade, with corner turrets, and the placement of the principal tower are reminiscent of Blithewood, the Robert Donaldson estate planned by Davis in 1834 and built near Fishkill, New York. It was pictured in the architect's *Rural Residences* of 1837. The entrance porch of Blithewood differs from that of the Kentucky villa, being of heavy masonry with corner buttresses and a battlemented parapet. Both houses have an L form—unlike Loudoun—because of which Ingelside shows to better advantage from the court (*Fig. 172*). Although about as large as the Hunt villa, because of its shape the Ingels house has a more homelike atmosphere. Circulation throughout the house is facilitated through the location of the stairway at the angle of the plan. Ingelside has a transverse central hall between the large drawing room and parlor, the stair vestibule behind the latter accessible from the hall (*Fig. 173*). The right flank of Ingelside is more interesting than the corresponding side of Blithewood, which recedes and goes back straight, housing kitchen, storerooms, and coachhouse. The wing of the Kentucky house juts out for the library and contains the dining room as well as services. Ingelside provides several dressing rooms on the chamber floor and makes use of the octagonal corner turrets as closets. The layout and facade of this Gothic Revival building have points in common with the design of the Greek Revival Innes house called Corinthia, built by the same architect soon after completing Ingelside. A detailed analysis has been given elsewhere,[25] and the two buildings may be compared through illustrations (*Figs. 171, 173; 128-129*).

Borrowed from Loudoun are the crisscross-beamed ceiling in the hall, the relationship of hall, drawing room, and parlor, the oriel opposite the fireplace in the drawing room, the parlor alcove in the lower portion of the tower, and the library beyond the stairway. The hall is lighted at the ends through tall double doors, which once may have contained colored glass. Stained glass in panes of solid hues enframe the windows

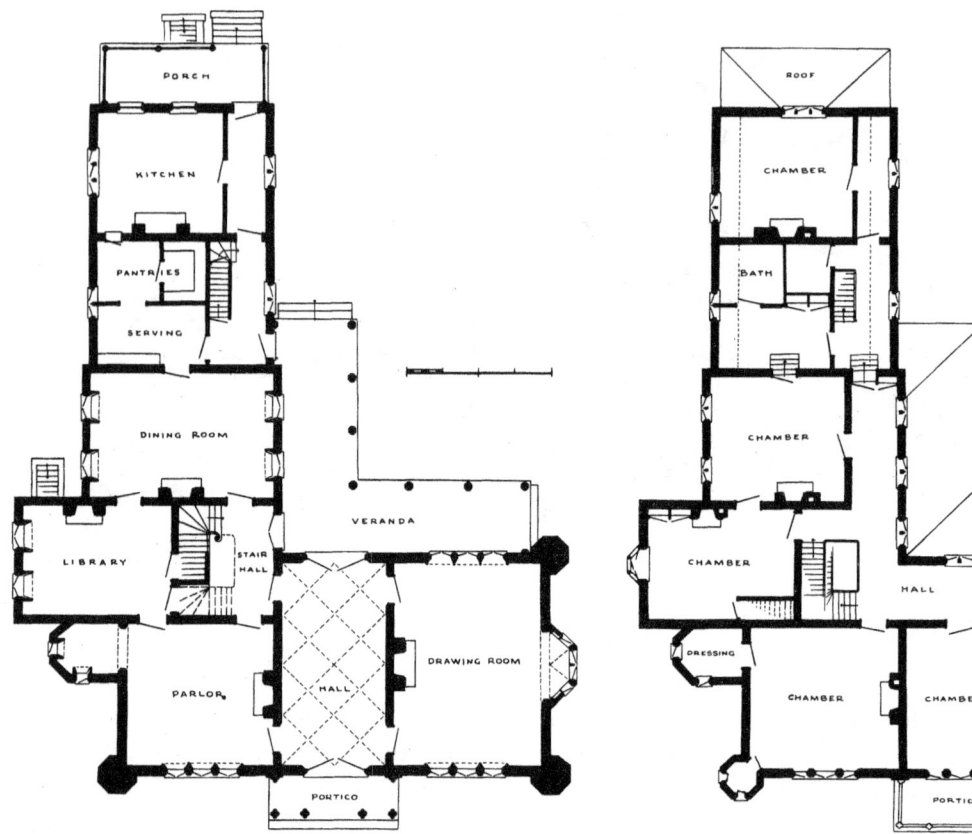

173. First and Second Floor Plans of Ingelside.

of the drawing-room oriel, and is to be found in the narrow windows of the upstairs closets. Interior door frames are like those of Loudoun, with carving in the narrow spandrels, but they are not recessed. The doors themselves have a similar arrangement of panels, although lacking the lobed headings with the bits of relief around them. Window shutters in the principal rooms fold back into casings that protrude into the room in the parlor alcove, library, and dining room. Dominating the drawing room is the large circular centerpiece modeled after a thirteenth- or fourteenth-century geometrical rose window. The white marble mantel in this room has a semicircular arched fireplace, with the undulating relief in the spandrels and cartouche in the carved style of contemporary neoclassic sculpture (*Fig. 174*). The chimneypiece in the library is of polished gray stone and has a half-round arch opening with flat spandrel panels and escutcheon keystone. In the other rooms are marblized iron mantels of the kind sold by Henry Ingels at his downtown place of business.[26] The centerpiece in the dining room comes from the same die as that in the Loudoun parlor (*Fig. 169*).

Behind the kitchen wing at Ingelside once stood a hipped-roofed, octagonal brick smokehouse, demolished in 1938. Farther back, a servants' cottage survives, sheltering three rooms on the ground floor and corresponding chambers under the roof. The gate lodge was enlarged for conversion into an apartment house many years ago, when the front of the estate was portioned off into building lots. The villa proper has been altered into apartments and the retracted lot used as a trailer camp since the 1940's.

ELLEY VILLA   The third of the three distinguished Gothic Revival houses of Fayette County is in the more popular Pointed Style and is closer to the ideals of Downing than to

174. Marble Mantel in the Drawing Room, Ingelside.

those of Davis. It was built by John McMurtry on an eight-acre tract located south of Maxwell Street and east of Rose Street for William R. Elley after 1850. The villa was adapted from Design XXV in *The Architecture of Country Houses,* first published in 1850 *(Fig. 175).* The author says of this plan that it was "no copy of any foreign cottage," but that every feature had been "suggested by the country life of those who live in residences of this size in the Middle United States."[27] Although the view illustrated was a plate made from a drawing by Alexander Davis, the originator of the design was Andrew Downing himself. The first concept of the house had been a sketch enclosed in a letter sent by the essayist to the architect on January 27, 1848.[28]

Downing's book at that time was in course of preparation, and he wished to include this scheme in it. A projecting entrance pavilion, with a steeply pitched bargeboarded gable over a bay window, is centered on a greater mass two rooms deep. The Tudor arch of the entrance porch opens onto a wide veranda to either side. The roof eaves come down very low over the windows to the second floor. Twin chimneys of three stacks each straddle the roof ridge. A greenhouse is at one end of the front gallery and a kitchen ell at the other. A detail of the verge board illustrated is identical to that carried out on the Elley villa *(Fig. 176).* In the residence by McMurtry, the noticeable change is the high-ceilinged second story proper to southern houses. Tall windows and small gables are added to either side of the entrance pavilion, and the conservatory is extended little farther than the end of the gallery *(Fig. 177).* The disposition of rooms is virtually the same in Design XXV and the Lexington house. Downing stressed the elegance of the central interior: "The entrance-hall being unoccupied by stairs, becomes a fine apartment, and being connected with a library of equal size, by large sliding doors, the effect of this suite of 44 feet, when thrown into one, will be very agreeable on entering the house. This

175. "A Country House in the Pointed Style." Andrew Downing, The Architecture of Country Houses (New York, 1850), Design XXV.

176. "Verge-Board." Downing, The Architecture of Country Houses, figure 137.

177. Elley Villa.

will be heightened by the position of the large bay-window at the end of the library."29 In the Elley villa there are folding doors between the hall and library (*Fig. 178*). The only conspicuous departure from the Downing plan in the Kentucky house is the opening up of the two rooms on the left side of the building, which serve as double parlors. The staircase is placed in a side hall behind the dining room and adjacent to several service rooms. The second-floor arrangements are practically the same, except that the plan in *Country Houses* indicates a door from the stair landing to the bathroom, which would be impossible because of the difference in floor levels. Stairways continue to the garret in both.

Colored glass enhances the oriel in the Elley library, and frosted glass with intaglio flower designs fills the transom and side lights to the front door. Matching centerpieces are in the ceiling of the hall and library, similar to decorations in the hall of the Bayles-Beck house and the drawing room of Botherum (*Fig. 164, 179*). An anthemion in a rectangular panel is enframed by a vine in high relief. The design of the white marble mantels in the parlors is of the Ingelside variety. That in the dining room makes use of several thin slabs of marble superimposed, the beveled edges cut along curved outlines, with a single console of contrasting depth supporting the projecting mantel shelf (*Fig. 180*).

Several dependencies and a racecourse once existed behind the Elley villa. A row of pine trees along Rose Street near the Maxwell intersection marked the entrance to the grounds, now reduced to the size of a city lot, the house facing Linden Walk. The place sometimes is referred to as Aylesford, a name given it by the Alford family while residing here after 1885. During the second quarter of the present century the villa was a fraternity house, and now it is in private hands once more. Its painted walls give the building a startling whiteness at odds with the spirit that created such a house.

The Elley villa is representative of several other houses in central Kentucky. The best known is Mound Cottage, the Brigadier General J. T. Boyle house on Maple Avenue in Danville.30 Similar is the Gentry house farther out the Harrodsburg-Danville Pike. Lacking the projecting entrance pavilion, these two seem more boxlike than the Elley villa. A house on the Frankfort Pike a few miles from Versailles substitutes a tower for the central gabled feature and has a long two-story wing at the back, but in other respects it is very much like the Lexington villa. The facade that most strongly resembled that of the Elley villa belonged to the

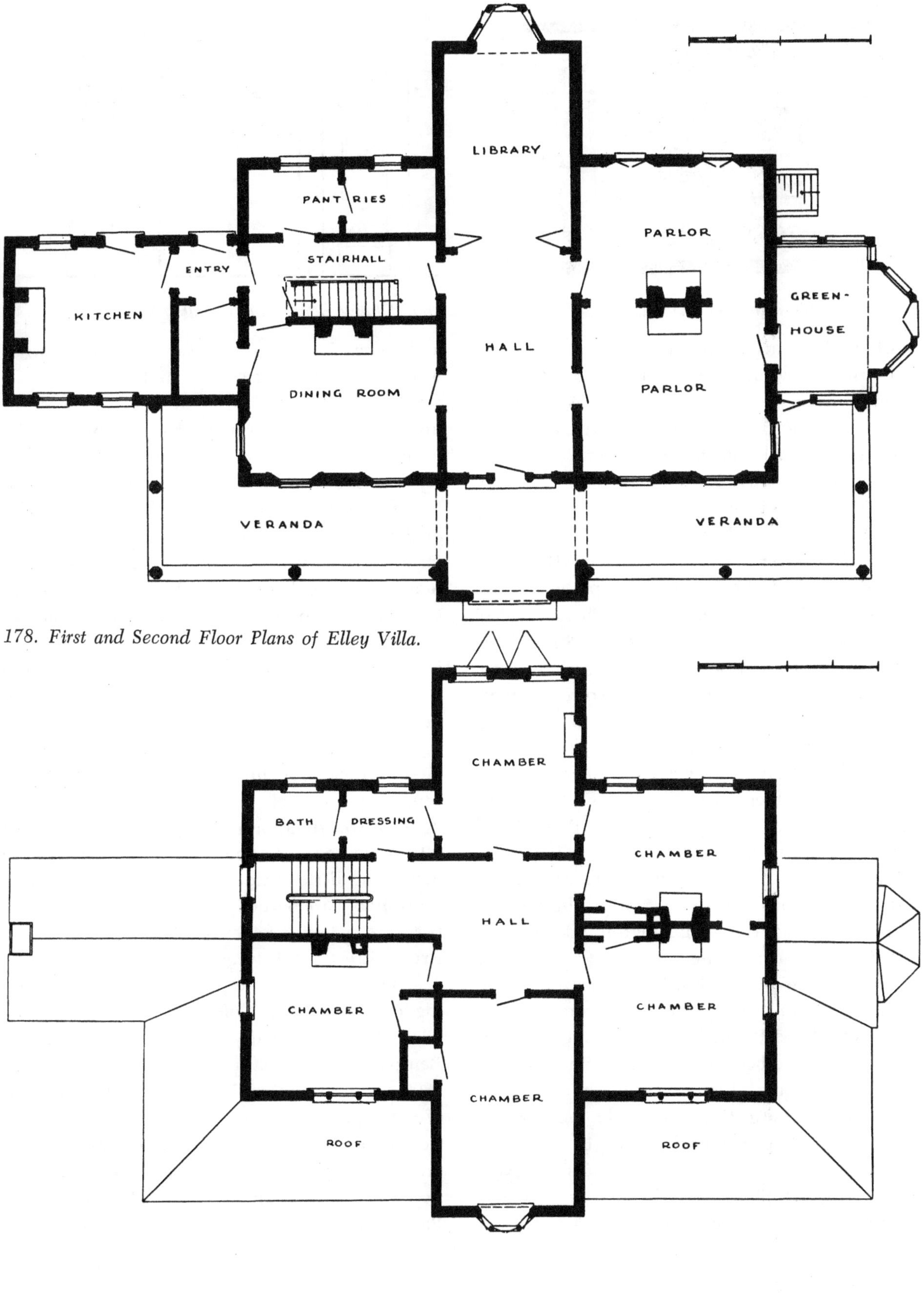

OF THE BLUEGRASS 129

178. *First and Second Floor Plans of Elley Villa.*

179. Centerpiece in Hall Ceiling, Elley Villa.

180. Dining Room Mantel, Elley Villa.

William M. Garrard house at the east end of Duncan Avenue in Paris, Kentucky, but the bay window over the entrance porch has been removed.[31] The Paris house, at present called Hidaway, has a front mass only one room deep, end chimneys, and a low-pitched roof.

Other Bluegrass houses of brick in the Pointed Style include a small dwelling on the west side of Spring Street between High and Maxwell streets in Lexington (perhaps post bellum), and the former Mentelle house (1858) near the city limits on East Main Street, the latter exhibiting delicate wood trim and cast-iron work. A greater amount of iron décor is lavished on the John B. Bibb house (1857) on Wapping Street in Frankfort, which has two tall gables loaded with heavily carved bargeboards toward the street.[32] Other examples are a house on the Lexington Pike near Paris, smaller than these, which has burned, a house similar to it on the Craig Mill Road near Midway, and a compact little house with a massive central chimney of four stacks, east of the Lexington Pike several miles above Nicholasville.

A unique phase of mid-nineteenth-century architecture in America resulted from the application of the Pointed Style to frame cottages. Such houses had been recommended by Downing, whose arguments often ran along the lines of economy. These cottages resemble the wooden churches popularized by Richard Upjohn, the architect of Trinity Church (1841-1846) in New York City. *Upjohn's Rural Architecture*, containing *Working Drawings and Specifications for a Wooden Church and Other Rural Structures*, was published in New York in 1852. The characteristic feature of these churches was walls of upright boards with vertical battens covering the joints. The type is often referred to as Carpenter's Gothic. John McMurtry built a small house of this construction at the northern end of the estate called The Elms, and after his heavy losses during the mid-1850's, he and his family moved into it.[33] The dwelling, referred to as Cottage Garden, now stands in South Broadway Park, but it is considerably altered. An existing house in this style in Fayette County is the Runyan place, several miles from Lexington below the Old Frankfort Pike. It is the original section of an irregular residence called Birch Nest. Other Carpenter's Gothic cottages in surrounding counties are the Thompson house (partially burned) on the Lexington-Paris Pike,[34] a little house on the southwest edge of Paris, the delightful little residence at Almahurst (with horizontal clapboarded walls) in Jessamine County,[35] and a house somewhat later than these on Bruen Street in Midway.

The Gothic vogue prompted some remodeling of old houses. One in Fayette County is Glen Rose, originally called Spring Hill by Benijah Bosworth, who built the house about 1800 on the Frankfort Pike about two miles west of Lexington. It was a one-and-three-quarters-storied brick structure, with a central hall separating pairs of rooms, each pair sharing a chimney. The alteration consisted of modifying a Palladian window over the front door by giving it a pointed arch, articulating the chimneys each into four stacks, extending the eaves of the roof, and attaching a bay window to the east end of the house.

THORN HILL   Remodeled in the pointed idiom in the 1850's was Thorn Hill, the early nineteenth-century house at Limestone and Fifth streets in Lexington, facing Rose Hill, remembered locally for having been the birthplace of John Cabell Breckinridge (statesman and Vice President of the United States), the home of Joseph Cabell Breckinridge (secretary of state under Governor Adair) and of Charlton Hunt (first mayor of Lexington). Perhaps Thorn Hill originally resembled the neighboring residence (1814) of the Reverend James McChord, the stairway arrangement indicating that the second floor may have been added. The kitchen wing certainly is much older, but the entire front mass may date from the middle of the nineteenth century. A good effect is produced by the tall chimneys, the three contiguous front gables, and the traceried portico (*Fig. 181*). The facade windows are all of three lights, those upstairs having pointed arches like that over the entrance at Glen Rose. A vestibule, leading into the parlor and drawing room, precedes the square stairhall which opens onto the rear gallery and into the dining room (*Fig. 182*). A pair of small sliding doors in the wall between the large kitchen and serving room recalls a similar arrangement at Ingelside. The broad chimney, gable, shuttered windows, and hooded door at the back of the house make a quaint composition. A two-storied servants' house stands a few feet from the east corner of the kitchen. Thorn Hill is a rule-of-thumb house, casual in its symmetry, inconstant in its measurements, having odd lengths and diversified angles which show up most pronouncedly in the front gables.

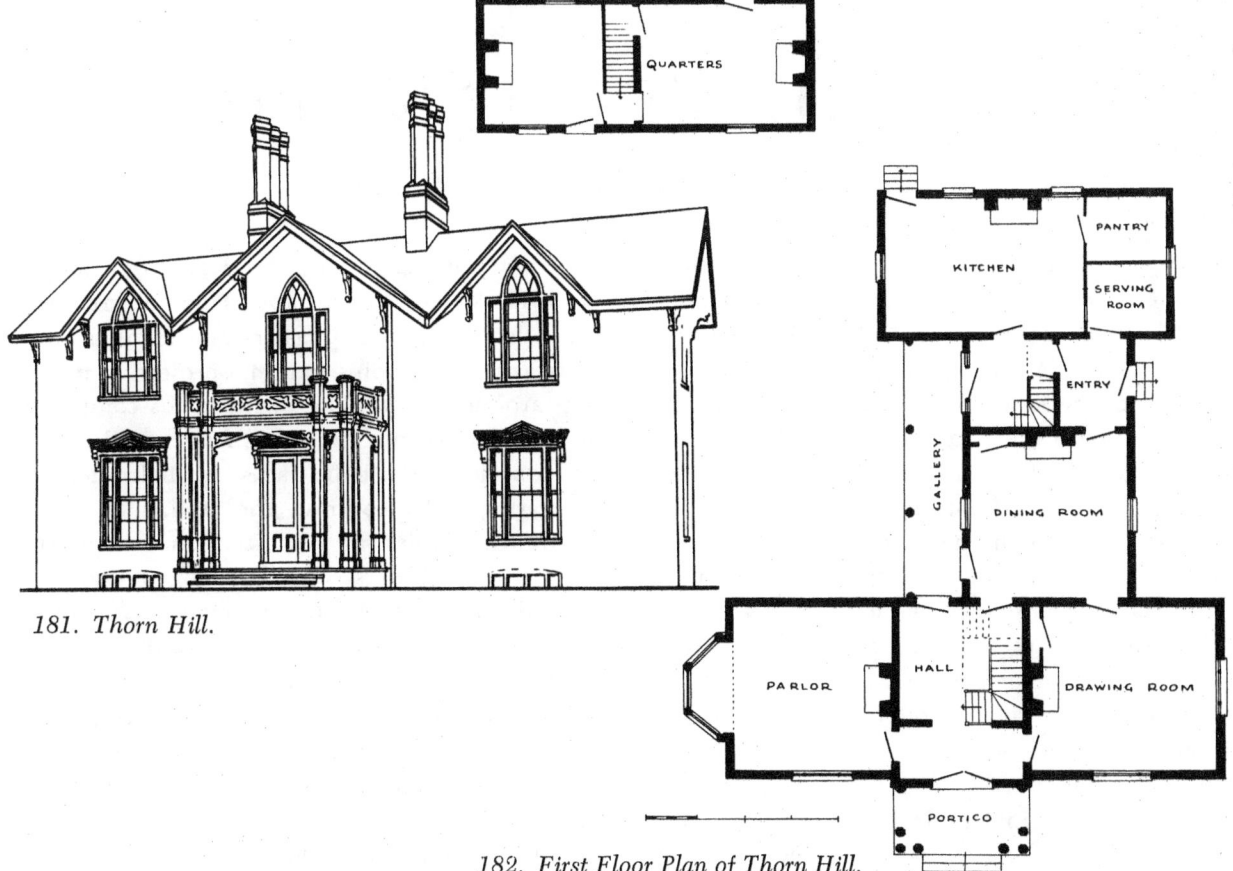

181. Thorn Hill.

182. First Floor Plan of Thorn Hill.

THE ITALIANATE 9

During the period of the revivals, a third style left a deep impression upon Kentucky domestic architecture. This third style was called Italianate, and drew its inspiration from the lesser houses of the Italian peninsula. Whereas the great Italian public buildings and palaces took on new characteristics with the passage of time, from the protoclassic of the Etruscans, through the Roman, medieval, and into later periods, the fundamental design of secondary dwellings remained practically unchanged from the beginning of historic times down to the nineteenth century. The type was well suited for adaptation to houses in democratic America.

The Italianate is related to one other contemporary style in America with which it should not be confused—the Renaissance Revival, which imitated buildings of the great sixteenth-century Italian architects. Renaissance Revival examples are ornamented with an abundance of architectural details, such as pilasters and entablatures, rustication and quoins, external projecting moldings around the windows, with hoods composed of lengths of cornice set above friezes, pediments on consoles, and balustrades in balconies or stairrailings. By contrast, the Italianate phase was much simpler. It was often casual concerning the matter of style, borrowing a doorway from the Greek Revival or its massing from the Gothic Revival. In line with the local tradition, it is no surprise that the Italianate, but not the Renaissance Revival, was found quite acceptable in central Kentucky. Like its two contemporaries, the Italianate style can be traced to beginnings in Britain.

The suitability of plain Italian houses for modern domestic uses was shown by the English-

ANTE BELLUM HOUSES

man Joseph Gandy (born 1771), who, at the age of twenty-three, had been sent by his father's employer to Italy for several years.[1] Afterward he earned his living through making renderings for the celebrated architect Sir John Soane and compiled two books of his own schemes for farm buildings, entitled *Designs for Cottages, Cottage Farms, and other Rural Buildings* and *The Rural Architect*. In these London publications of 1805 and 1806 are shown unadorned structures composed of long, low forms, with wide overhanging roofs, and occasionally an elevated loggia or tower. The models of these designs, undoubtedly, were Mediterranean. Another London volume of the same period, Rubert Lugar's *Architectural Sketches for Cottages* (1805), presents an asymmetrical design labeled "Italian Villa" (Plates XXVII-XXVIII). In the same author's *The Country Gentleman's Architect* (London, 1807), is a two-storied "Farm House," with a three-storied tower at the right and a projecting pavilion in the center, to the left of which a low wing housing the dairy connects with the pigpen and cowshed running at right angles. An octagonal beerhouse with a cupola forms the corner pavilion (Plates 6 and 14). The first Italianate house constructed in England predates the published works cited by several years. It goes by the name of Cronkhill, and was built by John Nash in 1802 for Mr. Walford, Lord Berwick's agent at Attingham, near Shrewsbury. This medium-sized residence was an informal, compact composition of square and round masses of various heights, capped by low roofs with deep bracketed eaves, and pierced by arched windows, the main block surrounded by an arcaded loggia.[2]

The Italianate mode appeared in America soon after its inception in England. Among its antecedents in the United States may be counted some of the work of Latrobe. For our purpose the naming of one example should suffice, and that is his design for the Pope house (1811) in Lexington (*Fig. 73*). Its eventual execution in Federal style is a good indication of the affinities (and confusion) between the Federal and Italianate. White Cottage, of the 1820's, refers to Italian (rather than Roman) architecture through its severe arcade and Palladian windows (*Fig. 103*), but it misses being Italianate because of its delicate, hand-wrought wood details. The Italianate style, properly speaking, like the contemporary revivals, depended upon machine production for its members. This factor is well illustrated in the first and second Ashlands, built respectively about 1814 and 1857 (*Fig. 188*). The Italianate showed a return to certain features of early brick buildings which had been eschewed by the revivals, such as round arches, belt courses, quoins, and polygonal rooms, though the last were occasionally used in the Gothic style (*Fig. 164*). Inspiration for much of Greek and Gothic Revival building came from designs printed in architectural books, and the Italianate was similarly stimulated. The first Italianate plan in an American publication was of "a small villa suitable for the summer residence of a genteel Family," appearing in *The Builder's Assistant*, by the English-born architect John Haviland (Philadelphia, 1818-1821), already cited as the first American publication to show the Greek orders. Plate 60 shows the front elevation of a symmetrical, two-storied composition of three parts, with a small cubic office attached to each end. The overhanging eaves of the low-pitched roof, covering the main mass, are supported on thin brackets. The gabled central pavilion is given an indented portico of two stories. It is stated that a house of this design had been built for John Cridland near Philadelphia. However, for the time being, this printed specimen stood alone. Italianate designs became common only after 1840. They were featured in the books of A. J. Downing, beginning with *Cottage Residences* (1842), in William H. Ranlett's *The Architect* (New York, 1847-1849), and Charles Wyllys Elliott's *Cottages and Cottage Life* (Cincinnati and New York, 1848).[3] Meanwhile, the architectural firm of Town & Davis of New York devised the elevation of a villa in what they termed the "Etruscan or American Style," which conjunction of names bespeaks an effort to naturalize the Italianate house in America. The rendering, made for exhibition in 1835, combines informally two heavy masses and two towers, all covered by wide, low-pitched hipped roofs on different levels. Another exhibition drawing of the following year is referred to as a "Tuscan Villa."[4] This one is a simple rectangular balanced form, to which are affixed delicate iron porches.

Italianate houses may be divided into two groups: first, those that are symmetrical, including the Cridland house by Haviland and Town & Davis' "Tuscan Villa" design; and, second, those that are not symmetrical, exemplified by the "Etruscan or American Style" design and Cronkhill in England. The first sometimes encroaches upon Greek Revival territory. The earliest of the asymmetrical or picturesque Italian villas in America is thought to be the Bishop Doane house in Burlington, New Jersey, built by the Philadelphia architect John Notman in 1837.[5] John Haviland, author of the Cridland house, was also from Philadelphia, which city may be said to have fathered the Italianate style, just as it had the Greek and Gothic Revivals.

The principal advocate of the Italianate in central Kentucky was a man whose work we have met before, Major Thomas Lewinski, architect of the two churches in medieval style on Market Street, designer of the portico added to the Gibson house, and creator of Mansfield and of the Greek Revival Bell and Johnson residences. Born in London of a Polish father and an English mother, Lewinski had been educated to become a Roman Catholic priest. Finding army life more to his venturesome nature, he joined the British regiments and fought in Spain. He came to the New World to continue his soldiering in South America, where he lost one eye. A well-rounded literary background equipped him to teach, and we find him at first in Kentucky as an instructor at the University of Louisville, where he married a Miss Carey of that city. Lewinski came to Lexington in 1842, when he was about forty years of age. He attached himself to Cassius Marcellus Clay, whom he defended in publishing the antislavery paper *The True American*. He taught French, and as commandant drilled the Lexington Rifles. A widower, he contracted a second marriage in 1846 to Mary Watkins, a niece of Henry Clay and sister of Thomas Watkins,

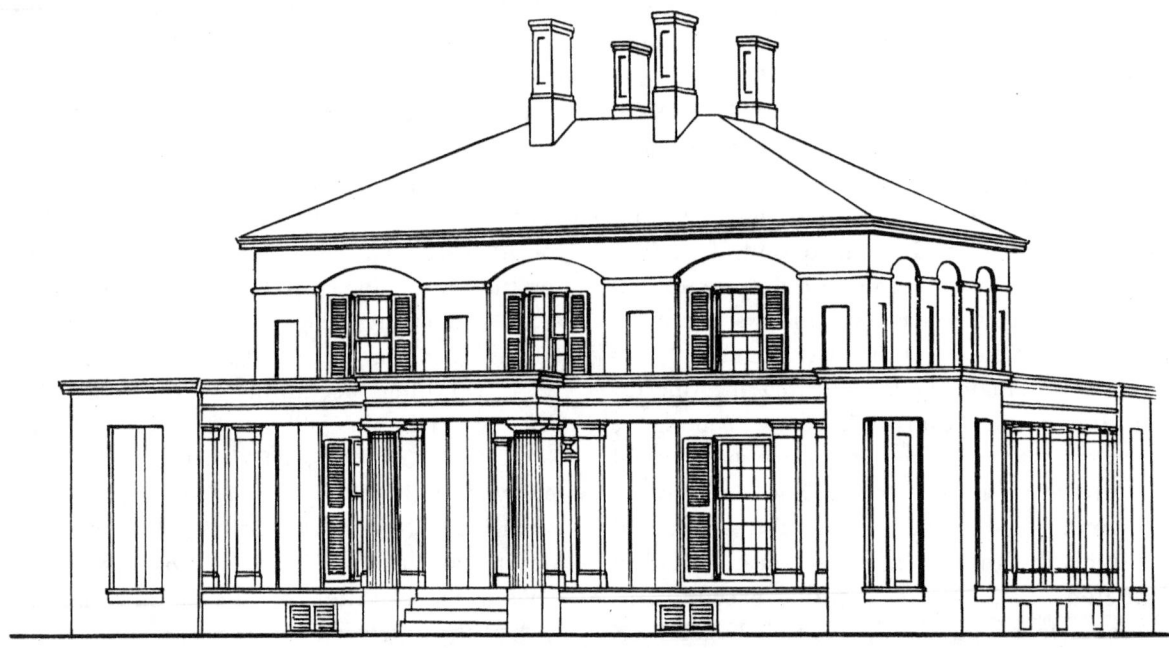

183. Clay Villa. Restored.

who had married one of John McMurtry's daughters. Lewinski was survived by two daughters at the time of his death in 1882.[6]

Lewinski seems to have practiced architecture in Lexington most actively during the mid-1840's. His professional diary covers the period from March 24, 1845, through July 5, 1847. However, he continued work in this field at least up to the time when he became secretary of the Lexington Gas Company, in the mid-1850's, and for a decade longer was sometimes engaged in remodeling. He functioned mainly as an architect, making drawings and specifications for buildings, and watching construction, but apparently acted as construction engineer himself only on the Henry Clay Monument, built in the Lexington Cemetery during the late 1850's.[7] It will be recalled that John McMurtry was the builder of the two Market Street churches. The two men were associated on other projects, including White Hall, the enlarged Cassius Clay mansion in Madison County.[8] Lewinski collected an architectural library and John McMurtry based the design of the formal villa Lyndhurst on a plan from Sloan's *The Model Architect,* which he would have seen in the Lewinski library.[9]

CLAY VILLA At the time Lewinski was working on the drawings for Mansfield for Thomas Hart Clay, he was busy also designing a house for another of Henry Clay's sons, James B. Clay. This residence is now located on Forest Avenue near East Main Street. The first entry about it in the Lewinski diary is dated June 11, 1845, stating that the architect "surveyed Building and took dimensions for steps to Portico." Subsequent remarks have to do with inspecting construction and making additional drawings for such details as doors, mantels, gates, lamps, "Ice House 'Cabinet d'aissance'," and furniture. Lewinski himself refers to the house as a "villa." The two-storied building is square and massive. The walls are enriched by applied segmental arches on wide, pilasterlike forms with sunken vertical panels, and the lower portion is enclosed by a porch or umbrage composed of brick corner pavilions connected by open galleries having

184. Sedgeley, Philadelphia. From Thompson Westcott, The Historic Mansions and Buildings of Philadelphia (Philadelphia, 1877), p. 450.

thick, square, coupled wooden piers supporting a deep entablature *(Fig. 183).* In some of its characteristics the villa may be compared to Sedgeley, the country house of William Crammond of Philadelphia, distinguished as the first Gothic Revival building in America and designed by Benjamin Henry Latrobe in 1799 *(Fig. 184).* Notwithstanding the difference in style, the two houses have in common hipped roofs, chimneys rising above interior walls, three bays on the flanks, and galleries between corner flankers. Lewinski's is the more heavyhanded of the two designs. Details of the Clay villa are Greek Revival. The projecting entrance bay, with its pair of correct Doric columns and simplified entablature, the pattern of the lights in the frontispiece and wide first-floor windows, and the library mantel seem to have been derived from Plates 77 and 73 in Edward Shaw's *Civil Architecture*—which Lewinski owned—and the external elements adapted from an elevation for a shop front. The plan of the main floor is similar to that of Mansfield, combining a central hall with four rooms of equal size *(Fig. 185*—compare *Fig. 158).* The hall is not divided, windows are in two walls of each room, and there were corner niches in the front library. Marble mantels in the double parlors have round arched fireplaces like those at Ingelside, and the one in the library is pilastered. Service rooms were in a lean-to or

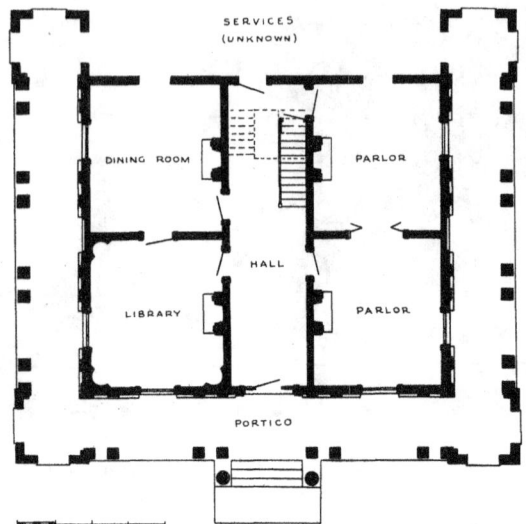

185. First Floor Plan of Clay Villa. Restored.

wing at the back, of which no trace remains; the absence of fireplaces in the basement eliminates the possibility of cooking belowstairs, as at Mansfield. The chamber floor follows the same plan as the first, except for having two dressing rooms at the front of the hall. The windows in the second story are quite low in the wall, reducing their efficiency in providing light and ventilation. A blind window was in the center bay of each flank, in both stories. Bracketed gables and wide eaves were added toward the close of the nineteenth century, and the staircase was continued to the garret. The partition between parlors was removed, and the folding doors were installed in the hall wall. In 1946 the house was stripped of its porches. The Clay villa belongs to the type designated "Tuscan" by Town & Davis.

CANE RUN   One of the finest of medium-sized Italianate villas in America is that designed by Lewinski and built by George Batcheller in 1853-1854 for Alexander H. Brand, three miles north of Lexington on the Newtown Pike. The house received its name from one of the headwater branches of Cane Run transversing the Brand farm. The bilateral symmetry of Lewinski's work of the 1840's here has given way to a new freedom in an informal composition of forms capped by low gabled roofs, the deep overhangs of which rest on slender brackets. There is an arcaded porch at the entrance, and the pile is dominated by a square tower (*Fig. 186*). The arched openings in simple masses have the flavor of John Nash's Cronkhill. The house is restrained in its use of ornament, and stress is laid upon an interesting arrangement of forms. The excellence of the architect's work is readily apparent in the disposition of rooms (*Fig. 187*). There is

186. Cane Run.

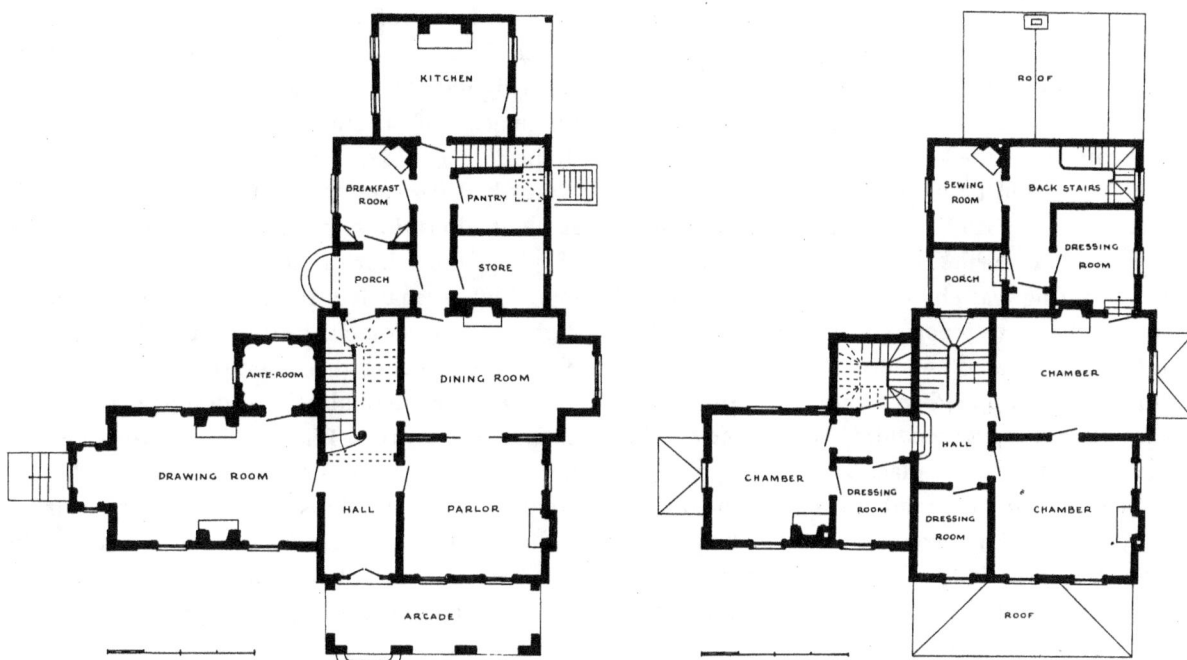

187. First and Second Floor Plans of Cane Run.

no monotony of plan, such as one finds in earlier Lewinski houses. One enters a long stairhall—divided by an arch—opening onto a porch at either end, and into the drawing room on one side and a parlor and dining room on the other, the last two divided by sliding doors. A breakfast room, kitchen, and other service rooms are housed in the back wing. The drawing and dining rooms have recessed windows at the far ends. The opening in the drawing room is on an axis with the hall door, the door to the parlor, and the window on the fireplace wall of this room. Twin marble mantels in the great room are identical to the chimneypiece in the drawing room at Ingelside (*Fig. 174*). An octagonal recess is in the ceiling of the Cane Run drawing room, the height of which (as at Ingelside and Loudoun) is greater than others in the house. The octagonal anteroom in the base of the tower repeats niches in alternate sides—as in the corners of the Clay villa library or Botherum drawing room—but here a regular polygonal shape is formed. Upstairs, the three major bedrooms have dressing rooms arranged in suites. A small sewing room is over the breakfast room. A staircase winds upward inside the square tower to a lookout, from which Brand is said to have surveyed the work on his plantation. Several brick dependencies of chaste design stand a short distance behind the main house. The property passed in 1881 to Joseph C. Anderson, who rechristened it Glengarry.

Lewinski designed another contemporary villa nearby for David S. Coleman, and it was built by the same contractor who constructed Cane Run. The Coleman house, called Highland Home, unfortunately burned on December 12, 1872, and no picture of it is known to be in existence. A new house was built on the site soon afterward. From specifications and records it is apparent that Highland Home was a house of similar size to Cane Run and may have resembled it in design.[10]

NEW ASHLAND   Following the death of Henry Clay in 1852, his home, Ashland, was purchased from the estate by his son, James B. Clay. For some years the walls of the house had been subsiding, and it was deemed no longer possible to make them safe through repairs. Consequently the house was torn down and rebuilt on the same site. The new building was completed by the middle of 1857. Perhaps the bricks and ash wood salvaged from the former house were used again in the new structure. The architect for the project was Thomas Lewinski, who had built the plain gardener's cottage on the estate in 1846.[11] Although the disposition of the original Ashland was retained, the style of the building was changed (*Fig. 188*). Quoins were added at the corners, cornices made heavier, chimneys elaborated, window headings arched, cast-iron hoods applied to those in the principal block, sashes throughout filled with large panes of glass, a platform placed in front of the entrance bay and a broad terrace at the back, and iron balconies affixed to the front windows of the end pavilions. Yet the front doorway and enframement of the Palladian window above were replaced following the old lines. The plan, which is assumed to have been identical with the original, fits together in an interesting arrangement of several rooms of odd geometric shapes (*Fig. 189*). The interior décor is in typically Victorian taste. One of the few subsequent alterations was the removal during the 1880's of the elliptical stairway, and its replacement by a massive structure having straight flights. The domed ceiling of this hall was obliterated during this alteration.

Lewinski may also have designed the house on the Tates Creek Pike one mile from Lexington, built in 1853 for John Clay, another of Henry Clay's sons. This rather plain, two-storied, L-shaped house, bearing some similarities to the cottage built at Ashland, was razed in 1956.

Among Lewinski's projects after he became

188. *First and Second Ashlands. Above, ca. 1814; below, 1857.*

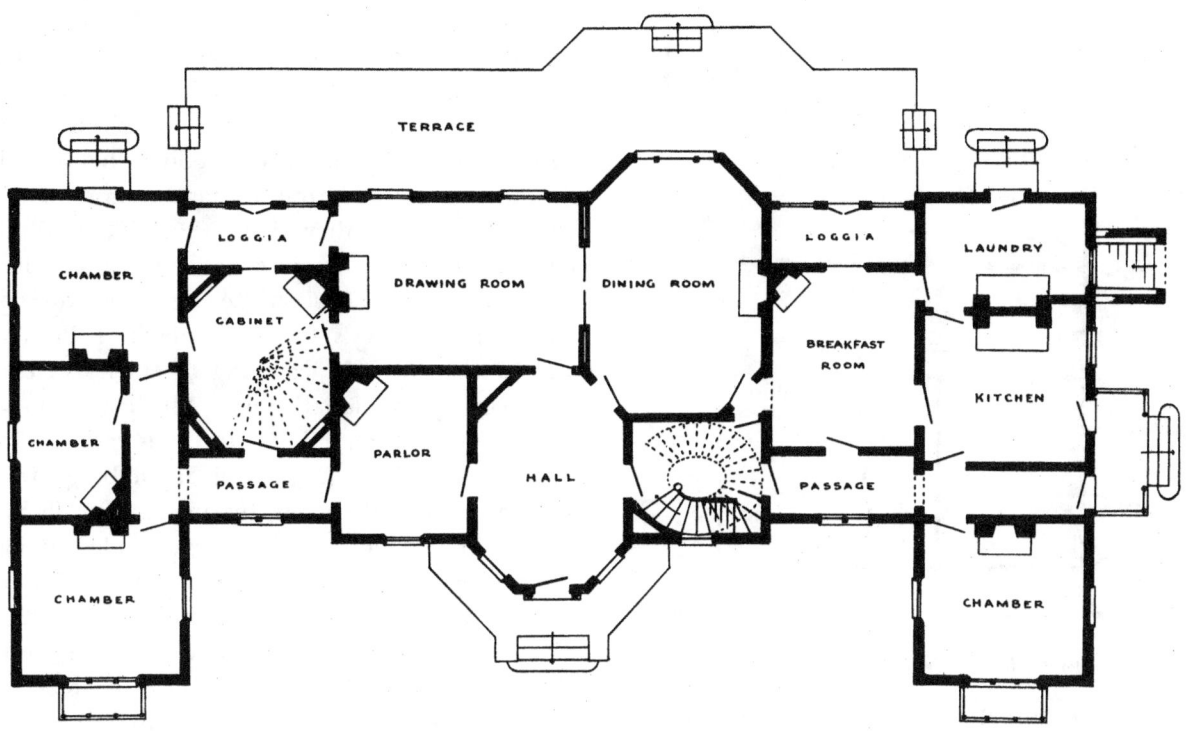

189. *Principal Floor Plan of Ashland.*

190. *Woolley House.*

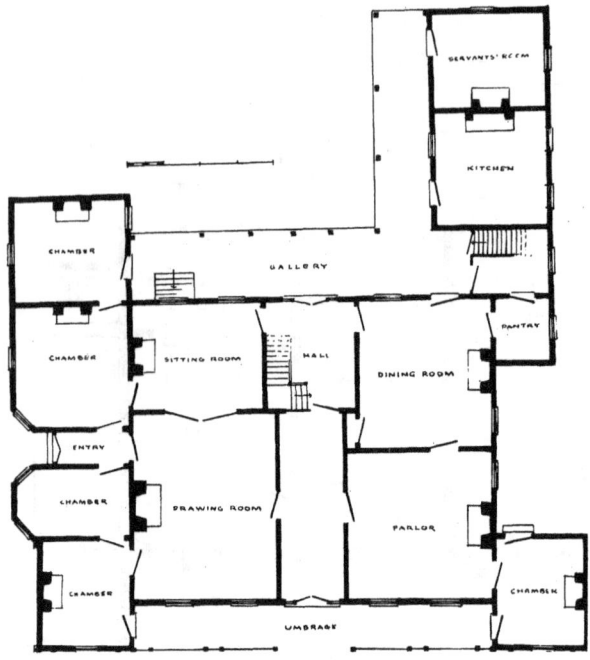

191. Principal Floor Plan of Woolley House.

secretary to the Lexington Gas Company was the remodeling of the other Fayette County residence associated with Latrobe, namely the John Pope house, purchased by John A. Woolfolk in March of 1865. Lewinski added a recessed entrance, a cast-iron porch across the front, a series of narrow arched windows—like those in the wings at Ashland—Moorish bay windows on the flanks, and bracketed eaves with a low gable centered on each side of the house.[12]

WOOLLEY HOUSE There are similarities between the remodeled Pope-Woolfolk house and the additions to Norton Cottage sponsored by Judge George Woolley about 1859. These similarities point to Lewinski as author of this undertaking also. Further, Lewinski had worked on Judge Woolley's former home in February and March of 1846, according to entries in the architect's professional diary. The main block of the building on High Street was more than doubled in height (*Fig. 190*); an umbrage was extended across the front, linking the two flanking pavilions, and a low wing was added along the east end, containing, among others, a couple of polygonal rooms (*Fig. 191*; compare *Fig. 89*). The square posts of the front umbrage were chamfered, like the original supports on the rear gallery. In addition, the posts had small brackets at the top, a feature proper to the Italian-Swiss chalet style. The extended bracketed eaves and iron crestings are accompanying accessories. Interior changes to the main story included the installation of a staircase in the

192. Swift House.

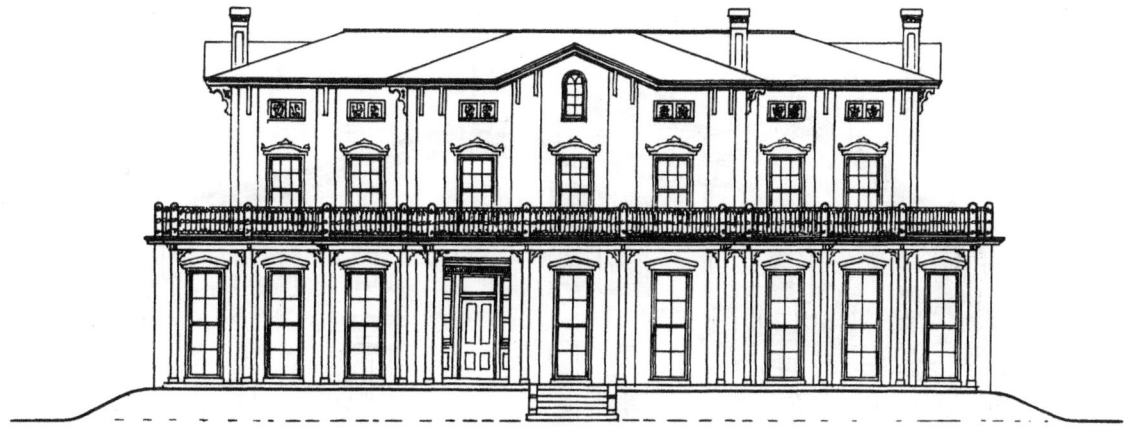

193. Weir-Fraser Villa.

square section of the hall at the back of the house—the steps ascending against the east leaf of the double doors to the passageway, which, of course, had to be fixed permanently—and the cutting of a wide doorway between the drawing room and the small room behind, formerly used as a bedroom. The enlargement provided an adequate number of new chambers, both in the wing and upper floors. In 1946 the entire building was razed.

SWIFT HOUSE In the same block of High Street as the Woolley residence, a second house may have attained its final form under Lewinski's direction. The repetition of arches and the chaste character of the portico on the Stephen Swift house suggest his workmanship. When first built, the Swift house must have been very much like the story-and-a-half Jacob Ashton house across the street, except that its windows were set in arched recesses and it had a small wing to one side (*Fig. 192*). During the mid-1840's the walls of the principal mass were carried up another story, with the upstairs fenestration also recessed, but here the arches were more depressed than those below. The axial windows to second floor and garret were combined in a vertical panel. This device is somewhat reminiscent of one employed by Alexander J. Davis, in which windows on two levels are united to look like one.[13] The converted facade bears some relationship to that of the Peck house farther east and on the opposite side of High Street (*Fig. 141*). The Swift house was demolished and the Calvary Baptist Church built on its site in 1905.

KINKEAD HOUSE Another house transformed into a villa at about the same time stands on the southeast corner of Walnut and Fourth streets, across from Elmwood. The work was carried out for Mrs. George Blackburn Kinkead after 1853.[14] Pilaster shafts on the front and a small distyle Doric portico reveal that the style of the original house was Greek Revival. The entrance was to the right of a three-bayed block, with a wing on this side of the house running back to a service ell. A new attic story was built over the entire house, with the exception of the service extension. Coupled consoles supported the eaves, and the chimneys were elaborated with panels and various projecting courses.

194. Richland.

195. Cloud House.

WEIR-FRASER VILLA   The dwelling erected on North Limestone above Third Street, after the burning of the hemp factory that stood there until 1846, was a duplicate of the Greek Revival residence on the adjoining corner lot, previously described as the Weir house. Both buildings probably were built by James Weir. The northern one was remodeled into an extensive Italianate villa for John Fraser about 1865.[15] Originally the house was a compact cubic block with

196. Lyndhurst.

a bold portico composed of a heavy entablature on thick cylindrical Doric columns and with squat pilastered wings to either side (*Fig. 143*). The structure was changed to a broad mass covered by a spreading roof, the front and sides surrounded by a light and airy umbrage (*Fig. 193*). The wings of the original house were heightened and were extended at the back so as to form a recessed porch across the three center bays. A small service wing was left attached to the southeast corner of the villa. Pilaster shafts were raised to the roof, with single or double brackets appended to support the wide eaves. Sashes of the lower windows were filled with extremely large panes of glass. An earth terrace was formed around the building, bringing the lawn almost up to the level of the porch floor. The choice of style may have been prompted by the changes to the Kinkead house a block away. The effect, however, was more like that of the enlarged Woolley house. The ironwork of the Fraser villa was confined more to a functional purpose, serving as the railing around the upper level of the veranda.

RICHLAND   South of the intersection of the Richmond Pike and Walnut Hill Road may be seen a blocky house called Richland, some part of which is said to have been built by General James Shelby at an early date. Acquired by his brother, Major Thomas Hart Shelby in 1848, the present building certainly postdates that year. The house became the home of the latter's daughter, Elizabeth, who married William B. Kinkead, the most likely person to have commissioned the structure as it now exists. The windows are like narrow slits in the great cube. Not even the low-pitched hipped roof shows as one approaches the house (*Fig. 194*). The severe form is relieved only by the chimneys, a bracketed cornice, a small Corinthian portico in front, and a porch with piers on the right flank. A two-storied service wing completes an L plan, in the angle of which is constructed a separate pavilion housing a high-ceilinged parlor lighted by a bay window. The drawing room in the main block on the left is divided by a screen of Corinthian columns. An elaborate square centerpiece is in both sections of the ceiling, the squares set on a diagonal with the room.

CLOUD HOUSE   Five miles from Lexing-

197. *"An Ornamental Villa." Samuel Sloan, The Model Architect (Philadelphia, 1852), Vol. I, Design IX, plate XXX.*

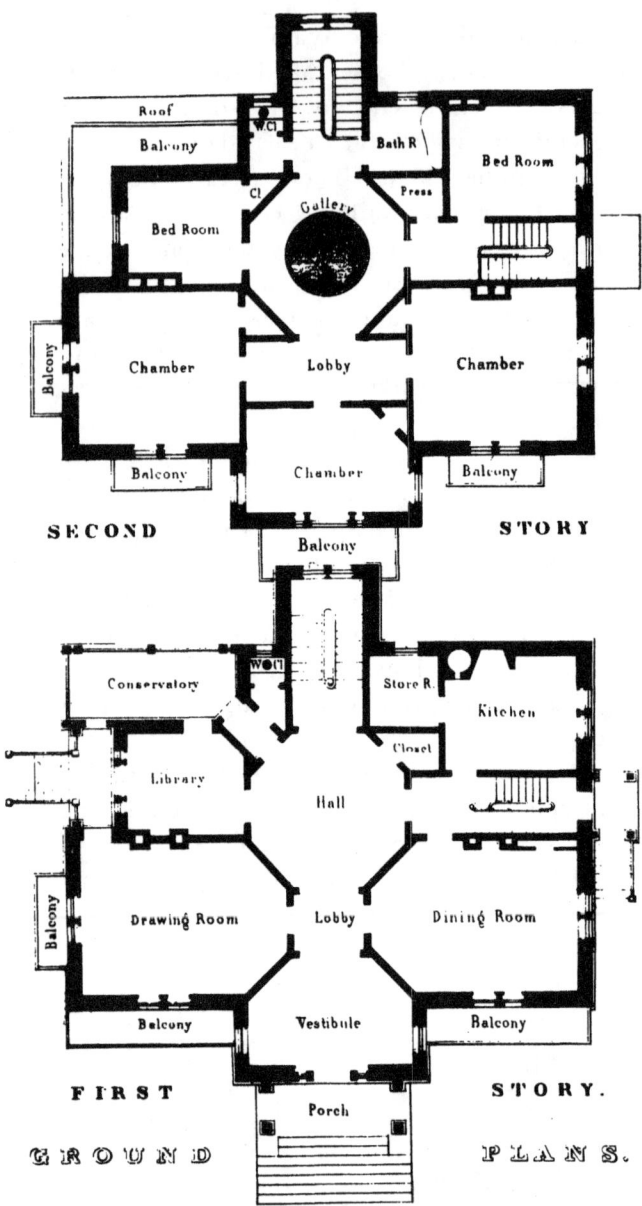

198. *Plans of Sloan's Ornamental Villa. Design IX, plate XXXVI.*

ton, on the south side of the Versailles Pike, William Jones built a villa for his mother-in-law, Mrs. Mary Cloud, in 1857. Having an Ionic portico, columned recessed doorway, and front fenestration consisting entirely of triple windows, the house resembles contemporary residences such as the Hayes house on the Sulphur Well Road and the Johnson house in Lexington (*Fig. 195*). It might, therefore, be classified with them as Greek Revival, but Mary Cloud's domicile has articulated chimneystacks and projecting bay windows, which automatically puts it into the romantic class. A fine spacious effect is achieved inside. The central transverse hall is broad and has wide double doors opening on both sides into the front parlors. A library on the right and dining room on the left sides of the house, behind, have presses flush with the chimney-fronts on the outer sides of the fireplaces, and connecting doors on the inner sides. The staircase rises in the hall next to the dining room and turns around a wide open well, continuing to the third floor. A door at the far end of the hall leads onto a rear gallery running alongside the rear service wing. The house was called Clover Land after 1877, and later was renamed Trevilla.

LYNDHURST William R. Fleming purchased an eleven-acre tract to the west of Rose Street, between High and Maxwell, in 1860,[16] on which he proposed building the finest villa in Lexington. The John Pope house, planned by Latrobe, was on one side, and the Higgins Mansion on the other, overlooking Town Fork of Elkhorn and the expanding city of Lexington beyond. White Cottage was on Main at the head of Rose Street. The gates to the Elley villa were across the intersection at the southeast corner of the Fleming property. The owner engaged the architect of the Elley residence to build his new home. John McMurtry produced an impressive, symmetrical mass virtually three stories in height, elevated on a high basement, with projections on four sides making it a great cruciform. The pile is dominated by a prismatic belvedere rising above the octagonal rotunda that was the core of the building (*Fig. 196*). Fleming came from Philadelphia, and it is not surprising that his villa bears an affinity to a design by the architect Samuel Sloan of that city, published in the first book of his two-volume work, *The Model Architect*, issued in 1852—a copy of which has been noted as belonging to Thomas Lewinski (*Fig. 197*). The author called this "an Ornamental Villa," or "a villa ornamented in the Swiss style." The "ornamental appendages," he admits, "are

OF THE BLUEGRASS

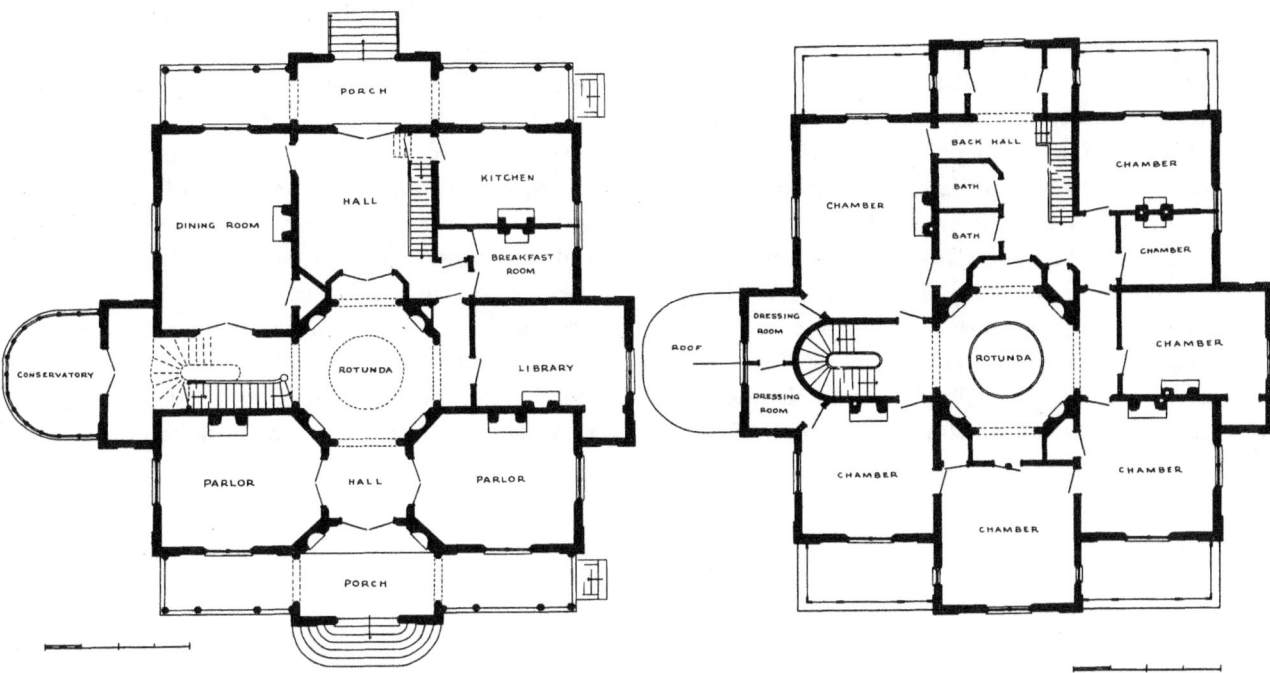

199. First and Second Floor Plans of Lyndhurst.

expensive. But it is to be hoped that the time is, or is coming, when such near-sighted utilitarianism will give way to more liberal views of life, and that he who builds for himself a home, will aim beyond mere physical comfort."[17] The design is recommended for "a wild and mountainous, or at best a hilly location." The simplification of the decoration undoubtedly was an adaptation to the quieter landscape setting above Town Fork. The Fleming villa is considerably larger than the house proposed by Sloan. Porches have been used in place of balconies, with slender cast-iron railings. The plan of the Sloan villa centers around an eight-sided hall (*Fig. 198*). McMurtry's layout carries this motif further, inserting wide openings in four sides, alternating with recessed niches (*Fig. 199*). He also extends the form through the roof, and circular wells in the second, third, and fourth floors permit light from the windows in the belvedere to illuminate the center of the house all the way down to the principal floor (*Fig. 200*). It has been said that marble balustrades, marble floors, and a fountain were to have gone into the rotunda. Wood was substituted for the material of the first and second features, and a gas chandelier with clusters of glowing bulbs at each floor level, suspended from the ceiling of the cupola, replaced the fountain spouting water upward from below. Rooms with splayed ends fitted into the angles of the rotunda in front, and the rear portion of the Fleming plan was more fully developed than that by Sloan. The largest room in the house was the dining room, located in the southeast corner, with the kitchen and breakfast room

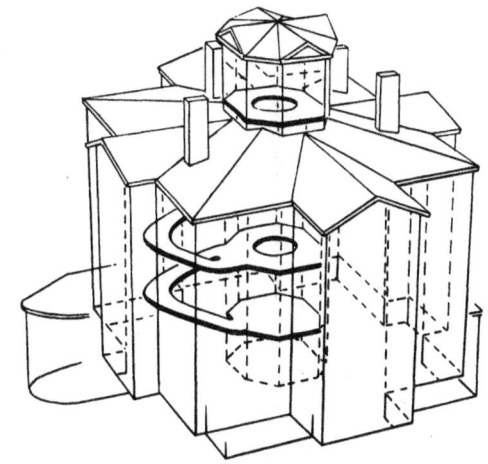

200. Space Diagram of Lyndhurst.

across the large back hall. Chambers were arranged in suites with dressing rooms on the second floor, where there were two bathrooms and a number of extra closets. The third floor was meant for servants or storage; the front room was reserved for billiards. Walls of the villa were composed wholly of hard-burned brick, which the architect said was found to be more durable than the stone usually used for foundations.[18] Fleming was unable to complete the villa, and the place was sold in 1867 for $35,000 to Robert R. Stone,[19] who gave it the name Lyndhurst, after his former home in Canada. McMurtry finished the house for its new owner, and estimated its cost at $25,000.[20] Interior fittings included Italian white marble mantels in the parlors—the spandrels of which are filled with carved figs, grapes, plums, and pomegranates—and the equally lush plaster cornices and centerpieces combining intricate acanthus leaves, beads, shells, and tiny faces. Robert Stone's furnishings equaled these fittings in splendor. Although the lot has dwindled to a fraction of its former size, the house itself has remained in the same family since its completion in the late 1860's, and so has retained much of its original character.

SUMMARY

IT WAS a far cry from the first single-room log cabin of the Revolutionary period to the last spacious hard-burned brick villa of the time of the Civil War. During this interim of over eighty years the residence in central Kentucky was transformed from a minimum shelter to a relatively sumptuous, romantic dwelling. Primitive functionalism had given way to a long metamorphosis, acted upon by a sequence of incoming fashion trends and technical advances, which finally culminated in a residence that enveloped space to produce the grandeur of visual effect.

We have seen in the houses of the region the resourcefulness of early settlers, quickly followed by substantial homes showing, in succession, lingering properties of the Middle Ages, adaptations from the European Renaissance, freshness of personal expression, strongly organized designs of modified classicism, varying degrees of correctness in the Greek and Gothic Revivals, and the informal freedom of the Italianate style. Each phase of building was based upon, yet attempted to surpass, its predecessors. The competitive spirit engendered progress. The result was a wide variety of house types, lending interest and character to the rolling Kentucky landscape.

In the midst of the changing architectural scene ran a thread of indigenous unity. The average size of ante bellum houses in the Bluegrass was established with the introduction of brick as a building material, in such late eighteenth-century examples as the original parts of Ellerslie and Hurricane Hall, and Stony Point. Ashland, built early in the second decade of the nineteenth century, set the limits for ground area covered. Although several times greater than the other houses mentioned, Ashland was not of palatial proportions. Its low wings helped maintain a human scale. The one residence of the prewar era in Fayette County that comes near to baronial magnitude is Loudoun, and it was designed by an out-of-state architect. The second unity was simplicity in decoration. Whether ornament was carved by hand or turned out by machine, it was applied sparingly. Gable ends, especially, were treated with great restraint.

Simple raking boards were used during the early phase and persisted into the Greek Revival period; or else there were parapets, which also appeared on castellated buildings. Sometimes the Greek made use of pediments, but of abbreviated members. However, cottages in the Pointed Style overstepped the rule in vergeboard finery. Porches and porticoes were somewhat more elaborate, yet never became ostentatious. Doorways and chimneypieces were consistently given modest articulation. Cornices inside rooms came into being only with the revivals, and in rare instances attained full entablature elaboration. Ornateness was indulged in only in one of the houses discussed—Lyndhurst—and here as a consequence of postwar interior decoration. The third unity was the predominant use of brick in building, once the period of unprocessed materials was over. The warm red color of Kentucky brickwork compliments the profuse summer greenery of the countryside. Brick walls were seldom covered with paint until nearly the end of the nineteenth century. Here, again, the one exception was Loudoun, which was sanded and painted at the recommendation of its New York architect.

Houses here never dominated nature, and seldom required much modification of it. Country houses were placed where they could look out over fields and streams, and even houses in town usually were surrounded by lawn on all sides. Mount Hope and the Hunt-Morgan house, each with one wall adjacent to the sidewalk, nevertheless enjoyed deep lots beyond. And everywhere there were trees. Lexington had the look of a town implanted in a forest. This respect and sympathy for the virgin beauty of the region was accompanied by excellence of craftsmanship. Both of these ideals were maintained until after the Civil War, and then began to decline.

Present-day domestic building in the Bluegrass region so far has failed to produce anything comparable to these early homes, in terms of good design and technical skill. Though technological advances have provided many comforts, modern builders overlook the important issue of the integration of sound construction and sensitivity of design for a satisfying artistic effect. To copy the old architecture today would be neither desirable nor possible, in the face of changed requirements and the lowering of craft standards. But the imagination, taste, and judgment exercised by past builders has left an architectural heritage in the Bluegrass which should be not only a source of pleasure but a standard which we may strive to equal or surpass.

REFERENCES

INTRODUCTION

1 Timothy Flint, *A Condensed Geography and History of the Western States* (Cincinnati, 1828), Vol. II, pp. 185-187.

2 J. Winston Coleman, Jr., "Lexington as Seen by Travellers, 1810-1835," *The Filson Club History Quarterly*, Vol. XXIX, no. 3 (July, 1953), pp. 267-281.

3 Published as part of [William] *Worsley and* [Thomas] *Smith's Kentucky Almanac, and Farmer's Calendar for the Year 1819* (Lexington, 1818). Lexington's first and second directories were reprinted privately by J. Winston Coleman, Jr., in 1953.

1 PIONEER BUILDING

1 John Filson, *The Discovery, Settlement and Present State of Kentucke* (Wilmington, Del., 1784), p. 33.

2 Thomas Ashe, *Travels in America Performed in 1806 for the Purpose of Exploring the Rivers of Allegheny, Monongahela, Ohio and Mississippi* (London, 1808), pp. 196-200.

3 Harold R. Shurtleff, *The Log Cabin Myth* (Cambridge, Mass., 1939).

4 Hugh Morrison, *Early American Architecture* (New York, 1952), pp. 504-505.

5 This and other remarks about the early stages of Winton are derived from a visit to the house and an interview with Mr. and Mrs. Howard Evans, the present owners (Mrs. Evans is a direct descendant of the original builder), on September 1, 1952, and from a leaflet on Winton subsequently issued by them.

6 Fayette County Deed Book *CoCt B*, pp. 153-155, 159, 161; *CirCt B*, p. 434; *CoCt 7*, p. 333; *CoCt Y*, p. 179.

7 Restored sketch based upon investigation of the ruins and a description of the structure given by the present resident on the farm, Mr. Elmer D. Swetnam, in 1953.

8 Thomas Tileston Waterman, *The Early Architecture of North Carolina* (Chapel Hill, N.C., 1941), pp. 7-8. The only other one seen by the author in central Kentucky is in a ruinous state at the Tempest and Sunshine house on the Leestown Pike in Scott County.

9 Fayette County Deed Book *A*, p. 230.

10 Henry Chandler Forman, *The Architecture of the Old South* (Cambridge, Mass., 1948), pp. 11, 15.

11 Charles E. Peterson, "French Landmarks Along the Mississippi," *Antiques* (April, 1948), p. 286.

2 FRAME HOUSES

1 Hugh Morrison, *Early American Architecture* (New York, 1952), pp. 33-34.

2 *Kentucky Gazette,* May 11, 1793, p. 4; April 9, 1796, p. 3; July 12, 1797, p. 2; July 26, 1797, p. 1.

3 Repeated in Julius P. Bolivar MacCabe, *Directory of the City of Lexington and County of Fayette for 1838 & 1839* (Lexington, 1838), p. 6.

4 [Joseph] *Charless' Kentucky, Tennessee, and Ohio Almanac, for the Year 1806* (Lexington, 1805), p. 18. Re-

printed by J. Winston Coleman, Jr., *Lexington's First City Directory* (Lexington, 1953), p. 3.

5 According to the elderly tenant, Mr. Charles A. Heeter, visited in August, 1956.

3 STONE HOUSES

1 C. Frank Dunn, "Historian's Search for Kentucky's Oldest House," *The Lexington Leader*, September 25, 1952, p. 28.

2 "In the Good Old Days," *The Lexington Leader*, March 9, 1954, p. 7. George W. Ranck, *History of Lexington* (Cincinnati, 1872), p. 26.

3 Patterson sold his holdings on High Street, consisting of 284¾ acres, to Richard Higgins and Lewis Sanders, July 29, 1813. Fayette County Deed Book *CoCt G*, pp. 493-494.

4 The tombstone in the family cemetery east of the house is inscribed: "Settled this place Feb 18, 1784."

5 Information courtesy of the late Mrs. Elizabeth Shryock Fields (granddaughter of Matthias Shryock), who accompanied the author on a visit to the house, June 26, 1945.

4 EARLY BRICK HOUSES

1 Reported to the author by an elderly bricklayer, who, working on the rebuilding of the wings of Woodstock in 1943, displayed in his handiwork, a rare case of maintaining the excellence of old craft standards.

2 *Kentucky Gazette*, July 12, 1797, p. 2.

3 *Kentucky Gazette*, June 1, 1813, p. 1; March 31, 1820, p. 3.

4 *Kentucky Gazette*, April 19, 1797, p. 1; May 7, 1802, p. 3; December 27, 1788, p. 1 (John Duncan); March 26, 1802, p. 3; May 8, 1815, p. 3; April 27, 1801, p. 3.

5 George W. Ranck, *History of Lexington* (Cincinnati, 1872), p. 222.

6 *Kentucky Gazette*, April 26, 1790, p. 2; December 12, 1809, p. 1.

7 Hugh Morrison, *Early American Architecture* (New York, 1952), p. 34.

8 *Kentucky Gazette*, April 14, 1792, p. 4; January 23, 1800, p. 3; March 14, 1798, p. 3.

9 *Kentucky Gazette*, October 12, 1793, p. 3.

10 *Kentucky Gazette*, May 31, 1788, p. 2; March 12, 1804, p. 3.

11 *Kentucky Gazette*, July 6, 1793, p. 4; December 21, 1793, p. 4; December 19, 1795, p. 4; June 11, 1811, p. 3; September 3, 1811, p. 3; April 20, 1813, p. 3; July 11, 1814, p. 3; May 1, 1815, p. 3; October 5, 1802, p. 4.

12 The elevation and floor plans are on a sheet of paper measuring 18½ x 23 inches, inscribed "Lexington —15," in the archives of the Transylvania Library. This design was not executed; the building constructed the following year (see *End Papers*) was designed by Matthew Kennedy.

13 Dates given here and in other lists in this chapter are largely derived (where acceptable) from the *Sunday Herald-Leader*, May 23, 1954, pp. 33, 38, compiled by C. Frank Dunn.

14 Henry Chandler Forman, *The Architecture of the Old South* (Cambridge, Mass., 1948), fig. 267, p. 179; fig. 109, facing p. 80; fig. 53, facing p. 47; fig. 62, p. 55.

15 Rexford Newcomb, *Old Kentucky Architecture* (New York, 1940), plates 33, 36; Elizabeth M. Simpson, *The Enchanted Bluegrass* (Lexington, 1938), pp. 61-70.

16 Details of Castlewood (wrongly attributed to Gideon Shryock) are reproduced in *The Architectural Forum* (September, 1934), pp. 210-216.

17 *Kentucky Gazette*, May 7, 1802, p. 3.

18 *Kentucky Gazette*, March 13, 1815, p. 3.

19 Beatrice St. Julien Ravenel, *Architects of Charleston* (Charleston, S.C., 1945), pp. 47-51.

20 *Kentucky Gazette*, December 21, 1793, p. 4; July 30, 1805, p. 4; September 19, 1809, p. 3; December 2, 1816, p. 3.

21 Elizabeth Patterson Thomas, *Old Kentucky Homes and Gardens* (Louisville, 1939), p. 79.

22 R. T. H. Halsey and Elizabeth Tower, *The Homes of Our Ancestors* (New York, 1937), pp. 210-211.

23 Clay Lancaster, "Primitive Mural Painter of Kentucky: Alfred Cohen," *American Collector* (December, 1948), pp. 6-8, 19.

24 *Kentucky Gazette*, June 20, 1839, p. 3.

25 Edna Talbott Whitley, *Kentucky Ante-Bellum Portraiture* (Richmond, Va., 1956), pp. 669-673. For accounts of early painters in the region, see also Samuel Woodson Price, *Old Masters of the Blue Grass* (Louisville, 1902).

26 Henry-Russell Hitchcock, *American Architectural Books . . . Before 1895* (3d ed., Minneapolis, 1946), p. 103.

27 *Kentucky Gazette*, April 25, 1798, p. 3.

28 *Kentucky Gazette*, January 30, 1810, p. 3.

29 *Kentucky Gazette*, March 27, 1810, p. 4; July 27, 1813, p. 4.

30 J. Winston Coleman, Jr., *The Court-Houses of Lexington* (Lexington, 1937), p. 15.

31 Elizabeth M. Simpson, *Bluegrass Houses and Their Traditions* (Lexington, 1932), p. 159. The statement that Latrobe was the architect is without foundation.

32 *Kentucky Gazette*, December 11, 1804, p. 3.

33 Information courtesy of the late Mrs. Willis (Elizabeth Shryock) Field.

34 The keystones were identical to that presented in *Fig. 30*. The corbel was cut down and used as a cornerstone on Mammoth Garage, Main Street facing Rose, the date altered from 1809 to read 1812.

35 Sketch of Christ Church, talk by Dean Massie to the Woman's Club, *The Lexington Herald*, December 19, 1915, sec. III, p. 1. Also information from Mrs. Field.

36 Information from Mrs. Field.

37 Bill filed in archives of Transylvania Library, dated December 15, 1804: Document no. 1805-U-40.

38 Information from Mrs. Field.

39 Thomas Tileston Waterman, *The Mansions of Virginia, 1706-1776* (Chapel Hill, N.C., 1945), p. 196.

40 Information courtesy of Mrs. Samuel M. Wilson, interviewed September 29, 1954.

REFERENCES

⁴¹ The property was acquired from Cabel Wallace by Pugh Price, January 14, 1804 (Fayette County Deed Book *A*, p. 260), and passed to Williamson Price in 1808 (Deed Book *D*, p. 514). Information courtesy of Professor and Mrs. E. Everett Elsey, letter of September 26, 1956.

⁴² Purchased by George Norton, December 2, 1817 (Fayette County Deed Book *Q*, p. 476) and resold to John L. Martin, May 11, 1819 (Fayette County Deed Book *S*, p. 280), it later became the property of George W. Morton, January 15, 1836 (Fayette County Deed Book *12*, p. 439). In 1840 (Fayette County Deed Book *17*, p. 352) the place came into the possession of the Christian family, who remained the owners for over a century.

⁴³ Fayette County Deed Book *CoCt C*, p. 159.

⁴⁴ Waterman, *Mansions of Virginia*, pp. 152, 164, 201, 215, 219.

⁴⁵ Fayette County Deed Book *DtCt C*, p. 271, January 24, 1800.

⁴⁶ Probably after Isabella Lake sold the property to John Carty, November 21, 1807 (Fayette County Deed Book *CoCt C*, p. 192).

⁴⁷ Fayette County Marriage Book *1*, p. 25 (Sowell [*sic*] Woolfolk to Sally Bowman, 1814); Simpson, *Bluegrass Houses and Their Traditions*, pp. 279-284.

⁴⁸ Fayette County Deed Book *T*, p. 102.

⁴⁹ *Architectural Record*, XLI (1917), pp. 435-447, 525-535.

⁵⁰ Simpson, *The Enchanted Bluegrass*, pp. 61-70.

⁵¹ Rexford Newcomb, *Spanish-Colonial Architecture in the United States* (New York, 1937), pp. 345-350.

5 THE GEOMETRIC PHASE

¹ Fayette County Deed Book *CoCt M*, p. 401.

² Information courtesy of the present owner, Mrs. Anderson Gratz.

³ Fayette County Deed Book *CoCt M*, p. 26. The property measured 97 x 168½ feet.

⁴ *Kentucky Gazette*, April 24, 1815, p. 3.

⁵ Clay Lancaster, "Some Octagonal Forms in Southern Architecture," *The Art Bulletin* (June, 1946), p. 104, figs. 2-3.

⁶ Hugh Morrison, *Early American Architecture* (New York, 1952), pp. 172-173.

⁷ Notice of payment of postage for plans (the present whereabouts of which are unknown). Transylvania University Minute Book *III*, p. 102.

⁸ Referred to in a letter from Latrobe (in Pittsburgh) to Clay, January 16, 1814, as "the large house in Short Street" and "the house on Market Street."

⁹ Writing to a man of this name in Lexington in a letter dated March 1, 1811, Latrobe refers to "my house on paper & yours in solid work."

¹⁰ Thomas Tileston Waterman, *The Mansions of Virginia, 1706-1776* (Chapel Hill, N.C., 1945), pp. 365-373.

¹¹ Talbot Hamlin, *Benjamin Henry Latrobe* (New York, 1955), pp. 315, 300, 381-382.

¹² Fayette County Deed Book *CoCt C*, p. 354; *CoCt D*, p. 455.

¹³ Ascertained from a watercolor drawing, showing the south wing of the house, made by Frances Peter about a century ago, now in the possession of the present owners of Winton, Mr. and Mrs. Howard Evans.

¹⁴ Information in a letter from C. Frank Dunn, October 7, 1953.

¹⁵ Waterman, *The Mansions of Virginia*, p. 97.

¹⁶ Cassius Marcellus Clay, *The Life of C. M. Clay* (Cincinnati, 1886), Vol. I, p. 74.

¹⁷ Rexford Newcomb, *Architecture in Old Kentucky* (Urbana, Ill., 1953), p. 66 (plan).

¹⁸ Five acres of land were purchased by John Brand from David Stout on January 15, 1811. Fayette County Deed Book *CoCt E*, p. 149.

¹⁹ Fayette County Deed Book *35*, p. 258.

²⁰ The drawing of the portico was made from a stereoscopic slide lent the author by Mrs. W. L. Dunkman in March, 1942.

²¹ Sketch plan of Coolavin reconstructed from description by Mrs. Dunkman.

²² Fayette County Deed Book *41*, p. 475. The name "Locust Grove" also designated the Thomas H. Waters house on East Short Street (so listed in the 1838 directory), not to be confused with the later name of Coolavin.

²³ Henri Walbert, *Residences & Plantations dans les Vallées de l'Ohio et du Mississippi au début du 19e Siècle* (Paris, 1948), pl. 5-6.

²⁴ Rexford Newcomb, *Old Kentucky Architecture* (New York, 1940), pl. 49.

²⁵ Frank J. Roos, Jr., *An Illustrated Handbook of Art History* (New York, 1937), p. 231.

²⁶ Roos, *An Illustrated Handbook*, p. 231.

6 CLASSICISM

¹ Fiske Kimball, "Thomas Jefferson and the First Monument of the Classic Revival in America," *Journal of the American Institute of Architects* (September-November, 1915), p. 48.

² Talbot Hamlin, *Greek Revival Architecture in America* (Oxford, 1944), p. 30.

³ Information related by Mr. Lewis A. Barker, present owner of the house.

⁴ Rexford Newcomb, *Old Kentucky Architecture* (New York, 1940), pl. 71.

⁵ Hugh Morrison, *Early American Architecture* (New York, 1952), pp. 475, 561.

⁶ J. Winston Coleman, Jr., *Masonry in the Bluegrass* (Lexington, 1933), p. 101.

⁷ *Kentucky Gazette*, March 17, 1812, p. 3; August 1, 1814, p. 3.

⁸ Fayette County Will Book *C*, p. 516.

⁹ Clay Lancaster, "The Early Architecture of Transylvania College," *The American Antiques Journal* (September, 1948), pp. 8-9.

¹⁰ *The American Antiques Journal* (September, 1948), pp. 11, 8 (illus.).

¹¹ Fayette County Deed Book *6*, pp. 629-630 (January 12, 1831).

12 Fayette County Deed Book *10*, p. 32 (March 26, 1834).

13 Deering Davis, *Annapolis Houses, 1700-1775* (New York, 1947), pp. 46-47 (illus.).

14 Thomas A. Knight and Nancy Lewis Greene, *Country Estates of the Blue Grass* (Cleveland, 1904), p. 158. See also Bettye Lee Mastin, "Old Calumet in Woodford County," *Sunday Herald-Leader*, January 5, 1958, p. 10.

15 Illustrated in Elizabeth Patterson Thomas, *Old Kentucky Homes and Gardens* (Louisville, 1939), p. 70. Buknore is shown in *The Lexington Leader*, September 3, 1952, p. 3.

16 Related to the author by Mrs. John Johnstone.

17 Other elements of Mount Vernon also were derived from the *Vitruvius Scoticus*. Thomas Tileston Waterman, *The Mansions of Virginia, 1706-1776* (Chapel Hill, N.C., 1945), p. 271.

18 Clay Lancaster, "Jefferson's Architectural Indebtedness to Robert Morris," *The Journal of the Society of Architectural Historians* (March, 1951), pp. 7, 10.

19 *Architecture de C.-N. Ledoux* (Paris, 1847).

20 Morrison, *Early American Architecture,* pp. 263-264.

21 Nola Nance Oliver, *Natchez, Symbol of the Old South* (New York, 1940), pp. 50-51.

22 The side addition and rear structure had been destroyed when the house was first examined by the author in 1937 and measured in 1940.

23 Rexford Newcomb, *Architecture in Old Kentucky* (Urbana, Ill., 1953), pp. 53-54, pl. 18-B.

24 Clay Lancaster, "Primitive Mural Painter of Kentucky: Alfred Cohen," *American Collector* (December, 1948), pp. 6-8, 19.

25 *Williams' Lexington City Directory, 1859-60* (Lexington, 1859), p. 3.

7 THE GREEK REVIVAL

1 Talbot Hamlin, *Benjamin Henry Latrobe* (New York, 1955), pp. 130, 132, 152, 157. The Thaddeus Burr house at Fairfield, Conn., had been given a Greek Doric portico in 1790, constituting a remodeling, whereas Latrobe's Philadelphia bank was an entirely new project, Greek Revival throughout.

2 Howard Major, *The Domestic Architecture of the Early American Republic: The Greek Revival* (Philadelphia, 1926), p. 29.

3 H. M. Pierce Gallagher, *Robert Mills* (New York, 1935), plate facing p. 116.

4 Agnes Addison Gilchrist, *William Strickland* (Philadelphia, 1950), pp. 15-19; Clay Lancaster, "Gideon Shryock and John McMurtry, Architect and Builder of Kentucky," *The Art Quarterly* (Autumn, 1943), pp. 257-265.

5 "The Cheapest and Best Furniture IN THE WEST," likewise, was now made by machinery, and "HANDWORK" declared "Behind the Times!" according to an advertisement by Patterson & Erd, "Home Manufacturers of SUPERIOR AND FASHIONABLE FURNITURE [on] MAIN-STREET, LEXINGTON, KY., a few doors below the Phoenix Hotel." *The Kentucky Statesman*, January 20, 1857, p. 2.

6 As, for instance, Philadelphia: Hood & Co. advertised in *The Kentucky Statesman*, January 6, 1854, p. 3, "IRON RAKING AND ORNAMENTAL IRON WORK," the address given as 121 North Tenth Street.

7 The Louisville Marble Mantel Manufactory advertised for sale "a full and complete assortment of MARBLE MANTELS, consisting of Egyptian, Italian and American marble"; the public was invited "to call at [the] . . . manufactory on the south west corner of Jefferson and Sixth Street . . . [to examine the] stock, and ascertain the very small difference in the cost of a marble mantel, when compared with those made of wood." The "STEAM MARBLE WORKS, RIDGE ROAD, Above Spring Garden Street, PHILADELPHIA," advertised an available supply of "Imported Garden Statuary and Vases . . . Tiles for Flooring . . . Mantels and Table Tops." John Struthers & Son of Philadelphia inserted an announcement of similar wares; a local concern, the "ITALIAN MARBLE WORKS" of S. Woodruff & Co., at Second and Upper Streets, made a bid for the same trade. *Lexington Observer & Reporter*, November 9, 1844, p. 3; February 6, 1847, p. 3; March 4, 1848, p. 3; November 7, 1846, p. 3.

8 An advertisement by George W. Norton announced the receipt of "100 Boxes of McCully's Window Glass and Glass Ware, of the following sizes, just received . . . 6X8, 8X10, 10X12, 10X16, 12X16, 18X24, 20X30, 24X36, 12X18, 10X20, 12X20, 13X20, 14X20, 14X22, 14X24, 28X42; all of which will be sold at lowest prices" (*The Kentucky Statesman*, February 24, 1854, p. 2). One notes the diversity of shapes and the increase in sizes over what was available half a century earlier (Chapter IV, notes 7-8).

9 Clay Lancaster, "Oriental Forms in American Architecture 1800-1870," *The Art Bulletin* (September, 1947), fig. 3 (facing p. 186).

10 Clay Lancaster, "Early Architecture of Transylvania College," *The American Antiques Journal* (September, 1948), pp. 11-13.

11 Philadelphia Art Alliance, *Philadelphia Architecture of the Nineteenth Century* (Philadelphia, 1953), p. 25, plate 22.

12 Lancaster, "Gideon Shryock and John McMurtry," fig. 2 (facing p. 258). Cf. Haviland, I, plate 24.

13 Clay Lancaster, "Major Thomas Lewinski: Emigre Architect in Kentucky," *Journal of the Society of Architectural Historians* (December, 1952), p. 13.

14 *Dictionary of American Biography*, Vol. XXI, pp. 479-481 (article by T. F. Hamlin).

15 Clay Lancaster, "Adaptations from Greek Revival Builders' Guides in Kentucky," *The Art Bulletin* (March, 1950), fig. 10 (following p. 68).

16 Lancaster, "Greek Revival Builders' Guides," fig. 14 (following p. 68).

17 The plasterwork of the lavishly decorated Gaineswood, near Demopolis, Alabama, was ordered from a catalog still in the possession of the Whitfield family. A page from it is reproduced in *House & Garden* (November, 1939), sect. I, p. 42. The motifs throughout this house have a decidedly Lafever flavor.

REFERENCES

18 Lancaster, "Greek Revival Builders' Guides," figs. 16-17 (following p. 68); Lancaster, "Gideon Shryock and John McMurtry," figs. 7-8 (facing p. 268).

19 Henry Caswall, *America and the American Church* (London, 1839), pp. 214, 220.

20 Letter from McMurtry to Gibson, July 11, 1848, listing these improvements, in the possession of Mrs. Davis Buckner of Rose Hill, Lexington.

21 Fayette County Deed Book *4*, p. 206.

22 Fayette County Deed Book *31*, p. 415.

23 Information courtesy of Mr. A. Haley, Lexington, 1948.

24 Robert Alexander Lancaster, *Historic Virginia Homes and Churches* (Philadlephia, 1915), p. 269.

25 Roger Hale Newton, " 'Sachem's Wood,' New Haven, Connecticut, One of the Earliest Greek Revival Mansions in the United States," *Old-Time New England* (October, 1942), pp. 33-36.

26 Information from the Hulett family, former owners of the house.

27 Bettye Lee Mastin, "Holley Place Is Copy of Burned Mansion," *Sunday Herald-Leader*, April 29, 1956, p. 46.

28 Illustrated in J. Winston Coleman, Jr., *Slavery Times in Kentucky* (Chapel Hill, 1940), facing p. 19.

29 Coleman, *Slavery Times in Kentucky*, facing p. 18. Restored sketch on map.

30 Elizabeth M. Simpson, *The Enchanted Bluegrass* (Lexington, 1938), pp. 197, 188 (illus.).

31 Detail shown in Lancaster, "Greek Revival Builders' Guides," fig. 6 (facing p. 68).

32 Information contained in letter to author from Mrs. Joseph Kerr (granddaughter of C. W. Innes), May 5, 1941.

33 Elizabeth M. Simpson, *Bluegrass Houses and Their Traditions* (Lexington, 1932), p. 298. Talbot Hamlin, *Greek Revival Architecture in America* (Oxford, 1944), pl. LXVIII (facing p. 233), fig. 30 (p. 246).

34 Information courtesy of Alfred Andrews.

35 The original image of the house was engraved on a silver tray made for Flournoy by G. W. Stewart, who flourished in Lexington between 1846 and 1852. It is inscribed "Presented to EJF by her husband". Now owned by Mr. Victor Bogaert of Lexington. It is illustrated in Noble W. and Lucy F. Hiatt, *The Silversmiths of Kentucky* (Louisville, 1954), p. 93. A photograph of Walnut Hall showing a single-story addition on the right flank is reproduced in J. Soule Smith, *Art Work of the Blue Grass Region of Kentucky* (Oshkosh, Wis., 1898), following p. 14.

36 Fayette County Deed Book *27*, p. 230; Deed Book *26*, p. 516.

37 Information courtesy of Dr. Alfred Peter.

38 *Civil Architecture* (4th ed., 1836), p. 154.

39 Dorothy and Richard Pratt, *Guide to American Homes—South* (New York, 1956), p. 195.

40 Rexford Newcomb, *Old Kentucky Architecture* (New York, 1940), plate 33.

41 *Antiques* (November, 1947), pp. 335, 342-343.

42 Newcomb, *Old Kentucky Architecture*, plates 91-92.

43 Fayette County Deed Book *17*, p. 507 (March 30, 1840).

44 Hugh Morrison, *Early American Architecture* (New York, 1952), p. 448 (figs. 373-374). Redwood Library was inspired by an elevation serving as the headpiece to Book IV of Edward Hoppus' *Andrea Palladio's Architecture in Four Books* (London, 1736).

45 Clay Lancaster, "Thomas Jefferson's Architectural Indebtedness to Robert Morris," *Journal of the Society of Architectural Historians* (March, 1951), fig. 1-2 (facing p. 4).

46 Information courtesy of Mrs. Lucas B. Combs, Lexington.

47 Fayette County Deed Book *24*, p. 50.

48 *House & Garden* (November 1939), sect. I. pp. 41-43.

49 Information about this house, and photographs of its dependencies (upon which are based the reconstructed drawings herein illustrated), have been made available to the author by the generosity of Mrs. Eleanor Parker Hopkins of Lexington.

8 THE GOTHIC REVIVAL

1 Kenneth Clark, *The Gothic Revival* (London, 1928), chap. 5.

2 Theo B. White, ed., *Philadelphia Architecture in the Nineteenth Century* (Philadelphia, 1953), plate 11.

3 It was destroyed in 1853.

4 Roger Hale Newton, *Town & Davis, Architects* (New York, 1942), pp. 214-216.

5 Clay Lancaster, "The Architecture of Sunnyside," *American Collector* (October, 1947), pp. 13-15.

6 Robert Peter, *History of Fayette County, Kentucky* (Chicago, 1882), p. 121.

7 *The Architecture of Country Houses* (New York, 1850), p. 257.

8 Clay Lancaster, *Back Streets and Pine Trees* (Lexington, 1956), pp. 2-5.

9 *The Kentucky Gazette*, December 7, 1837, p. 3.

10 Lancaster, *Back Streets and Pine Trees*, pp. 9-11.

11 Lancaster, *Back Streets and Pine Tree*, pp. 16-17.

12 Fayette County Deed Book *23*, p. 131.

13 Fayette County Deed Book *25*, p. 442.

14 Date incised in the stonework over the basement door.

15 "Observations on Architecture," *Lexington Daily Press*, May 27, 1887, p. 1.

16 Information related to the author by Mrs. Laura Hall Bohmer, to whose place on the Versailles Pike the gates were later moved.

17 Clay Lancaster, "Major Thomas Lewinski: Emigre Architect in Kentucky," *Journal of the Society of Architectural Historians* (December, 1952), p. 18.

18 Newton, *Town & Davis*, pp. 82-118, 153-164.

19 Fayette County Deed Book *62*, p. 520 (July 31, 1850).

20 Used, for instance, on Charles Alger's villa (1845), Berkshire, Mass. Newton, *Town & Davis*, Plate 16.

[21] Professional Diary of A. J. Davis, Metropolitan Museum of Art, Print Room, p. 116.

[22] *Lexington Daily Press*, June 2, 1887, p. 2.

[23] Downing, *The Architecture of Country Houses*, p. 59.

[24] *Lexington Observer and Kentucky Reporter*, September 16, 1848, p. 3. The foundry was started by Joseph Bruen about 1815 (*Kentucky Gazette*, February 26, 1816, p. 4), and a brick building was built to house it in 1830 (*MacCabe's Directory*, 1838-1839, pp. 31-32). Henry Boone Ingels was Bruen's son-in-law.

[25] Lancaster, *Back Streets and Pine Trees*, pp. 44-46.

[26] *Lexington Observer and Kentucky Reporter*, January 20, 1855, p. 1.

[27] Downing, *The Architecture of Country Houses*, pp. 304-305.

[28] In the Print Room, Metropolitan Museum of Art.

[29] *The Architecture of Country Houses*, p. 306.

[30] Pictured in Rexford Newcomb, *Old Kentucky Architecture* (New York, 1940), plate 125.

[31] Pictured in Thomas A. Knight and Nancy Lewis Greene, *Country Estates of the Blue Grass* (Cleveland, 1904), p. 175.

[32] Elizabeth Patterson Thomas, *Old Kentucky Homes and Gardens* (Louisville, 1939), p. 38.

[33] Lancaster, *Back Streets and Pine Trees*, pp. 65-66.

[34] *The Lexington Leader*, April 13, 1956.

[35] *Sunday Herald-Leader*, January 11, 1942, p. 53.

9 THE ITALIANATE

[1] John Summerson, *Heavenly Mansions and Other Essays on Architecture* (New York, 1948), pp. 114-115.

[2] Illustrated: John Summerson, *John Nash, Architect to King George IV* (London, 1935), pl. III.

[3] Clay Lancaster, "Italianism in American Architecture before 1860," *American Quarterly*, pp. 138-142; figs. 5-6, 8.

[4] Roger Hale Newton, *Town & Davis, Architects* (New York, 1942), figs. 23, 21.

[5] Carroll L. V. Meeks, "Henry Austin and the Italian Villa," *The Art Bulletin* (June, 1948), p. 166. Illustrated: Downing, *A Treatise on . . . Landscape Gardening* (1841), figs. 29-30 (pp. 314-315).

[6] Clay Lancaster, "Major Thomas Lewinski: Emigre Architect in Kentucky," *Journal of the Society of Architectural Historians* (December, 1952), pp. 13-14, notes 2-8 (p. 20).

[7] Lancaster, "Major Thomas Lewinski," p. 19.

[8] Lancaster, "Major Thomas Lewinski," pp. 19-20, fig. 15 (facing p. 16).

[9] Although dispersed, the Lewinski library is known to have contained copies of Edward Shaw's *Civil Architecture* (4th ed., Boston, 1836), Thomas Kelly's *The Pointed Arch, or Gothic Style* (London, 1836), and the first volume of Samuel Sloan's *The Model Architect* (Philadelphia, 1852), now owned by Mr. William Combs of Lexington; the fifth and sixth volumes of plates of J. F. Blondel's *Cours d'Architecture* (Paris, 1777), now owned by Mr. Alfred Andrews of New York City; John Henry Parker's *A Companion to the Fourth Edition of a Glossary of Terms Used in Grecian, Roman, Italian and Gothic Architecture* (London, 1846) and Edward Cresy and G. L. Taylor's *Architecture of the Middle Ages in Italy* (London, 1829), presented to the author by Miss Kathleen Mulligan of Lexington.

[10] Lewinski is mentioned as the architect of these two villas in the suit of William Pullen [subcontractor of brickwork] *vs.* D. S. Coleman, Fayette Circuit Court, File 1267, July 31, 1854.

[11] Entry in Lewinski's diary under April 24, 1846: "Completed design for gardener's cottage for the Honbl. H. Clay."

[12] Information that Lewinski was the architect for the remodeling was contained in a letter to the author from Miss Mamie B. Woolfolk of Memphis, Tenn.

[13] Referred to as "Daviséan windows." Newton, *Town & Davis*, figs. 30, 33, 34, 35, 36, 41, 44.

[14] Information courtesy of Miss Jacqueline Kinkead, interviewed August 12, 1955.

[15] Information courtesy of Dr. John W. Scott.

[16] Fayette County Deed Book *35*, p. 611.

[17] *The Model Architect*, Vol. I, p. 41.

[18] McMurtry's observation that hard-burned brick could outlast stone was gained from his European journey. *Lexington Daily Press*, November 16, 1887, p. 2.

[19] Fayette County Deed Book *44*, p. 369.

[20] *Lexington Daily Press*, June 2, 1887, p. 2.

GLOSSARY

Abacus—the square topmost member of a Doric capital (*see diagram*)

Acanthus—a prickly herb, the leaves of which inspired architectural ornaments for the Greeks

Acroteria—(Greek, pl.) summit or extremity ornaments on pediments

Alcove—(Arabic *al-qubbah*: arch) a recessed portion of a room

Anta (Antae, pl.)—a pier produced by thickening a wall at its termination

Antapodia (pl.)—literally, in front of the basement (podium), projecting cubic forms

Antefix—an ornament on the eaves originally masking tile joints

Anteroom—literally, a room before; a small room that functions in connection with a larger room

Anthemion—(Greek) flower, the "honeysuckle" motif

Antis—*see* In Antis

Apron—a vertical member below a window sill

Arcade—a series of arches, usually on columns or piers

Arch—(Latin *arcus*: arc of a circle) the curved top of an opening composed of wedge-shaped blocks (voussoirs)

Architrave—the first or lowest horizontal member of an entablature (*see diagram*)

Archivolt—the inner vertical molding around an arch, corresponding to the straight architrave in an entablature

Arcuated—pertaining to the use of arches

Arris—an edge separating the channels in the shaft of a Doric column (*see diagram*)

Articulate—to divide into components

Attic—the top story above a main cornice, sometimes confused with garret

Banister—(corruption of baluster) the spoke of a stair-railing

Balcony—a projecting platform surrounded by a balustrade

Baluster—(Latin *balustium*: pomegranate) an upright form that supports a railing

Balustrade—a series of balusters and railing

Bargeboard—the carved or decorated raking board of an overhanging gable

Baroque—the flamboyant classic style of the seventeenth century

Baseboard—the molding or plank around the base of an interior wall

Batten—a strip of wood nailed across a series of adjacent boards binding them together

Battlement—a parapet with notched spaces or crenels

Bay—any architectural unit

Bay Window—a projecting form for admitting light

Bead—a small cylindrical molding

Bead-and-Reel—an ornamental molding made up of small half-spheres alternating with coupled spindle shapes

Belt—a projecting flat stringer at the level of the upper floor of a building

Belvedere—(Italian *belvadara*: fine view) a pavilion affording a panorama; a cupola

Blind Arch—an applied arch, not open through

BLIND WINDOW—a false window consisting usually of recessed fixed shutters, for external effect only

BOMBÉ—(French) a bulging form

BOSS—(French *bosse*: knob) an ornament at the intersection of vault ribs

BRACKET—a projecting member supporting an overhanging form

BREAKFRONT—an elevation (as of a mantel) with advancing and receding planes

BUTTRESS—an external masonry mass for added support

CAMPANIFORM—bell-shaped

CAPITAL—the head of a column (*see diagram*)

CARPENTER'S GOTHIC—a simple type of Gothic Revival executed in wood

CARTOUCHE—a scrolled raised plaque for an inscription

CASEMENT—a window that swings open on hinges (as opposed to a sash window)

CAST IRON—ironwork formed in the melted stage in molds

CELLA—the enclosed part of a classic temple

CENTERPIECE—a ceiling ornament from which the chandelier hangs

CHAIRRAIL—a molding placed horizontally on a wall at the height of the back of a chair

CHALET—an Alpine-type house with low-pitched roof and deep eaves

CHAMBER—(French *chambre*: room) a bedroom

CHAMFER—a surface formed by cutting away the edge of two planes meeting at a right angle

CHANNEL—a vertical groove in the shaft of a Doric column, somewhat wider than a flute and meeting in an edge or arris (*see diagram*)

CHIMNEYBREAST—the fireplace chimney projecting into a room

CHIMNEY STACK—the shaft of a chimney rising above the roof

CLAPBOARD—an overlapped weatherboard applied horizontally

CLASSIC—pertaining to the culture of the ancient Greeks and Romans

CLERESTORY—a row of windows high in a wall

CLOSED STRINGER—*see* STRINGER

CLUSTERED PIER—a support formed of engaged colonnettes, in plan a trefoil or quatrefoil

COLLEGIATE STYLE—another name for castellated

COLONNADE—a range of columns

COLONNETTE—a small, slender column

COLOSSAL ORDER—the use of columns more than one story in height

COLUMN—a classic support having base (except in the Doric order), shaft, and capital (*see diagram*)

COMMON BOND—brickwork composed of several layers of bricks laid sidewise (stretchers) bonded by a row laid endwise (headers), repeated in regular succession

COMPOSITE—the Roman order formed by combining Ionic volutes with Corinthian acanthus leaves

CONSOLE—a bracket of classic form, usually scrolled at top and bottom

CORBEL—a bracket

CORINTHIAN—the classic order distinguished by campaniform capitals ornamented with acanthus leaves

CORNICE—the topmost, projecting member of an entablature, sometimes used singly (*see diagram*)

COUPLED COLUMNS—columns grouped in pairs

COUPLED WINDOWS—a pair of windows separated only by a stanchion

CRENEL—one of the embrasures in a battlement

CRESTING—an openwork ornament along the top of a horizontal ridge

CROCKET—(French *croc*: hook) an ornament, often resembling foliage, spaced along a gothic gable or spire

CROW-STEPPED—a sloping parapet over a gable with stair-step outline

CRUCIFORM—in the shape of a cross

CUPOLA—a prismatic superstructure with windows on all sides for admitting light

DENTIL—a small rectangular block used in a series resembling teeth

DEPENDENCY—a detached outbuilding

DISTYLE—having two columns

DOGRUN—*see* DOGTROT

DOGTROT—a breezeway open on two opposite sides, also called a dogrun or 'possomtrot

DORIC—the common Greek order, distinguished by a heavy column without base, a channeled shaft, and a capital made up of an echinus and square abacus (*see diagram*)

DORMER—a window form that projects through a sloping roof

DOVETAIL—a flaring tenon shaped like a dove's tail

DRAWING ROOM—a withdrawing room or reception room

DRIPMOLD—a hood mold with pendant sides

ECHINUS—the cushion form supporting the square abacus of a Doric capital (*see diagram*)

EGG-AND-DART—an ornamental classic molding with alternating forms resembling an egg and a dart

ELL—an extension or wing at right angles to a building, usually at the rear

ENFRAMEMENT—a frame or molding encircling an opening

ENGLISH BOND—a brickwork pattern made up of alternating courses of all-header and all-stretcher bricks

ENTABLATURE—the horizontal part of an architectural order, supported on columns, composed of architrave, frieze, and cornice (*see diagram*)

ESCUTCHEON—(Latin) a shield

FACADE—the front of a building

FANLIGHT—a half-circular or half-elliptical window, usually over a door

FEDERAL—the early nineteenth-century architectural style

FENESTRATION—the window system or arrangement

FINIAL—a crowning ornament, as on a post

GLOSSARY

FLANK—the side of a building

FLANKER—architectural element attached to the side of a building

FLEMISH BOND—a type of brickwork composed of alternating bricks laid sidewise (stretchers) and endwise (headers), creating a checkerboard-like pattern

FLUE—a chimney duct for the passage of smoke

FLUSH—with exposed surfaces even or on the same level

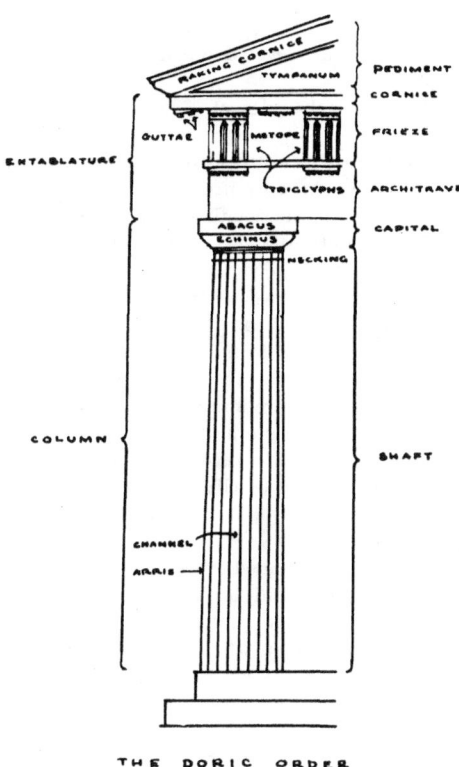

THE DORIC ORDER

FLUTE—a groove or concave depression used decoratively, as on a column shaft

FRAME—a casing around an opening; a system of construction in which the supporting system is made up of timbers

FRET—an ornamental network of geometric lines

FRIEZE—the second member of an entablature, in classic architecture usually containing relief carvings (*see diagram*)

FRONTISPIECE—the portal or entrance elaboration

FUNNEL—a wide-mouthed vessel for running liquids into a narrow channel

GABLE—the triangular shape at the end of a building made by a sloping roof

GALLERY—a long narrow room or covered porch

GARÇONNIERE—(French) the boys' quarters

GARRET—the top story under the slope of the roof

GOTHIC—the later medieval style in Europe, distinguished by pointed arches

GOTHIC REVIVAL—in America the nineteenth-century style inspired by the European gothic

"GREEK EARS"—projections near the top of enframements to doors or windows

GREEK REVIVAL—the style inspired by antique Greek buildings, employed in America during the first six decades of the nineteenth century

GRILLE—a protective grating in an opening, usually made of iron

GUTTA (GUTTAE, pl.)—(Latin: drop) a small pendant conic ornament, usually occurring in a series (*see diagram*)

HALF TIMBER—a framing of wood with filling between the timber members

HEADER—a brick laid with the small end exposed

HERRINGBONE—rows of bricks laid in reverse directions, making a sort of zigzag pattern, used for paving

HIP—the outer ridge formed by two sloping roof planes

HOOD—a jutting member over an opening to shed rainwater

ICEHOUSE—a structure built below groundlevel for storing ice

IMPOST—a block on top of a post or column providing a wider bearing surface than a capital for the springing of an arch

IN ANTIS—literally, between antae (piers), said of columns supporting the upper wall in a doorway recess

IONIC—the classic order distinguished by volutes on the capital

ITALIANATE—in the Italian manner, a mid-nineteenth-century architectural style

JAMB—an upright forming the side of an opening

JOINERY—construction work in wood

KEYSTONE—the centermost voussoir of an arch, often given special architectural treatment

LAMBREQUIN—an interior ornament or valance spanning the head of a window arch or opening to an alcove

LEADED GLASS—window glass held in place by lead muntins

LEAN-TO—an extension to a building under a pent roof usually continuous with the plane of the main roof

LEVEL-CROWN VAULT—a vault the summit of which maintains a constant height

LINTEL—the horizontal member bridging two vertical supports

LOGGIA—(Italian) a roofed open gallery, usually elevated

LOUVERS (pl.)—sloping slats placed horizontally in an opening to exclude rain or direct sunlight but allowing the passage of air

LUNETTE—a half-moon window, or wall space beneath an arch or vault

MEANDER—an endless geometric fret design
MERLON—a solid interval between crenels of a battlement
METOPE—the space between two triglyphs in a Doric frieze, usually carved in relief (*see diagram*)
MOLDING—a long strip of material having a definite profile used for decorative purposes
MULLION—a thin support between window lights, usually of stone or wood
MUNTIN—a slender window bar, usually of wood or lead

NECKING—a molding at the top of the shaft of a column (*see diagram*)
NEWEL POST—the main upright support at the base of a stairrailing
NOSING—the horizontal molding across the top of the riser of a step

OBELISK—a tall tapering square form capped by a pyramid, an ancient Egyptian monument
OPEN-NEWEL STAIRCASE—a spiral stairway encircling a void
OPEN STRINGER—see STRINGER
ORDER—a defined column and entablature combination viewed as the unit of a style (*see diagram*)
ORIEL—a large bay window

PALLADIAN MOTIF—an opening of three lights, the centermost arched
PANEL—a flat member held within a framework
PARAPET—a wall section rising above a roof
PARLOR—(French *parler*: to speak) a room primarily for conversation
PARTITION—a division wall between interiors
PAVILION—a small building or individual mass or wing of a building of complex form
PEDESTAL—a base or small foundation, usually a single block of stone with moldings at top and bottom
PEDIMENT—the triangular form of a classic gable (*see diagram*)
PENT—a small attached room or pavilion usually covered by a roof of a single slope
PERISTYLE—a range of columns on all sides of a court or around a building
PIER—a plain upright support, somewhat greater than a post
PILASTER—a flat upright member applied to a wall, treated like a column with base, shaft, and capital
PILLAR—a thick column
PINNACLE—an ornamental peak or small spire
PLATE GLASS—rolled sheet glass
PLINTH—a square block at the base of a column
POINTED STYLE—the cottage version of the Gothic Revival, distinguished by steeply pitched gables with bargeboards
PORTAL—a doorway
PORTE-COCHÈRE—(French) a carriage entrance
PORTICO—a classic porch

'POSSOMTROT—a breezeway; see DOGTROT
POST—a plain free-standing support
PRESSES (pl.)—built-in closets or cupboards
PROSTYLE—having columns in front

QUATREFOIL—a four-lobed gothic ornament
QUOINS—projecting end blocks used decoratively

RAISED BASEMENT—an elevated house with basement floor at groundlevel
RAKING—sloping, as the edge of a gable or pediment (*see diagram*)
RAMP—an upturned member, as of a stairrail
RECESSED DOORWAY—an entrance placed behind the plane of the front wall, the opening usually enframed by an entablature and pilasters, or moldings with "Greek ears" at the upper corners
REEDING—a surface treated with a series of adjacent, parallel convex moldings
RENAISSANCE—literally "rebirth," meaning the rebirth of classical culture, as that following the medieval period
RENAISSANCE REVIVAL—the imitation of the Renaissance style during the middle and late nineteenth century
RIB—a projecting band on a ceiling or vault
RIBBING—an arrangement of ribs; on stonework smaller in scale than reeding
ROMAN DORIC—see TUSCAN
ROMANESQUE—the early medieval style distinguished by heavy walls and round-headed windows
RUSTIC—in its natural state, not shaped by man
RUSTICATION—stonework in which the blocks have beveled or rabbeted edges making the joints more conspicuous

SADDLEBAG—a shape with constricted waist, as the plan of a saddlebag cabin
SADDLE JOINT—a cutting the top of which slopes off to each side, used in log construction
SASH—the unit of a window that raises and lowers
SCREEN—a barrier or superficial division between spaces
SEGMENTED ARCH—an arch that is less than half of a circle or ellipse, meeting the jambs in angles
SERPENTINE—undulating or winding like a serpent, said of lines or surfaces
SERVICE—the kitchen, pantry, and servant functions, including back stairs, passageways, etc.
SHAFT—an upright form such as the main body of a column (*see diagram*)
SHAKE—a split wood shingle
SHINGLE—a thin slab of wood or other material for covering roofs
SHIPLAP—an overlap, such as clapboards
SHOULDER—the outer angle of a setback, as of a chimney
SHUTTER—a hinged or retractable panel or screen for a window, often louvred
SILL—the base member of a window or door
SMOKEHOUSE—a windowless building for smoking meats

GLOSSARY

Soffit—the underside of a lintel, staircase, or similar surface
Spandrel—the triangular space between the curve of an arch and its rectangular enframement
Splay—a sloping surface, as the side of a window
Stairhall—a passage containing steps to other floors
Stanchion—a vertical support, as in a window
Stockade—a line of posts set upright close together to form a defense
Stretcher—a brick laid lengthwise
Stringer—the member along the outer face of a flight of steps; a closed stringer is a straight board masking the step ends; the open stringer is where the step outline is revealed; also any band, such as a belt
Stucco—a type of cement used to form a hard covering for exterior walls

Temple-Type—in the form of a temple; a building with a portico spanning the entire front
Terracotta—a hard-baked clayware used for external architectural embellishment, usually a reddish color
Tessellation—a checkerboard pattern of squares
Tetrastyle—having four columns
Tracery—the open patternwork in a gothic window
Transom—a window over a door
Transverse Hall—a passage that cuts through a building from front to back
Tread—the horizontal top plane of a step
Trefoil—a three-lobed ornamental gothic motif
Triglyphs—rectangular blocks in a Doric frieze incised with two vertical grooves and having chamfered sides (*see diagram*)
Triple Window—a window of three lights, the centermost usually three times the width of the side lights
Truncated—the form left after part has been removed

Truss—a construction of members forming a rigid triangular framework
Tudor Arch—a low-pitched pointed arch, theoretically four-centered
Turret—a small tower, usually at the angle of a larger structure
Tuscan—the Roman Doric style (the column is more slender than in the Greek and has a base and plain shaft)
Tuscan Revival—a phase of the Italianate distinguished by a symmetrical form
Tympanum—the space enclosed by an arch or pediment

Umbrage—(Latin *umbra*: shadow) a porch or veranda
Unbonded—a masonry wall having all-stretcher (sidewise) bricks exposed

Valley—the meeting of two sloping roof planes forming a reentrant angle
Vault—an arched ceiling
Veranda—(East Indian) an open gallery or porch
Vestibule—a small outer room or entrance hall
Villa—a somewhat pretentious country residence
Volute—a spiral form, as in an Ionic capital
Voussoir—a wedge-shaped stone composing an arch

Wattle-and-Daub—the filling used in medieval half-timber houses consisting of withes or twigs and clay or plaster
Winder—a wedge-shaped step turning the corner of a staircase
Winding Staircase—a newel or open-newel staircase
Wrought Iron—forged iron

ALBUM OF PHOTOGRAPHS

Upright Forms. Left, the stone chimney of the Bowman cabin; lower left, the pinnacles of Ingelside; lower right, the crenelated turrets of Loudoun. Unless otherwise indicated, the photographs in this section were made by the author.

Town Houses (now razed). Upper left, the Gist-Peck house; lower left, the classic cottage; both old photographs from the collection of the late Charles R. Staples. Upper right, the Swift house, photog-

rapher unknown; lower right, the Cochran house, old photograph from the collection of the late Dr. Waller Bullock, courtesy of the Transylvania College Library.

Portals. Above, the fan doorway, from the front hall, of the Hunt-Morgan house; below, the gate to the service court of the same building. On the facing page: upper left, the portico and fan doorway of Rose Hill, photograph courtesy of J. Winston Coleman, Jr.; lower left, the doorway of Waveland. Upper right, the portico of Botherum; lower right, the cast-iron porch of the Johnson house.

Suburban Houses Which Have Given Way to City Growth. Upper left, Coolavin, from the collection of the late Dr. Waller Bullock, courtesy of the Transylvania College Library; lower left, The Elms, old

photograph courtesy of Mrs. P. G. Savage. Upper right, White Cottage, old photograph courtesy of J. Winston Coleman, Jr.; lower right, Glendower, photograph made in 1940.

Interior Decoration. Above, the mantel in the west parlor of Lyndhurst; below, detail of the oriel and the painted ceiling in the drawing room of Loudoun. On the facing page: above, the stairhall of Hurricane Hall; middle, detail of the screen and ceiling in the parlors of Gibson house; below, the gold lambrequin and mirror formerly in the drawing room of Loudoun.

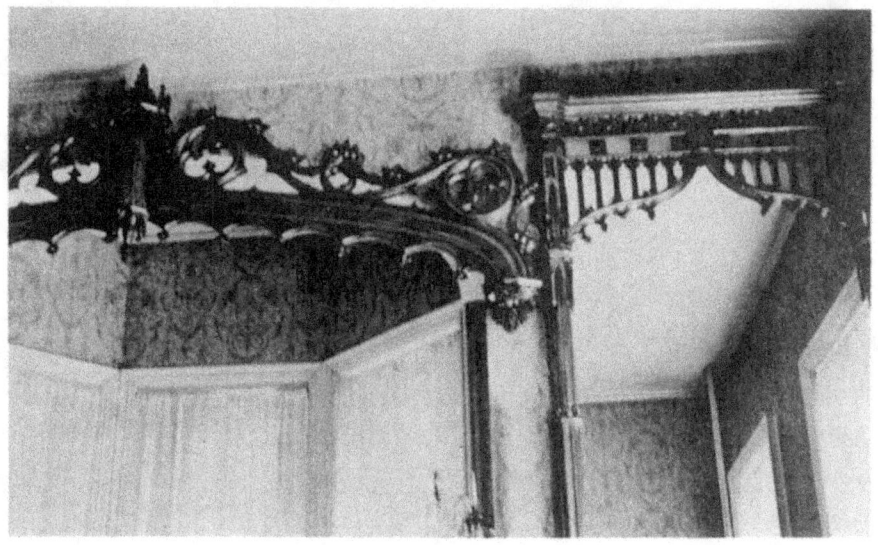

Country Houses. Upper left, the Grimes house; lower left, Hurricane Hall; upper right, Grassland; lower right, Fairlawn. Photographs courtesy of J. Winston Coleman, Jr.

Entrance Details. Above, the portico ceiling of Lemon Hill; below, ironwork detail on a North Broadway house near Second Street. On the facing page: above, the rear entrances of Alberti Place (largely destroyed), photograph made in 1943; middle, portal detail on the Peck house; below, west doorway of Botherum.

Ceiling Centerpieces. Above, in the front hall of the Benjamin McCann house; middle, in the drawing room of Ingelside; below, in the west parlor of Lyndhurst.

BIBLIOGRAPHICAL INDEX

THE FOLLOWING bibliography is selective, listing only the more comprehensive sources of information on early Bluegrass houses. Additional descriptive material on individual houses is cited in the index proper. Special attention is called to the old maps, views of Lexington, and collections of photographs, which, although they are not cited in the bibliographies for individual houses, are of great value in any study of ante bellum building in Fayette County.

Lethem's *Review of Lexington* (no. 14 in the numbered list of references, below) offers a comprehensive view of commercial buildings through line drawings and text, and does not wholly overlook the domestic building of the city. *Art Work of the Blue Grass Region of Kentucky* (22), like other books in the regional "Art Works" series, is of value mostly for its numerous illustrations, many of which are of residences. Of even greater importance for its photographic views is Knight and Greene's *Country Estates of the Blue Grass* (10), which, although it plays up the absorbing preoccupation of the region, shows a goodly number of horsemen's domestic establishments as well. More recently, a book of photographs by Richard Garrison (3), with introduction by Sydney S. Combs and comments by J. Winston Coleman, Jr., was issued by the Kentucky Society.

During the second quarter of the present century, descriptive treatments of ante bellum houses began to appear. An inestimable contribution was made by Mrs. Elizabeth M. Simpson in her two volumes (19, 20). If Mrs. Simpson has a tendency to glamorize, she is to be forgiven on the grounds of a genuine appreciation for her subject. She admits that she is recording traditions, and traditions are sometimes more revealing than formal history. Among the other descriptive accounts cited below, the WPA guide to Kentucky (26) contains a chapter on architecture by Professor Rexford Newcomb of the University of Illinois.

Professor Newcomb was the first to consider Kentucky houses as examples of serious architecture, without regard to their traditions or the fame of their former occupants. Measured drawings of a few buildings had been published in architectural periodicals (cited in the index), but no attempt had been made to give a systematic view of ante bellum building in this area prior to Mr. Newcomb's work (16). The text of *Old Kentucky Architecture* is disappointingly brief, and many errors are to be noted in the drawings (not delineated by the author himself). A second book by Professor Newcomb, *Architecture in Old Kentucky* (15), demonstrates what a regional survey of architecture should be.

Until now, the only attempt to deal systematically with the early architectural development of Fayette County was made by the present author in *Ante Bellum Suburban Villas and Rural Residences of Fayette County Kentucky and Some Outstanding Homes of Lexington* (Lexington, 1955), a brief essay accompanied by a map of approximately 30 by 40 inches, on which are drawn in perspective more than 300 county residences and about 30 town houses, restored to their condition in the 1860's. Some 40 floor and plot plans are inserted along the margins. Stress was laid on the county architecture because the Middleton, Wallace and Company view of Lexington of the mid-1850's—though inaccurate in many details—gives a better picture of the urban architecture than anyone could hope to reconstruct today.

Local newspapers (beginning as early as 1787) comprise the richest source of information on Lexington building not cited in the following bibliography. Frequent contributors on architectural subjects in recent years have been J. Winston Coleman, Jr., C. Frank Dunn, Joe Jordan, and Bettye Lee Mastin. Numerous citations of their valuable work appear in the index bibliographies of individual houses. Two articles by C. Frank Dunn (in the Lexington *Herald-Leader*, June 26, 1949, and May 23, 1954) list the dates of numerous early Fayette houses. These dates have been adopted in the present volume, except where contrary evidence is presented.

MAPS AND VIEWS

Doct. Luke Munsell's (Large Map of 1818.) Improved to the present time from Authentic Documents by the (Author.) Published by Corey G. Fairbank Cincinnati and Luke Munsell Danville Ky, 1834, Engraved by Doolittle & Munsell, Cincinnati.

    A street plan of Lexington (with that of Louisville and Maysville) is shown on the lower margin. The sites of some thirty buildings (including six residences) are indicated. Copy owned by H. C. Sadler, Lexington.

City of Lexington, Fayette Co, Ky., 1855 Surveyed and Published by Hart and Mapother, Civil Engineers & Co. No 9 Court Place Louisville . . . Lith. of Robyn Co. Louisville, Ky.

    A plan of the city giving streets, with buildings shaded, by which is gained some idea of their shapes. The names of some of the owners are indicated. Traced by Claude Jackson in 1939 and engraved and published by Haag and Sons, engravers, Lexington.

"View of Lexington, Kentucky."

    Published in *Ballou's Pictorial Drawing-room Companion*, Vol. VIII, no. 17 (whole no. 199), Saturday, April 28, 1855, p. 268. An engraved view of the city looking southwest from the portico of Morrison College with College Square (Gratz Park) in the foreground, showing Saint Peter's Church (and a little beyond) on the left, to the corner of Third Street and Broadway on the extreme right. This sketch was reproduced as a lithograph for the official Souvenir Program of the Lexington Sesquicentennial Jubilee Celebration in 1925.

View of the City of Lexington, Ky. Drawn on Stone & Printed in Oil Colors by Middleton, Wallace & Co. Lithos. 115 Walnut St. Cincinnati, O. Published by J. T. Palmatary.

    A view of the mid-1850's from the southwest, showing Maxwell Springs Fairgrounds (site of University of Kentucky campus) in the foreground, extending north to Fifth Street (several omissions near upper boundary), and from the beginning of Versailles Pike on the west to the present location of Walton and Clay avenues on the east. Copy owned by James M. Malloy, Lexington.

Topographical Map of the Counties of Bourbon, Fayette, Clark, Jessamine and Woodford, Kentucky, from Actual Surveys, revised and corrected by E. A. and G. W. Hewitt, published by Smith, Gallup & Co., New York, 1861.

    The locations of the houses in the county are indicated by their names and those of the owners or tenants. Also on this map is a plan of Lexington, similar to the Hart and Mapother listed above, though without names of owners. Copy in Duncan Tavern, Paris, Kentucky.

EARLY DIRECTORIES

(Joseph) *Charless' Kentucky, Tennessee, and Ohio Almanac, for the Year 1806* (Lexington, 1805), pp. 18-25.

    Republished by J. Winston Coleman, Jr., as *Lexington's First City Directory* (Lexington, 1953).

BIBLIOGRAPHICAL INDEX

William Worsley and Thomas Smith, *Worsley & Smith's Kentucky Almanac, and Farmer's Calendar for the Year 1819* (Lexington, 1818), pp. 37-47.

    Republished by J. Winston Coleman, Jr., as *Lexington's Second City Directory* (Lexington, 1953).

Julius P. Bolivar MacCabe, *Directory of the City of Lexington and County of Fayette for 1838 & 1839* (Lexington, 1838).

    Lists twenty-five of the distinguished residences of Lexington, giving their names, locations, and owners, and includes invaluable descriptions of some of the city's more important public buildings.

COLLECTIONS OF PHOTOGRAPHS

Andrews Collection, Avery Library, Columbia University.
    Photographs of early Kentucky architecture made by Alfred Andrews about 1940. 54 plates mounted 33 x 25 cm.

Bullock Collection, Transylvania University Library.
    Collected by Dr. Waller Bullock, and including the collection of Judge James Hillary Mulligan.

Coleman Collection, Winburn Farm, Russell Cave Pike.
    Made and collected by J. Winston Coleman, Jr.

Dunn Collection, Kentucky State Historical Society.
    Collected by the late C. Frank Dunn and presented to the society by Mrs. Dunn.

Lancaster Collection, Lexington Public Library.
    Collected by A. B. Lancaster and presented to the library by his daughter, Mrs. Mary Frazier Lancaster Henderson. Many of the photographs made by Captain Jinks.

Staples Collection.
    Collected by Charles R. Staples; divided among the Lexington *Leader*, the Lexington Public Library, and Dr. Thomas D. Clark.

Lafayette Studio Collection, Lexington.
    Consists of several large albums of photographs copied from various sources by Robert Long.

BOOKS AND BROCHURES

1. American Guide Series, *Lexington and the Bluegrass Country* (Lexington, 1938).
2. Henry Caswell, *America and the American Church* (London, 1839).
3. J. Winston Coleman, Jr., *Old Homes of the Blue Grass* (Lexington, 1950).
4. Sydney S. Combs (texts by C. Frank Dunn and Charles R. Staples), *Blue Grass Homes* (Lexington, 1948).
5. Sydney S. Combs, *Our Proud Heritage* (Lexington, 1950).
6. Talbot Hamlin, *Benjamin Henry Latrobe* (New York, 1955).
7. Talbot Hamlin, *Greek Revival Architecture in America* (New York, 1944).
8. Charles Kerr (ed.), *History of Kentucky*, 5 vols. (Chicago & New York, 1922).
9. Fiske Kimball, *Domestic Architecture of the American Colonies and of the Early Republic* (New York, 1927).
10. Thomas A. Knight & Nancy Lewis Greene, *Country Estates of the Blue Grass* (Cleveland, 1904).
11. Clay Lancaster, *Back Streets and Pine Trees: The Work of John McMurtry, Nineteenth Century Architect-Builder of Kentucky* (Lexington, 1956).
12. Elise Lathrop, *Historic Houses of Early America* (New York, 1927).
13. William A. Leavy, "A Memoir of Lexington and Its Vicinity," edited by Nina M. Visscher (*The Register of the Kentucky State Historical Society*, April, 1942 —January, 1944).
14. John Lethem, *A Review of Lexington, Kentucky, As She Is* (New York, 1887).
15. Rexford Newcomb, *Architecture in Old Kentucky* (Urbana, Illinois, 1953).
16. Rexford Newcomb, *Old Kentucky Architecture* (New York, 1940).
17. William Henry Perrin, *History of Fayette County, Kentucky* (Chicago, 1882).
18. George W. Ranck, *History of Lexington, Kentucky* (Cincinnati, 1872).
19. Elizabeth M. Simpson, *Bluegrass Houses and Their Traditions* (Lexington, 1932).
20. Elizabeth M. Simpson, *The Enchanted Bluegrass* (Lexington, 1938).
21. J. Frazer Smith, *White Pillars* (New York, 1941).
22. J. Soule Smith, *Art Work of the Blue Grass Region of Kentucky* (Oshkosh, Wisconsin, 1898).
23. Charles R. Staples, *The History of Pioneer Lexington, 1779-1806* (Lexington, 1939).
24. Elizabeth Patterson Thomas, *Old Kentucky Homes and Gardens* (Louisville, 1939).
25. Henri Walbert, *Residences & Plantations dans les Vallées de l'Ohio et du Mississippi au début du 19e Siècle* (Paris, 1948).
26. Works Progress Administration, *Kentucky, A Guide to the Bluegrass State* (New York, 1939).

UNPUBLISHED DOCUMENTS

27. Alfred Andrews, "Greek Revival Houses in Kentucky" (thesis, Columbia University, 1942).
28. C. Frank Dunn, "Old Houses of Lexington," 2 vols. (typescript, Kentucky State Historical Society).
29. Thomas Lewinski, Account Book, covering the period from March 24, 1845, through July 5, 1847, found among the effects of the late Elijah Watkins, purchased by Judge James H. Mulligan in 1903, later owned by W. K. Massie of Lexington (several copies made by Samuel M. Wilson in 1936).

ARTICLES OF SPECIAL INTEREST

30. Alfred Andrews, "Gideon Shryock—Kentucky Architect," *Antiques*, November, 1947, pp. 348-349.
31. Clay Lancaster, "Adaptations from Greek Revival Builders' Guides in Kentucky," *The Art Bulletin*, March, 1950, pp. 62-70.
32. Clay Lancaster, "Builders' Guide and Plan Books and American Architecture from the Revolution to the Civil War," *Magazine of Art*, January, 1948, pp. 16-22.

33. Clay Lancaster, "The Early Ironwork of Central Kentucky," *Antiques*, May, 1948, pp. 354-358.
34. Clay Lancaster, "Gideon Shryock and John McMurtry, Architect and Builder of Kentucky," *The Art Quarterly*, autumn, 1943, pp. 257-275.
35. Clay Lancaster, "Kentucky's Architectural Firsts," *Antiques*, November, 1947, pp. 331-334.
36. Clay Lancaster, "Latrobe and the John Pope House," *Gazette des Beaux-Arts*, April, 1946, pp. 213-224.
37. Clay Lancaster, "Major Thomas Lewinski: Emigre Architect in Kentucky," *Journal of the Society of Architectural Historians*, December, 1952, pp. 13-20.
38. Clay Lancaster, "Some Octagonal Forms in Southern Architecture," *The Art Bulletin*, June, 1946, pp. 103-111.
39. Clay Lancaster, "Through Half a Century, Palladianism in the Bluegrass," *Gazette des Beaux-Arts*, June, 1944, pp. 347-370.
40. Clay Lancaster, "Three Gothic Revival Houses at Lexington," *Journal of the Society of Architectural Historians*, January-June, 1947, pp. 13-21.
41. Clay Lancaster, "The Homes of Francis Hunt," *Antiques*, January, 1950, pp. 42-44.
42. Josephine F. McDonald, "Some Old Kentucky Houses," *Country Life in America*, April, 1926, pp. 49-51.
43. Rexford Newcomb, "Architecture in Kentucky," *Kentucky Progress Magazine*, fall, 1931, pp. 4-13, 42-43.
44. Rexford Newcomb, "The Architecture of Old Kentucky," *Kentucky State Historical Society Register*, July, 1933, pp. 185-200.
45. Rexford Newcomb, "Gideon Shryock," *The Architect*, October, 1928, pp. 41-46.
46. Rexford Newcomb, "Gideon Shryock—Pioneer Greek Revivalist of the Middlewest," *Kentucky State Historical Society Register*, September, 1928, pp. 221-235.
47. Rexford Newcomb, "Kentucky Architecture," *The Octagon*, March, 1940, pp. 8-10.
48. Rexford Newcomb, "The Small Houses of Old Kentucky," *Kentucky Progress Magazine*, spring, 1934, pp. 112-117.
49. "Ohio River Valley Estates," *House & Garden*, September, 1940, pp. 34-39.

The following combined index and bibliography lists the names of houses mentioned in the text and of their builders or early owners, with cross references to the specific names used to designate the various examples in this volume. When additional material is available for a given house, the index entry is followed by a bibliographical entry, in which the numbers in parentheses refer to the numbered references listed just above and are followed by page numbers when necessary. In the citation of materials not in the numbered list, these symbols are used:

AC	*American Collector*
AF	*Architectural Forum*
AM	*Antiques*
BHG	*Better Homes & Gardens*
C-J	Louisville *Courier-Journal*
CLA	*Country Life in America*
DP	Lexington *Daily Press*
H-L	Lexington *Herald-Leader*
KG	Lexington *Kentucky Gazette*
KM	*Kentucky Magazine*
KS	Lexington *Kentucky Statesman*
LH	Lexington *Herald*
LL	Lexington *Leader*
LO	Lexington *Observer and Kentucky Reporter*
LT	Lexington *Transcript*
SS	*Scenic South*

Abbotsford: Scott's mock castle, 114
Adam brothers: mentioned, 67-68
Adams, William: *Vitruvius Scoticus*, 75
Airy Mount (Woodford County): murals by Cohen, 27
Alberti house: log section, 10; described, 87-88
Alberti, John Charles: mentioned, 87
Alberti, John Leer: enlarged Alberti house, 87
Alleghan Academy or Hall: later names for Pettit house, 96
Allen house (near Georgetown): mentioned, 94
Allen (Thomas M.) house: mentioned, 33
Allen, James Lane: mentioned, 33; stories with characters modeled on Fayette householders, 45, 119; lived at Oakwood, 168
Allen, Richard: builder of Falconer house, 33

Allen, Washington: constructed Waveland, 89
Almahurst (Jessamine County): mentioned, 130
American Builder's Companion, The: by Benjamin, 82
Anchor and Hope: mentioned, 33
Anderson, Joseph C.: owner of Cane Run, 137
Arcadia (Danville): mentioned, 102
Architect, The: by Ranlett, 133
Architectural books. See Builder's guides
Architectural Instructor, The: by Lafever, 83
Architectural Sketches for Cottages: by Lugar, 133
Architecture of Country Houses, The: by Downing, 116, 127-128
Armstrong, Robert H.: stucco work, 26
Ashe, Thomas: described Indian catacombs, 1

Ashland: doorway fan, 28; tall windows, 48; compared to Woodlands, 53; Latrobe plans for wings, 53; original house described, 56-57; mentioned, 133; new house described, 137-138
—bibliog. (19) 399-408; (5) 20; (15) 54-56; (24) 85; (3) 76; (49); (42); (35); (37); (9) 274; (12) 390-391; H-L 1/11/53, 4/29/51, 10/1/50, 4/2/50, 3/14/54; LL 5/11/50; BHG 5/24, 35-36; CLA 6/04, 158-162; SS 6/50; LO 7/1/1857
Ashton (Jacob) house: mentioned, 43, 58, 108; described with Greek Revival alterations, 85; compared to Swift house, 141
—bibliog. (28) 25
Aspen Hall (Harrodsburg): mentioned, 101
Athens (Kentucky): early brick houses, 37, 41

BIBLIOGRAPHICAL INDEX

Auvergne: described, 107
Auvergne (Bourbon County): twin of Buknore, 74
Aylesford: later name for Elley Villa, 128
Ayres (Samuel) house: belt course, 22

"Bacon's Castle" (Virginia): gable parapets, 23
Baker house (near Nicholasville): described, 98
Barker house: mantel, 68
Barr log house: mentioned, 5, 7
Barry, Catherine: purchased Pope house, 56
Batcheller, George: constructed Cane Run, 136
Bates log house: mentioned, 7
Baxter house: belt course, 22; compared to Price house, 32
Bayles-Beck house: described, 118
—*bibliog.* H-L 5/28/50; (11) 21-23; (28) 54
Bayles, Jessee: owned site of Bayles-Beck house, 118
Beatty log house: mentioned, 5
Beauties of Modern Architecture, The: by Lafever, 83-84, 108
Beck, James Burnie: owner of Bayles-Beck house, 118
Belair: mentioned, 87
—*bibliog.* (19) 122-129; (4); (5) 42
Bell (David) house: described, 102-103
—*bibliog.* LL 8/13/57
Bell (John) house. See Stoneleigh
Bell Place: later name of Sayre house, 96
Bell, Susan: owner of classic cottage, 77
Belt course: on early brick houses, 22; medieval feature, 115
Benjamin, Asher: *Builder's Assistant*, 28, 45; *American Builder's Companion*, 82
Berry frame house: mentioned, 13
Berry house (Dedman Road): mentioned, 37
Berry house (Tates Creek Pike): belt course, 22
Berry log houses: storage cabin, 3; saddlebag cabin, 8-9
Bibb house (Frankfort): mentioned, 130
Biddle, Owen: builder's guides, 28
Birch Nest: mentioned, 130
Bird Hill: ruins described, 4; mentioned, 10
Bird, Abraham: built Kenney house, 33
Blacksmith: defined, 20-21
Blithewood (near Fishkill, N. Y.): compared to Ingelside, 125
Bob, John: brickmaker, 18
Bodley (Thomas) house: description, 50; place in old Transylvania square scheme, 50; plan compared to Winton, 58; Greek Revival portico, 85

Bodley house (*continued*):
—*bibliog.* (15) 52; (19) 159-164; (5) 14; (24) 84-85; (28) 72; H-L 7/18/58
Boggs (Robert) house: mentioned, 5; described, 16-17; chamfered posts, 24
—*bibliog.* (4) 7; (15) 48
Books, architectural. See Builder's guides
Boone Creek: adjacent to Fayette County, xi; mentioned, 3
Boone, Daniel: mentioned, xi
Bosworth, Benijah: built Spring Hill, 130
Botherum: mentioned, 18; Tudor arch, 117; described, 118-120; centerpiece like Elley Villa, 128
—*bibliog.* (15) 133; (19) 180-185; (24) 91; (11) 34-38; (16) 12; (5) 24; LL 10/23/47; H-L 3/2/52, 3/14/54, 10/30/55; (38); LH 12/9/34
Bourbon County: related to Fayette, xi
Bowman house: mentioned, 98
Bowman log buildings: cabin, 8; barn, 9; cabin and barn, 40
Bowman, Abraham: built Bowman cabin, 8; daughters married Sowyel Woolfolk and John Keen, 40
Bowman, George H.: owner of Cedar Hall, 101
Bowyer (George A.) house: mentioned, 109
—*bibliog.* (11) 23
Boyce, William: owned site of Peck house, 102
Boyle, J. T.: built Mound Cottage, 128
Bradford, Daniel: bookstore, 28
Bradford, Fielding: mentioned 36
Bradford, John: newspaper, 12; bookstore, 28; built Fairfield, 36
Brand, Alexander H.: built Cane Run, 136
Brand, James W.: partner of Kennedy, 69
Brand, John: built Rose Hill, 63; purchased Kennedy house, 71
Brand, William Moses: built Elmwood, 93
Brandon (Virginia): compared to Ashland, 56
Breckinridge, John Cabell: born at Thorn Hill, 131
Breckinridge, Joseph Cabell: resided at Thorn Hill, 131
Brewton house (Charleston, S. C.): mentioned, 26
Brick houses: introduced into Kentucky, 19, 20, 21
Brickmaking: in Fayette County, 18
Brickwork: types in early houses, 22
British Architect, The: by Swan, 28
Britling, The: later name for McMurtry house, 117
Brown, Joshua: built Headley house, 33

Brown, William: builder's guides, 82
Bryan house (Bryant Road): mentioned, 44
Bryan house (Jessamine County): temple-type house, 103
Bryan house (Military Pike): belt course, 22; brick cornice, 23; mentioned, 33
Bryan (Betty) house (Jessamine County): resemblance to Lemon Hill, 106
Bryan, David: built Cave Place, 51
Bryan, Joseph: built Waveland, 89
Bryan, William: owner of Cave Place, 51
Bryan's Station: Joseph Rogers house, 43
—*bibliog.* (19) 360-366; H-L 1/15/52
Buenna Hill: described, 93; compared to Maple Grove, 107
—*bibliog.* (11) 44
Builder's Assistant, The: by Benjamin, 28, 45
Builder's Assistant, The: by Haviland, 81-82, 133
Builder's guides: early books available, 27-29; Greek Revival, 81-84
Builder's Pocket Treasure, The: by Pain, 28
Builders, early, in Lexington: proportion to population, xii
Buknore (Bourbon County): compared to Fayette houses, 73-74
Bulfinch, Charles: Federal style protagonist, 68
Bullock (Waller) house: mentioned, 42
"Burnt Records": mentioned, 30
Bush house: mentioned, 33
Bush, Alexander: resided in McCann house, 91
Butler (James C.) house: iron grilles, 83; described, 108-109; mentioned, 117
—*bibliog.* (11) 17-19; LH 12/9/34; (28) 99

Cabins. See Log houses; Slave cabins
Cahokia (Illinois) courthouse: mentioned, 9
Caldwell (George) house. See Elk View
Caldwell (Matthew) house. See Caldwell-Wilson house
Caldwell-Wilson house: described, 7; mentioned, 10
Calvary Baptist Church: built on site of Swift house, 141
Cane Run: described, 136-137
—*bibliog.* (15) 159; (17) 127; (37); H-L 2/10/52, 11/23/58
Capitol at Frankfort. See Statehouse (Frankfort) by Shryock
Carr log house: mentioned, 7
—*bibliog.* LL 9/2/51
Carter house: log cabin, 3; main house described, 97-98
Carvings: early woodwork, 26; in Mount Hope, 49
Cassell house: mentioned, 42-43

Castellated style: variety of Gothic Revival, 116
Castlelawn. *See* McCann (Benjamin) house
Castleman, David: built Castleton, 107
Castleton: described, 107
—*bibliog.* (10) 92; (19) 17-27; (24) 95-97; (4); (5) 35; LL 5/7/50; H-L 1/9/49; LH 10/1/04
Castlewood (Madison County): carved woodwork, 26
Castlewood Park: site of Loudoun, 124
Cave Place: described, 51
—*bibliog.* (19) 71-81; (24) 98-99; (5) 25; H-L 5/25/52, 7/1/51
Cedar Grove (Cleveland Road): mentioned, 13, 37
Cedar Grove (Paris Pike): mentioned, 33
Cedar Hall: downspout funnels, 24; parlor doorway, 73-74, 84; described, 101
—*bibliog.* (19) 343-348; (24) 100-101; (4); (5) 31; (16) Pl. 101; (15) 133; H-L 8/21/49, 3/14/54, 5/26/46; KS 12/24/1858; LL 5/4/50; (11) 32
Cemetery gateway, old (Lexington): mentioned, 117
Charless' Kentucky Almanack: Lexington city directory, xii, 12
Chimneypieces. *See* Mantels
Christ Episcopal Church: designed by Lewinski, 120
Christian house: belt course, 22
Church Building Act of 1818, English: effect on British architecture, 115
Cincinnati: mentioned, xi; Taft house at, 66
Civil Architecture: by Shaw, 82, 135
Clark County: related to Fayette, xi
Clark, John: builder of Auvergne, 107
Clark, John S.: purchased Walnut Hall, 99
Clark, Joseph: purchased Kirklevington, 92
Classic cottage: front door, 28; described, 77-78; mentioned, 103
Classic elements: in early houses, 25, 67; orders, 67
Classicism: in Fayette County, 67-78
Clay Hill (Harrodsburg): Lowery carvings, 26; mentioned, 101-102
Clay (Henry) house. *See* Ashland
Clay (John) house: mentioned, 138
—*bibliog.* H-L 6/6/46; LL 3/5/49
Clay (James B.) villa: described, 135-136
—*bibliog.* (15) 147; (37); (39); (29) 6/11/1845 ff.; H-L 5/27/51; LL 7/6/50
Clay, Cassius M.: owner of Morton house, 62; associated with Lewinski, 134, 135
Clay, Thomas H.: built Mansfield, 113
Clemens log house: mentioned, 7
Clérisseau: collaborated with Jefferson, 68

Cleveland (Eli) cabins: described, 3-4; mentioned, 42
Cleveland-Rogers house: described, 42; portico compared to Lewis Manor, 61
Clifton: described, 101
—*bibliog.* (19) 62-63; LL 9/29/01
Cloud (Mary) house: described, 143-144
—*bibliog.* (4)
Clover Land: another name for Cloud house, 144
Coachhouses: at Hunt-Morgan house, 48; Grassland, 73
Cochran (James W.) house: mentioned, 85, 108; described, 104
Cockerell, Samuel Pepys (English architect): mentioned, 67, 68
Cohen, Alfred: murals in Woodford County, 27, 77
Cole house: mentioned, 37
Coleman, David S.: built Highland Home, 137
Coleman, Horace: built Sugar Tree Grove, 44
Collection of Designs in Architecture, A: first American builder's guide, 28
Colonial Home: described, 94
Common-bond brickwork: use in early brick houses, 22
Conservatory of Music, Lexington: occupied Gibson house, 87
Contrasts: by Pugin, 115
Coolavin: doorway fan, 28, 29; described 64
—*bibliog.* (28) 143
Coons house: mentioned, 13, 37
Cooper house: belt course, 22; resembles Stony Point, 84
Corinthia: described, 94-95; newel like McCauley house, 99-100; compared to Ingelside, 125
—*bibliog.* (11) 44-47; (40); (33); LH 12/9/34
Cottage Garden: McMurtry home, 130
Cottage Residences: by Downing, 116, 133
Cottages and Cottage Life: by Elliott, 133
Country Gentleman's Architect, The: by Lugar, 133
Cove Spring: twin doors, 40
Crammond, William: builder of Sedgeley, 115
Crenshaw (David) saddlebag cabin, 8-9
Cridland house (Philadelphia): mentioned, 133
Cronkhill: first Italianate house in England, 133, 134; compared to Cane Run, 136
Crowstep gable: on Doland house, 23

Darnaby house (Briar Hill Road): mentioned, 37
Darnaby house (Cleveland Road): mentioned, 10
Darnaby house (Winchester Pike): mentioned, 106

Darnaby log house: described, 9
Davis, Alexandar J.: first Greek house, 89; designed Glenellen, 115; books by, 115-116; buildings designed by, 121; designed Blithewood, 125; design in Downing book, 127; window design, 141. *See also* Town & Davis
Dedman house: mentioned, 107
Delta: mentioned, 97
Designs for Cottages: by Gandy, 133
Detached kitchens: at Rankin house, 7; Hurricane Hall, 32; Fairfield, 36; Union Dale, 43; Winton, 58; Rose Hill, 64; Grassland, 73
Devore house: mentioned, 13
Dewees, Farmer: owned White Cottage, 75
Diamond Point (Harrodsburg): temple-type house, 103
Dimmick, Horace E.: executed ornamental painting, 27
Doans house (Burlington, N. J.): first picturesque Italianate house in America, 134
Dogtrot: type house described, 9; at Sugar Tree Grove, 44
Doland house: crowstep gable, 23; described, 77
Downing house: mentioned, 37
Downing & Grant: wallpapers, 27
Downing, Andrew J.: biographical sketch, 115-116; books on architecture, 116; influenced Elley villa, 127-128; Italianate design, 133
Downing, F., & Co.: early decorating, 27
Dudley house (North Broadway Extended): brick cornice, 23; mentioned, 43
Dudley house (Winchester Pike): mentioned, 43
Duncan Park: site of Morton house, 61
Dunreath: mentioned, 106
—*bibliog.* (19) 306-313; (15) 134; (4); LL 7/30/51, 5/7/48; H-L 1/9/49

Edgewood: mentioned, 106
Egyptian elements: in Greek Revival, 81
Elbert house: mentioned, 37
Elk View: described, 13
Elkhorn Creek: its tributaries, xi; South Elkhorn mentioned, 8. *See also* Town Fork
Elkton: former name of Fairlawn, 96
Ellerslie: belt course, 22, 23; stairhall, 25; described, 30; compared to Price house, 31
—*bibliog.* (12) 391-392; (28) 185; H-L 4/22/51, 4/16/41, 1/4/48, 6/9/46
Elley (William R.) villa: described, 126-129
—*bibliog.* (15) 154-155; (11) 49-54; H-L 4/16/50; (40); (34); (32); AC 5/48, 18; LL 1/6/38
Elliott, Charles Wyllys: *Cottages*, 133

BIBLIOGRAPHICAL INDEX

Elms, The: doorway from Shaw book, 82; described, 100-101; cottage at, 130
—*bibliog.* (11) 29-32; (31); KS 9/26/1856
Elmwood: described, 93
—*bibliog.* (19) 227-233; (17) 187; LL 10/2/47; (28) 90
Elsing Green (Virginia): window treatment, 33
English-bond brickwork: filling for frame houses, 12
Eothan: another name for Vaucluse, 45
Episcopal Theological Seminary: occupied January (later Gibson) house, 86
Erwin, James: owner of Woodlands, 52
Euphrasia Hall: built on site of Glendower, 66
Evans log house: described, 7

Fairfield: described, 36-37
—*bibliog.* H-L 7/30/50, 10/11/53; LL 8/25/52; C-J 9/14/56
Fairlawn: described, 96
—*bibliog.* (19) 186-194; (24) 94-95; (15) 140-141; (5) 39; (28) 201; LL 5/6/50, 5/11/49; H-L 3/14/54; LH 9/29/01
Fairview: mentioned, 33
Falconer house: mentioned, 33
Fan doorways: of medieval origin, 24, 46; outstanding examples in Fayette County, 46; Cave Place, 51; Woodlands, 52-53; not attributable to Latrobe, 53; Pope house, 55; Poplar Grove, 57; smaller Price house, 58; Ashton house, 58; Lewis Manor, 61; Norton cottage, 64
Farmington (Louisville): mentioned, 66
Farra house: chamfered posts, 24; described, 35; mentioned, 38; stairway compared to Ridgely house, 39
Farrar, Joseph R.: owned Tuckahoe, 44
Fayette County: described, xi-xii; early houses in, xii-xiii
Featherstone house: brick cornice, 22; mentioned, 37
Federal Hill (Bardstown): Adam details, 24; chimneys between rooms compared to Woodlands, 52; entrance compared to Coolavin, 65
Federal style: mentioned, xiii, 46; sketch of, 68
Ferguson, Abraham L.: built Lemon Hill, 104
Fields house: mentioned 42
Fields house (Richmond, Ky.): carved woodwork, 26
Filson, John: described Indian relics, 1
Fleming, William R.: built Lyndhurst, 144
Flemish-bond brickwork: chimney on log house, 10; use in early brick houses, 22
Flournoy, Victor: built Walnut Hall, 98
Foley house: mentioned, 40

Forest Home: mentioned, 40, 43
Forkland: described, 107
—*bibliog.* (19) 268-277
Fort Springs: stone inn, 18
Foster house (Boston): colossal orders, 69
Foster log house: mentioned, 5
Foundation for the Preservation of Historic Lexington and Fayette County, The: headquarters in Hunt-Morgan house, 48-49
Frame houses: in Fayette County, 11-14
Fraser, John: enlarged Weir house, 142
Frazer, Oliver: daughter's painting at Eothan, 27; resided at Eothan, 45
Fry cabin: described, 4
Funnels, downspout: early examples, 24

Gaineswood (Demopolis, Ala.): mentioned, 110
Gandy, Joseph: designs for farm buildings, 133
Garçonnières: in Louisiana, 53; in Winton, 58
Garrard house (Paris, Ky.): resembles Elley villa, 130
Gaugh, Michael: biographical sketch and work, 29-30
Gentry house (near Danville): mentioned, 128
Gess log house: described, 9
Gibson (Tobias) house: belt course, 22; centerpiece design, 84; described, 86-87; portico compared to Mansfield, 113
—*bibliog.* (20) 282-290; (11) 26-28; H-L 2/3/52, 11/13/38, 2/3/57; (29) 7/21/1846 ff.; (37); (2) 215
Gibson (William) house: belt course, 22; resembles Stony Point, 32
—*bibliog.* (28) 223
Gilmore, Robert: builder of Glenellen, 115
Gist house: belt course, 22; mentioned, 33
Gist, Levi: owned Gist-Peck house, 59
Gist-Peck house: mentioned, 14; carved woodwork, 26; described, 59-60; compared to Doland house, 77
Glass, window: in early houses, 21
Glen Rose: formerly Spring Hill, mentioned, 43, 130; porch like Thorn Hill, 131
Glendower: described, 66
—*bibliog.* (19) 3-16; H-L 4/15/51
Glenellen (near Baltimore): mentioned, 115
Glengarry: later name for Cane Run, 137
Gloucester (Natchez): mentioned, 76
Good Samaritan Hospital. *See* Protestant Infirmary
Gothic Revival: mentioned, xii; discussed, 114-131
Grange, The (near Paris, Ky.): compared to Fayette houses, 66

Grassland: described, 72-73; compared to Peck house, 102; stairway compared to Leafland, 106
—*bibliog.* (4); (5) 44; H-L 7/20/58
Gratz Park: as Transylvania campus, described, 50-51; presented to Lexington in 1884, 51
Gratz, Benjamin: owner of Mount Hope, 49
Gratz, H. Howard: owner of White Cottage, 76
Graves house: Edgewood, 106
Gray, Richard: built Manchester, 41
Gray, Thomas: English graveyard poet, 114
Greek Revival: mentioned, xiii; history and characteristics, 79-84; in Kentucky, 84-113; compared to Gothic Revival, 116
Greentree: later name for Fairlawn, 96
Greenwood: mentioned, 44; mantel discussed, 68-69
Grimes (Charles) house: described, 18
—*bibliog.* H-L 9/28/58; *Life* 4/25/55

Half-timber construction: origin, 11; in Fayette County, 11-12
Haligan house: mentioned, 33
Hall house (Parkers Mill Road): belt course, 22; resembles Stony Point, 32
Hall (Augustus) house: mentioned, 110
Halloway house (Richmond, Ky.): doorway from Dakin design, 83; centerpiece design, 84; mentioned, 101
Hamilton, Archival L.: purchased Kirklevington, 92
Hammond house (Annapolis): compared to Kennedy house, 71
Hardware for houses: early period, 6, 21
Harmony Grove: mentioned, 43
Harmony Hall: mentioned, 42
—*bibliog.* H-L 7/29/56
Harp log house: mentioned, 3
Harrison, Carter Henry: sold Clifton, 101
Hart (John) house: belt course, 22; mentioned, 32
Hart (N.G.S.) house: belt course, 22; compared to Stony Point, 32
—*bibliog.* (28) 259
Hart (Thomas) house: belt course, 22, 23; plan related to Lake house, 37; place on old Transylvania square scheme, 50
Hart, John: built Hartland, 97
Hartland: described, 97; compared to McMurtry house, 117
—*bibliog.* (4); (3) 50
Haverhill parlor (Metropolitan Museum): wallpaper, 27
Haviland, John: *Builder's Assistant*, 81-82; Italianate design, 133, 134
Hayes (Samuel T.) house: described, 107; compared to Johnson house, 108

BIBLIOGRAPHICAL INDEX

Hayes, William: built Woodstock, 41
Hazel Dell: belt course, 22
Headley house: mentioned, 33
—*bibliog.* (4)
Headley, Hamilton A.: built Kirklevington, 91
Helm Place: later name for Cedar Hall, 101
Henderson house: mentioned, 37
Henderson log house: mentioned, 5
Henry, Patrick: mentioned, 59
Hickey, Thomas: built Coolavin, 65
Hidaway: later name for Garrard house, Paris, 130
Higgins (Joel) Mansion: described, 85-86; mentioned, 104
—*bibliog.* (28) 295
Highland Hall: described, 97
Highland Home: mentioned, 137
—*bibliog.* (37)
Hilldale: mentioned, 43-44
—*bibliog.* H-L 4/18/54
Hills, Chester: builder's guides, 82
Holley house (Scott County): mentioned, 91
Holmes, Robert: paints offered for sale in 1795, 21
Homewood (Baltimore): mentioned, 66, 113
Horn Quarter (Virginia): mentioned, 88-89
Howe, Edward: paint oils pressed, 21
Hudson, Joseph: paints offered for sale in 1793, 21; wallpapers, 26
Hughes, Jacob: owned Leafland, 106
Hughes, Thomas: built Fairlawn, 96
Hunt house: mentioned, 80; described, 110-112
—*bibliog.* (41); LL 6/3/53; (28) 315
Hunt, Charlton: resided at Thorn Hill, 131
Hunt, Francis K.: built Hunt house, 110; built Loudoun, 121
Hunt, Henrietta: mentioned, 47
Hunt, John W.: built Hunt-Morgan house, 47; mentioned, 69
Hunt-Morgan house: doorways, 24, 26, 47; described, 47-50; stairway compared to Bodley house, 50; place in old Transylvania square scheme, 50; fan of doorway compared to Plancentia window, 52; fan doorway compared to Poplar Grove, 57; plan compared to Winton, 58; mentioned, 108
—*bibliog.* (19) 149-158; (24) Pl. 90-91; (16) 7; (15) 51; (3) 62; (4); (5) 43; (41); H-L 6/22/41, 10/9/55, 10/16/55; AM 11/47, 345
Hunter log cabin: mentioned, 4
Hurricane Hall: chamfered posts, 24; stairhall, 25; cornice, 25-26; wallpaper, 27; described, 33-35; compared to Steel's Run, 36
—*bibliog.* (19) 262-267; (15) 50; H-L 3/30/52

Icehouses: at Rose Hill, 64; Grassland, 73
Indians: few in Kentucky, xi; constructions, 1
Ingels, Henry B.: built Ingelside, 124
Ingelside: described, 124-126
—*bibliog.* (19) 195-202; (16) 12; (15) 152-153; (40); (34); (33); (14) 102; (11) 39-44; AC 4/48, 9; 5/48, 18; LH 12/9/34; H-L 4/15/42, 5/21/50
Innes (James) house: mentioned, 43
Innes, Charles W.: built Corinthia, 94
Innes, Robert: built Buenna Hill, 93
Ironwork, architectural: in early houses, 20-21
Italianate: mentioned, xiii; discussed, 132-146

Jackson house: mentioned, 33
—*bibliog.* LL 8/25/52
Jacquemort & Bénard: wallpaper in Woodlawn, 27
January, Thomas: built first section of Gibson house, 86
Jefferson, Thomas: home mentioned, 25, 48; designed Brandon, 56; Federal style protagonist, 58
Jessamine County: related to Fayette, xi
Johnson & Warner's bookstore: mentioned, 28
Johnson house (Russell Cave Pike): compared to Stony Point, 32
Johnson (Edward P.) house: centerpiece, 84; described, 108
—*bibliog.* (37) 6
Johnson, Madison C.: built Botherum, 118
Jones log house: described, 9
Jones, William: commissioned Cloud house, 144

Keen (John) house: mentioned, 7; stairway, 24; described, 40
—*bibliog.* (19) 278-284; (15) 49; (12) 392; (4); LL 5/16/47; H-L 4/20/52
Kennedy house: described, 71-72; compared to Grassland, 73; forerunner of Greek type, 102; compared to Peck house, 102
Kennedy, Matthew: mentioned, 29; built Transylvania 1816 building, 51; sketch of architectural work in Bluegrass, 69-71
Kenney house: mentioned, 33
Kentuckian Hotel: occupies McConathy house, 104
Kentucky Agricultural and Mechanical College: agricultural school in Woodland Park, 52
Kentucky River: adjacent to Fayette County, xi
Kilmore: later name for Lewis Manor, 61
Kinkead (Mrs. George B.) house: described, 141

Kinkead, William B.: enlarged Richland, 143
Kirklevington: doorway design, 83; described, 91-92

Lafayette High School: occupied The Elms, 101
Lafever, Minard: books of Greek Revival designs, 82-84; designs used in Kentucky, 83, 84, 87, 90, 92, 101, 105, 108
Laird house: described, 107
Lake (Isabella) house: square posts, 24; described, 37; mentioned, 38
Land grants: contributed to settling Fayette County, xi
Latrobe, Benjamin H.: biographical sketch, 53; work in Kentucky, 53; design for Pope house, 54-55; designed wings for Ashland, 56-57; Federal style protagonist, 68; introduced Greek Revival to America, 79-80; introduced Gothic Revival, 115; Italianate influence, 133; architect of Sedgeley, 135
Laughed, David: built Hurricane Hall, 33
Leafland: described, 106; compared to Maple Grove, 107
Leavy, William: saw advertisement, 21; built The Elms, 100
Lemon Hill: described, 104
—*bibliog.* (20) 200-206
Lewinski, Thomas: remodeled Pope house, 55, 140; built gardener's cottage at Ashland, 57; rebuilt Ashland, 57, 138; owned book by Shaw, 82; added portico to Gibson house, 86; designed Johnson house, 108; designed Hall house, 110; designed Mansfield, 112; designed Lexington churches, 120-121; Italianate advocate, 134; biographical sketch, 134-135; designed Clay villa, 135; designed Cane Run, 136; designed Highland Home, 137; work for Woolley, 140
Lewis (Thomas) Manor: described, 60; compared to Coolavin, 65; mentioned, 75
—*bibliog.* (19) 314-318; (15) 65; (4); LL 8/25/52; H-L 6/8/52
Lexington: early history and description, xii, 12
Lexington White Lead Manufactory: paints manufactured, 21
Liberty Hall: mentioned, 98
Liberty Hall (Frankfort): Adam details, 24; chimneys between rooms compared to Woodlands, 52; upstairs drawing room compared to Pope house, 55
Lime: early use in mortar, 20
Limestone: used in early Fayette buildings, 19-20
Limestone (town). *See* Maysville
Lintel, Laurence: lime merchant, 20

BIBLIOGRAPHICAL INDEX

Locks: early, 21
Locust Grove (Coolavin): renamed, 65
Locust Grove (Leestown Pike): chamfered posts, 24; stairway, 25; twin doors, 40
Locust Hill: belt course, 22; chimney, 24; compared to Price house, 32; mentioned, 33
Locuston: described, 13-14; portico compared to Vaucluse, 45
Log houses: history, 1; features, 2; in Fayette County, 2-10
Long, Samuel: constructed Bodley house, 29, 50; shop mentioned, 69
Loudoun: mentioned, 115; built by McMurtry, 121; described, 121-123; compared to Ingelside, 124-125
—bibliog. (19) 203-211; (5) 30; (16) 12; (15) 153-154; (40); (34); (41); (11) 38-39; AC 5/48, 18; (14) 102; LH 12/9/34; LL 10/4/47, 10/25/54; H-L 11/26/50, 1/13/52
Louisville: mentioned, xii
Lowery, Mathew P.: carvings at Harrodsburg, 26
Lowry, James: locksmith advertisement, 21
Lugar, Robert: books on architecture, 133
Lyndhurst: Tudor arch mentioned, 117; described, 144-146
—bibliog. (15) 159; (39); (11) 67-75; (14) 102; LH 12/9/34; LL 10/4/47, 10/25/54; H-L 11/26/50, 1/13/52
Lynnwood (Mercer County): mentioned, 91

MacBean, Poyzer & Co.: Lexington booksellers, 28
McCalla, John M.: built Mount Hope, 49
McCann (Benjamin) house: doorway design, 83; centerpiece, 84; hall door design, 84; described, 91
—bibliog. (15) 134-135; (19) 349-351; (4); (5) 41; (11) 48; LL 5/4/48; H-L 5/4/41
McCann (Neal) house: described, 12
McCauley (John) house: centerpiece design, 84; parlor doorway, 84; described, 99; compared to The Elms, 100; parapets like Rogers house, 113
—bibliog. (11) 32-34; H-L 4/23/50; LL 7/10/48
McChord (James) house: alterations to, 45; compared to Thorn Hill, 131
—bibliog. (20) 97-105; (28) 400; H-L 7/15/56
McChord Presbyterian Church: designed by Lewinski, 120-121
McConathy frame house: mentioned, 13
McConathy house (High Street): mentioned, 104, 110

McConnell house (Woodford County): Cohen murals, 27
McConnell (James) stone house: claimed Kentucky's oldest, 15
—bibliog. LL 9/25/52
McCoy (Neil) house: fan doorway, 26, 51
—bibliog. H-L 10/30/49
McLear log house: mentioned, 6
McMahan house: belt course, 22; compared to Stony Point, 32
McMurtry house (North Broadway): plan related to Lake house, 38; plan compared to Butler house, 109
—bibliog. (11) 5-7
McMurtry house (South Broadway): described, 117; porch compared to Loudoun, 122
—bibliog. (11) 19-20
McMurtry, John: enlarged Mount Hope, 49; constructed The Elms, 82, 100; enlarged Gibson house, 86-87; constructed McCann house, 91; constructed Buenna Hill, 93; constructed Corinthia, 95; constructed McCauley house, 99; financial difficulties, 101; constructed Butler house, 108; work for Sayre Institute, 108; reputed architect of Rogers house, 113; biographical sketch, 116-117; designed Botherum, 119; constructed Lewinski churches, 121; designed Ingelside, 124; constructed Elley villa, 127; lived at Cottage Garden, 130; association with Lewinski, 135; designed and constructed Lyndhurst, 144
Malvern Hill: later name for Vaucluse, 45
Manchester: mentioned, 41
—bibliog. (3) 18; (5) 34
Mansfield: described, 112-113; basement kitchen, 113; plan compared to Clay villa, 136
—bibliog. (19) 375-382; (37); (5) 40; (24) 86; (16) 10; (15) 132; (29) 4/29/1845 ff.; (3) 38
Mantels: early carved wood, 26; stone, 26
Maple Grove: described, 107
Maplewood: mentioned, 44
Marshall house: mentioned, 44
Marshall house (Washington, Ky.): mentioned, 68
Marshall, Thomas A.: owned Weir house, 103
Martain (James) house: belt course, 22; twin doors, 40
Masonic Hall, Grand: mentioned, 69
Maysville: mentioned, xi
Meadows, The: described, 73
—bibliog. (19) 104-113; (28) 441; LL 10/16/47; H-L 7/1/51
Medway (South Carolina): crowstep gable, 23
Mentelle house: mentioned, 130

Meredith, Samuel: built Winton, 58
Metropolitan Museum of Art: owns Davis drawings for Loudoun, 123
Mills, Robert: Greek Revival architect, 80
Model Architect, The: by Sloan, 135, 144-145
Modern Builder's Guide, The: by Lafever, 83, 90, 92
Monticello (Jefferson's home): mentioned, 25; windows, 48; early scheme for resembles Lemon Hill, 105
Moore house: cabin, 3; frame wing, 13; belt course, 22, 23
Moore, James: sketch of, 45
Moore, William G.: owned Thomas-Moore house, 99-100
Morgan, Calvin C.: mentioned, 47
Morgan, Charles: mentioned, 4
Morgan, Frederic L.: owns former Shryock book, 28
Morgan, John Hunt: mentioned, 47
Morgansa: mentioned, 33
Morris house (New York City): pre-Revolution colossal-order portico, 69
Morris (David) house: mentioned, 37
Morrison College. See Transylvania University
Morrison, James: purchased Plancentia, 52
Morton (William) house: described, 61-63; plan compared to Rose Hill, 63; compared to Mansfield, 113
—bibliog. (19) 213-220; (15) 65-66; (4); (5) 27; H-L 2/17/52, 1/4/48
Mound Cottage (Danville): mentioned, 128
Mount Airy (Woodford County): Lowery carvings, 26; compared to Cleveland-Rogers house, 42
Mount Brilliant: original section, 33; Greek Revival portico, 85
—bibliog. (19) 130-140; (24) 82-84; (4); (5) 26; (3) 64-66; (15) 141; (21) 56-57; H-L 5/20/51; LH 9/29/01; *Life* 4/25/55
Mount Hope: carved woodwork, 26, 42; fan doorway, 47; described, 49-50; place in scheme of old Transylvania square, 50
—bibliog. (15) 50; (19) 386-390; (24) 87; (5) 38; (3) 34-36; (16) 7; (42); (12) 389-390; (28) 231; H-L 7/21/46
Mount Vernon (Washington's home): mentioned, 75
Mountrose: mentioned, 44
Mulberry (South Carolina): flankers compared to Woodlands, 53
Muldrow (Hugh) log house: described, 5-6

Nails: early use in Fayette, 20
Nash, John: designed Cronkhill, 133
New Geneva (Pennsylvania): early glass from, 21

Newport Parish Church (Virginia): crowstep gable, 23
Noble, Elijah: purchased Plancentia, 52
Norman, John: *Builder's Assistant*, 28
Norton (John) cottage: chamfered posts, 24; doorway, 26; described, 64. *See also* Woolley house (High Street)
—*bibliog.* (28) 462; LL 4/22/46, 6/26/50
Notman, John: designed Doane house in New Jersey, 134
Nutter log house: mentioned, 7

Oakwood: mentioned, 108
—*bibliog.* (19) 99-103; (24) 98; (4); (5) 23; H-L 4/26/50
Octagon House (Washington, D. C.): entrance pavilion compared to Woodlands, 53
O'Neal (Arthur) house: mentioned, 13
Orders, architectural: classic, 67; American, 68; colossal, 69

Pain, William: builder's guides, 28
Paints and pigments: early selection, 2
Palladian motif: Bodley house window, 50; Winton doorway, 29; Transylvania 1816 main building doorways, 29; second story door to McCoy house, 51; Morton house, 62; Paradise doorway, 66; windows in White Cottage, 75; window in Doland house, 77; in classic cottage, 77; window in Ashton house, 85
Paradise: described, 66
Parapet wall: on early houses, 23
Parker, Alexander and James: hardware merchants, 21
Parker, John: built Stony Point, 32
Parlange (Louisiana): mentioned, 76
Patchen Wilkes: later name for White House, 44
Patterson (Robert) cabin: history and description, 3
—*bibliog.* LL 5/18/39
Patterson house: stone part, 15-16; brick part, 41
Paul, Peter: stone cutter, 26
Pavements: early brick, 22
Payne, Edward C.: owned site of Fairlawn, 96
Payne, Henry: built Jackson house, 33
Pearson cabin: mentioned, 5
Peck (Henry J.) house: described, 102; mentioned, 109
Peck, John: owned Gist-Peck house, 59
Peter, Robert: resided at Winton, 59
Pettit (William B.) house: described, 95-96
—*bibliog.* (19) 319-324; (3) 52; (15) 134; (4); (5) 45; (11) 48; H-L 6/4/50, 6/17/51, AM 11/47
Philadelphia: architectural importance, 79, 80, 115
Pine Grove: mentioned, 33
Piscatorial Retreat: mentioned, 18

Pittsburgh: early glass from, 21
Plancentia: described, 51-52; compared to Woodlands, 52, 53
—*bibliog.* H-L 2/1/53
Pleasant Lawn (Woodford County): Cohen murals, 27; described, 76-77
Pleasant Retreat: mentioned, 43
Pointed Style: variety of Gothic Revival, 116
Pope (John) house: kitchen intended on ground floor, 25; described, 53-55; Italianate aspects, 133; remodeled by Lewinski, 140
—*bibliog.* (15) 52-53; (39); (35); (36); (13) 42-43; (8) II, 1096; (6) 105-108; H-L 1/13/52, 11/17/46; LH 4/15/17
Poplar Grove: fan doorway, 26; described, 57
Poplar Hill Farm: stone house, 17
Practical Builder, The: by Pain, 28
Prather house: belt course, 22
Preston, Margaret: owner of Ellerslie, 30
Preston, William: owner of Glendower, 66
Prestwould (Virginia): plan compared to Ellerslie, 30
Price house (Liberty Road): mentioned, 58
—*bibliog.* H-L 5/23/54, 4/15/56; (4)
Price house (Old Frankfort Pike): mentioned, 33
—*bibliog.* (19) 35-42; H-L 9/1/46
Price (Pugh or Williamson) house: belt course, 22; described, 31-32
Price, Daniel W.: purchaser of Coolavin, 65
Protestant Infirmary: occupied White Cottage, 76
Public Library, Lexington: erected 1904, 51
Pugin, Augustus W.: influence on Gothic Revival, 115

Quarles, Jane: wedding at Hurricane Hall, 35
Quarles, Roger: purchased Hurricane Hall, 33

Rafinesque, Constantine: described Indian relics, 1; reputed designer of White Cottage garden, 75
Ramsey, James C.: brushes, 21
Ranch house: White House compared to, 45
Rankin (Adam) house: described, 6-7; chamfered posts, 24
—*bibliog.* H-L 2/23/41
Ranlett, William H.: *The Architect*, 133
Red House: another name for Bell house, 103
Redwood Library (Newport, R. I.): compared to Lemon Hill, 105
Renaissance Revival: related to Italianate, 132

Retreat: belt course, 22; resembled Stony Point, 32
Revett, Nicholas: collaborated with James Stuart, 79
Richland: described, 143
—*bibliog.* (4)
Ridgely (Frederick) house: belt course, 22, 23; described, 38; place on old Transylvania square plan, 50
—*bibliog.* (28) 514
Ridgeway (St. Matthews): compared to Fayette houses, 66
Riley house: mentioned, 37
Roberts, O. P.: advertises house plans, 29
Rodes house: mentioned, 44
Rogers (Joseph) house. *See* Bryan's Station
Rogers (Mrs. C. C.) house: described, 113
—*bibliog.* (15) 132; (11) 20-21; (4)
Rogers, Jeremiah: mentioned, 42
Romanticism: opposed to Classicism, 114
Roofs: on early houses, 22, 23-24
Rose Hill (North Limestone): external kitchen stairway, 8; doorway and portico, 47; drawing room window, 48; described, 63-64; Greek portico added, 85
—*bibliog.* (19) 221-226; (24) 92-93; (3) 32; (16) 44-48; (15) 63; (25) Pl. 4; (21) 58-61; (4); (5) 28; (28) 522; AF 6/35, 567-578; H-L 3/18/51
Rose Hill (Parkers Mill Road): belt course, 22
—*bibliog.* H-L 4/14/54
Royster house: mentioned, 37
Runyan house: mentioned, 130
Rural Architect, The: by Gandy, 133
Rural Architecture, Upjohn's: designs of wooden churches, 130
Rural Residences: by Davis, 115, 125
Russell (Robert S.) house: mentioned, 17

Sachem's Wood (New Haven): Davis' first Greek Revival house, 89
Saddlebag cabin: described, 8-9; at Stony Point, 32
Saint Peter's School: occupied old houses, 110, 112
Sanders, Lewis: builder of Plancentia, 51
Sawmill: first in America, 11; in Kentucky, 11
Sayre Female Institute: occupied enlarged Johnson house, 108
Sayre house: described, 96
—*bibliog.* (37); H-L 4/4/48
Sayre, David A.: built Sayre house, 96; purchased Johnson house for school, 108
Scarlet Gate: later name for Oakwood, 108
Scott, Robert: owned Plancentia, 52

BIBLIOGRAPHICAL INDEX

Sedgeley: first Gothic Revival building in America, 115; compared to Clay villa, 135
Shady Grove: belt course, 22; twin doors, 40
Shady Side: mentioned, 89
 —*bibliog.* (3) 78; (15) 141; LL 5/12/49
Shaw, Edmund: builder's guides, 82; design used for Clay villa, 135
Sheffer, John H.: built Dunreath, 106
Shelby, Elizabeth: mentioned, 143
Shelby, Isaac: built Arcadia, 102
Shelby, James: built house at Richland, 143
Shelby, Thomas H.: built Grassland, 72
Shelby, Thomas H., Jr.: built Belair, 97; owned Richland, 143
Showalter house (Georgetown): mentioned, 101
Shryock (Frederick) house: mentioned, 6; described, 17
Shryock (Matthias) house: belt course, 22
Shryock, Cincinnatus: son of Matthias, 29
Shryock, Gideon: son of Matthias, 29; associated with Strickland, 80; introduced Greek Revival to Kentucky, 80; used Lafever motifs, 84; reputed architect of Weir house, 103
Shryock, Matthias: owner of Benjamin book, 28; biographical sketch and work, 29
Sidener house (Greenwich Road): mentioned, 41
Sidener house (Muir Station Road): mentioned, 13, 37
Slave cabins: at Hurricane Hall, 35; Rose Hill, 64
Slickaway. *See* Fort Springs
Sloan, Samuel: *Model Architect*, 135, 144-145
Smith, Elijah: owner of Norton cottage, 64
Smith, Francis: mentioned, 9
Smith, George: mentioned, 9
Smith, Levi T.: owner of Norton cottage, 64
Smith, William: owned White House, 44
Smith-Darnaby house: described, 9
Smokehouses: at Hurricane Hall, 35; Woolfolk house, 40; White House, 45; Grassland, 72; in Woodford County, 73; Ingelside, 126
Soane, John (English architect): mentioned, 67
Southern National Bank (Louisville): design from Lafever book, 84
Spears house (Paris): described, 94
Spring Hill: mentioned, 43, 130
Spring Valley: compared to Price house, 32
Springhurst: mentioned, 98
 —*bibliog.* (22); H-L 4/26/50

Spurr house: mentioned, 97
Stairways: outside, 8, 43, 58; in early houses, 25; circular type not attributable to Latrobe, 53; elliptical at Ashland, 57; at Grassland, 72
Stark (John) house: plan related to Lake house, 37-38; balances Mount Hope on old Transylvania square, 50
 —*bibliog.* (28) 564-566
Statehouse (Frankfort) by Gideon Shryock: first Greek Revival building in Kentucky, 80; temple type, 103
Steel's Run: described, 36
Stephens, Luther: builder of courthouse, 29; owned site of Gist-Peck house, 59
Stone house: mentioned, 7
Stone houses: in Fayette County, 15-18
Stone, Robert R.: owner of Lyndhurst, 146
Stoneleigh: described, 17; mentioned, 21; twin doors, 40
 —*bibliog.* LL 3/31/52
Stony Point: belt course, 22; square posts, 24; described, 52
Strawberry Hill (England): home of Walpole, 115
Strickland, William: Greek Revival architect, 80; pupil of Latrobe, 115
Stuart (Robert) house: described, 30-31
Stuart, James: protagonist of Greek Revival in England, 79
Stucco: used during early period, 26
Studman, Thomas: whitesmith, 21
Styles of architecture: in the Bluegrass, xii. *See also* Federal, Greek Revival, Gothic Revival, Italianate
Sugar Tree Grove: mentioned, 19, 44
 —*bibliog.* (4)
Sullivan, William: builder of Poplar Grove, 57
Sutton, David: architect of early courthouse, 29; mentioned, 60
Swan, Abraham: builder's guides, 28
Swift house: described, 141

Tandy, Gabriel: built Morgansa, 33
Taylor, Stark: built Pleasant Retreat, 43
Thomas, Barak G.: owned site of Thomas-Moore house, 94
Thomas-Moore house: described, 93-94
Thompson house (Bourbon County): mentioned, 130
Thompson, Clifford: built original part of Shady Side, 89
Thompson, William Z.: married Jane Quarles, 35
Thorn Hill: related to McChord house, 45; described, 131
 —*bibliog.* (28) 592-594
Tilton, Robert: built Williams house, 44
Todd, John: mentioned, 30
Todd, Levi: built Ellerslie, 30; mentioned, 31

Tools: early building, 21
Totten's School for Boys: in McCauley house, 100
Town and Country Builder's Assistant, The: by Norman, 28
Town & Davis, architects: mentioned, 115, 121, 133-134
Town Fork of Elkhorn: mentioned, xi, 6
Town, Ithiel: partner of A. J. Davis, 115, 121; invented hollow brick wall, 122. *See also* Town & Davis
Transylvania University: first buildings, xiii; Patterson cabin at, 3; 1815 elevation for proposed building, 22; 1816 main building, 29, 69-70; description of campus 1816-1829, 50; 1827 Medical Hall, 69; Morrison College, 69, 81; Morrison compared to Weir house, 103
Treatise on . . . Landscape Gardening, A: by Downing, 116
Trevilla: later name of Cloud house, 144
Trotter, James G.: owner of Woodlands, 52
Tuckahoe: later became White House, 44
Tuscan style: related to Italianate, 134, 136

Union Dale: external staircase on kitchen, 8; brick cornice, 23; described, 43
University of Kentucky. *See* Kentucky Agricultural and Mechanical College
Upjohn, Richard: book on vertical board churches, 130

Valley Retreat: belt course, 22
Vaucluse: painted mantel frieze, 27; doorway fan, 28, 46; described, 45
 —*bibliog.* (19) 28-34; (15) 49; (4); (5) 46; (3) 20-22; AM 11/47, 335-339
Villa: use of term, 116
Vitruvius Scoticus: by Adams, 75

Waite, Ezra: stucco worker of Charleston, 26
Wakefield (Virginia): doorway compared to Coolavin, 65
Wallace, Samuel: built house in Woodford County, 73
Wallis house: mentioned, 44
Wallpaper: in early houses, 27; in Hurricane Hall, 35
Walnut Hall: described, 98-99; compared to Weir house, 103
 —*bibliog.* (15) 141-142; (19) 239-248; (4); (5) 32; (24) 93-94; (22); (21) 54-55; KM winter 39, 8 ff.; LL 5/5/50; LH 11/13/04; H-L 1/11/53, 10/26/52, 5/6/51, 1/2/49
Walpole, Horace: built Strawberry Hill, 115

Warfield, Benjamin: probable builder of Forkland, 107
Warfield, Elisha: purchased Ridgely house, 38; built The Meadows, 73; built Mrs. C. C. Rogers house for daughter, 113
Warfield, Lloyd: owned Morton house, 62
Warner, Elijah: owned Woodlands, 52
Watkins, Mary: marriage to Lewinski, 134
Watkins, Thomas: Lewinski's brother-in-law and McMurtry's son-in-law, 134-135
Watts (David) place: ruins on farm mentioned, 3; log house described, 4-5; brick house, 37
Waveland: doorway design, 83; described, 89-91; compared to Hartland, 97; compared to Baker house, 98
—bibliog. (15) 134; (7) fig. 30; (4); C-J 12/22/57
Webb (Charles) house: described, 10; chimney mentioned, 24
Weir house: described, 103
—bibliog. (16) pl. 101; (15) 132; (4); (3) 74; (28) 674
Weir, James: built Weir houses, 103, 142
Weir-Fraser villa: described, 142-143
Welcome Home: mentioned, 33
Wells (Isaac) house: belt course, 22; resembles Stony Point, 32
West, Edward: invented nail-cutting machine, 20

Westover (Virginia): window treatment, 34
Wheelock house: plan related to Lake house, 38
White Cedar Springs: mentioned, 33
White Cottage: described, 75-76; related to Italianate style, 133
—bibliog. (28) 686; H-L 11/18/51; LL 4/15/42, 8/16/31; DP 4/1/1875
White House: described, 44-45
—bibliog. (19) 255-261; (4); LL 8/25/52
Whitesmith: defined, 20
Whitney, Payne: owned Fairlawn, 96
Wickliffe, Robert: mentioned, 30; owned Glendower, 66
Wilgus, Asa: constructed Pope house, 54
Williams house: mentioned, 44
Williams house (Jessamine County): compared to Gist-Peck house, 60-61
Williams, Daniel J.: built Pleasant Lawn, 76
Wilson (John) frame house: mentioned, 13
Wilson (Robert) house: mentioned, 33
Wilson (Sam) log house. *See* Caldwell-Wilson house
Winslow, Hallett M.: builder of courthouse, 29
Winton: log houses, 4; external stairway, 8; doorway, 29; described, 58-59
—bibliog. (19) 51-59; (5) 36; H-L 5/11/52
Woodland: mentioned, 37
Woodland Park: site of Woodlands, 52

Woodlands: carved woodwork, 26; polygonal flankers, 28, 29; described, 52-53
—bibliog. (14) 29
Woodlawn (Madison County): wallpaper, 27
Woods: varieties used in Fayette during early period, 20
Woodstock: described, 41-42
Woolfolk (Sowyel) house: mentioned, 7; stairway, 25; described, 39-40; service wing like Woodstock, 41; gallery posts resemble Grassland, 72
—bibliog. H-L 10/21/51
Woolfolk, John A.: owner of Pope house, 140
Woolfolk, John H.: owned Weir house, 103
Woolley house (High Street): described, 140-141
Woolley house (Second at Market): porch model for Bodley house, 50; mentioned, 110
Woolley, George: purchaser of Norton cottage, 64; enlarged Norton cottage, 140
Works in Architecture of Robert and James Adam, The: mentioned, 68
Worley log house: mentioned, 6
Wythe house (Williamsburg): window treatment, 34

Young Builder's General Instructor, The: by Lafever, 83, 105
Young Carpenter's Assistant, The: by Biddle, 28

1816-1829   CONJECTURAL RESTORATION

www.ingramcontent.com/pod-product-compliance
Lightning Source LLC
Chambersburg PA
CBHW060314240426
43661CB00059B/2756